Key Concepts in
Crime and Society

Recent volumes include:

Key Concepts in Race and Ethnicity
Nasar Meer

Key Concepts in Migration
David Bartram, Maritsa Poros and
Pierre Monforte

Key Concepts in Sociology
Peter Bramham

Key Concepts in Childhood Studies 2e
Allison James and Adrian James

Key Concepts in Youth Studies
Mark Cieslik and Donald Simpson

Key Concepts in Family Studies
Jane Ribbens McCarthy and Rosalind
Edwards

Key Concepts in Drugs and Society
Ross Coomber, Karen McElrath, Fiona
Measham and Karenza Moore

**Key Concepts in Classical
Social Theory**
Alex Law

Key Concepts in Social Work Practice
Aidan Worsley, Tim Mann, Angela
Olsen and Elizabeth Mason

The SAGE Key Concepts series provides students with accessible and authoritative knowledge of the essential topics in a variety of disciplines. Cross-referenced throughout, the format encourages critical evaluation through understanding. Written by experienced and respected academics, the books are indispensable study aids and guides to comprehension.

Key Concepts in
Crime and Society

ROSS COOMBER, JOSEPH F DONNERMEYER,
KAREN MCELRATH AND JOHN SCOTT

Los Angeles | London | New Delhi
Singapore | Washington DC

Los Angeles | London | New Delhi
Singapore | Washington DC

SAGE Publications Ltd
1 Oliver's Yard
55 City Road
London EC1Y 1SP

SAGE Publications Inc.
2455 Teller Road
Thousand Oaks, California 91320

SAGE Publications India Pvt Ltd
B 1/I 1 Mohan Cooperative Industrial Area
Mathura Road
New Delhi 110 044

SAGE Publications Asia-Pacific Pte Ltd
3 Church Street
#10-04 Samsung Hub
Singapore 049483

Editor: Chris Rojek
Assistant editor: Gemma Shields
Production editor: Victoria Nicholas
Copyeditor: Sharon Cawood
Proofreader: Neil Dowden
Marketing manager: Michael Ainsley
Cover designer: Wendy Scott
Typeset by: C&M Digitals (P) Ltd, Chennai, India
Printed in Great Britain by Henry Ling Limited at
    The Dorset Press, Dorchester, DT1 1HD

Library of Congress Control Number: 2014948904

British Library Cataloguing in Publication data

A catalogue record for this book is available from
the British Library

MIX
Paper from
responsible sources
FSC
www.fsc.org   FSC™ C013985

ISBN 978-0-85702-255-4
ISBN 978-0-85702-256-1 (pbk)

At SAGE we take sustainability seriously. Most of our products are printed in the UK using FSC papers and boards.
When we print overseas we ensure sustainable papers are used as measured by the Egmont grading system.
We undertake an annual audit to monitor our sustainability.

contents

contents

v

Section Three: Responses to Crime 145

key concepts in
crime and society

about the authors

Ross Coomber, PhD, is Associate Professor, Criminology and Criminal Justice, Griffith University, Australia. Until recently he was Professor of Sociology and Director of the Drug and Alcohol Research Unit at Plymouth University (UK). He has been involved in researching a wide range of issues relating to drug use, drug supply and formal and informal interventions in many societies around the world for over 25 years. He has taught a final-year undergraduate module, *Drugs and Drug Use in Society*, for 20 years. He has published extensively within the drug field and is the author of *Pusher Myths: Re-Situating the Drug Dealer* (2006) and co-editor of *Drug Use and Cultural Contexts 'Beyond the West'* (2004) (both Free Association Books) among others.

Joseph F Donnermeyer, PhD, is Professor Emeritus in the Rural Sociology programme, School of Environment and Natural Resources at The Ohio State University. He received his MA and PhD degrees in Sociology from the University of Kentucky (Lexington), and prior to his appointment at OSU was an assistant professor in the Department of Agricultural Economics at Purdue University in West Lafayette, Indiana. Dr Donnermeyer's specialisation is rural criminology, a field in which he has written over 100 peer-reviewed journal articles, book chapters and books on issues related to rural crime, including a co-authored monograph – *Rural Criminology* (2014, Critical Criminology Series, Routledge). He is a trainer in various executive development and leadership programmes through the Ohio Association of Chiefs of Police, the Ohio Fire Chiefs Association and other trade organisations. Currently, he holds adjunct appointments at Queensland University of Technology (Brisbane) and the University of New England (Armidale, New South Wales), and is a research associate with the Research Center on Violence, West Virginia University (Morgantown).

Karen McElrath earned a PhD in Criminology from Florida State University and has held faculty positions at Duquesne University, the University of Miami and, most recently, at Fayetteville State University where she is the Dudley E. Flood Endowed Professor of Criminal Justice. She returned to the USA in 2013, after spending 17 years in Northern Ireland where she worked at Queen's University in Belfast. Karen has taught classes in the areas of drug use/policy, research methods and criminology/criminal justice. She is the author of one book, the editor/co-editor of four books, including *The*

American Drug Scene, now in its 7th edition (Oxford University Press). Karen has published several scholarly journal articles and has actively engaged with communities, non-profit organisations and government bodies. Her current research interests focus on stigma, social control and drug treatment, changing patterns of opioid use (namely heroin) and the school-to-prison pipeline.

 **John Scott** is a Professor in the School of Justice, Queensland University of Technology, Australia. His current projects include research on rural crime and research on the social supply of cannabis. Gender, especially masculinity, has been a major focus of his research. His previous book (co-edited with Minichiello), *Male Sex Work and Society* (2014, Harrington Park Press), examines these fields and follows a longer-term research focus on the sex industry.

preface

Two of the co-authors involved in this book (Coomber and McElrath) previously worked on another of the recent additions to the Sage Key Concepts series (*Key Concepts in Drugs and Society*) and, whereas previously SAGE had approached us, this time round we took the idea to them.

This came about for two primary reasons: first, the format and approach; that is, the provision of an affordable text that effectively bridges the gaps between the kinds of texts commonly available to those new to engaging with crime-related issues – full-blown books on discrete topics such as Police and Policing or Gangs – and dictionaries or encyclopaedias that provide snippets of introductory insight. Even introductory texts that cover a greater breadth of material and issues often struggle to provide a sufficiently critical stance on the topics dealt with and ultimately provide little more than a basic overview of the areas, seeking to cover almost everything about crime-related issues they can. Second, we already had experience of writing a Key Concepts volume and felt that we appreciated the niche of providing critical introductory stances on a wide range of concepts and issues we considered to be 'key' to anyone studying crime in society. In other words, it was an opportunity to once again engage in an approach that we liked and were convinced of its value.

As well as bridging this gap between depth and breadth in an accessible way (the Key Concepts approach is now proven and can be cited as a success within its own terms as a workable market model), the other gap that will be bridged is that of national provincialism. The text shies away from overly parochial views of crime in society and reflects, wherever possible, a truly international perspective that a readership from the UK, Canada, the USA and Australia – among others – will relate to and find relevant. The text aims at being 'international' in the sense that examples are drawn from the USA, the UK and other countries (e.g. Australia, Canada) but also presents topics in a country-neutral way. In this sense, the aim has been, wherever possible, to utilise terminology and examples that 'travel' rather than appear ethnocentric to any one set of national perspectives. This is achieved in part through the make-up of the author group. Coomber was based in the UK whilst writing this book but is now based in Australia, Donnermeyer and McElrath are based in North America and Scott is based in Australia. In addition, each of the authors is aware of the contemporary international crime-related research context and the 'hot topics' therein. The text also aims to bridge the sometimes confused gap between criminology and crime and deviance in the sense that students on criminal justice or criminology courses, as well as those on sociology, urban studies and anthropology courses, will find the text relevant – hence the title *Crime and Society*.

The other advantage to a relatively introductory text with a much greater number of concepts covered in reasonable depth is that overlapping cross-referenced coverage helps build up a stronger, more informed world view that draws on the key concerns/issues for each area and also provides the student/reader with an immediate understanding of the topics being considered, while allowing them to understand the main areas of contention within them and/or what the strengths and weaknesses of those key concepts are.

The challenge of the Key Concepts series is to decide on which concepts to include and any group of authors would make some different choices. Enclosed in this book are the ones that we made. There are 'classic' issues that could barely be avoided, such as definitions around 'crime' and 'deviance', but also less obvious others (to some authors perhaps) such as Researching crime, Normalisation or Environmental crime and green criminology.

Forty interconnected but also relatively disparate concepts can be organised in a range of ways. We chose to order the book into three different sections: 1. Understanding Crime and Criminality; 2. Types of Crime and Criminality; and 3. Responses to Crime. In this way, we try to provide insight into how crime has been understood in the ways it has; what types of crime are prominent and why; followed by consideration of how and why crime has been responded to in the ways that it has.

In Section One, which has a focus on understanding crime, we start with providing definitions of Crime and of Deviance but also provide insight into the way crime has been seen to develop historically in pre-industrial society, in modern society and in post-modern society. From there, we consider the Social construction of crime and deviance, the way that crime has been theorised (Crime and theory) and how crime researchers go about researching crime (Researching crime). Understanding how crime is conceptualised and responded to is raised when we look at Social Control, Governance and Governmentality, and some of the specific concrete forms that society uses to manage crime in this respect are described in looking at the criminal justice system. Key to the running of criminal justice systems are Crime statistics and how they are used, and a critical understanding of statistics and how they are subject to a range of influences can also be seen when we consider the concepts of Prevalence, incidence and incident of crime; Risk from crime; Risk of becoming criminally involved; Why people commit crime; and Fear and the fear of crime. A theme that runs through many of the concepts is that of Poverty and exclusion and the ways that this increases the likelihood of being involved in crime, but also of being a Victim of crime. Although there are a range of demographic lenses that we could have chosen to consider crime through, we felt that understanding how crime can be normalised for some groups was important as a contrast to always seeing it as 'outside' the norm, and to also consider the important differences and aspects of crime as it relates to Gender, Age, Ethnicity and Class.

In Section Two, we have chosen to focus on a number of specific types of crime. Although crimes committed within these categories would often be small-scale (but not always), the concepts are built around crime areas considered of conceptual importance as a 'thing in and of itself'. So, in this sense organised crime can take many different forms but it is often presented and considered as though it was a simply definable thing that presents society with clear and definable risks. However, as we see in relation to the various forms of supposedly organised crime presented in this section, simple definitions and categorisations are both elusive and often problematic for a range of reasons. Drug markets (Drug-related crime and violence) are often overly homogenised and simplified to the point where they distort useful understanding, and Gangs can take so many forms that even those studying them can become confused as to the essence of what they are looking at. Human trafficking and slavery has more resonance in the twenty-first century than many would expect, but while it is often international and organised, it very often isn't quite as organised or international as the terms would evoke. Sex Work can overlap with human trafficking and slavery and organised criminality but it can also be organised by grass-roots activism or local authority approaches to reducing harms, as well as have varying levels of legality/illegality attached to it.

Crime also happens in places and spaces – both physical and virtual. Consideration of crimes committed on the environment generally and specifically are considered in Environmental crime and green criminology, whereas crime in rural and urban areas often manifests very differently because of the nature of those spaces and the places they have become. Internet/cyber crime is both space- and place-free in the sense that an internet criminal can commit cyber fraud or crime from almost any physical location, while, at the same time, the impact of their crimes can be truly international and transnational and left to run and build its own momentum. Terrorism and War crime are also organised and international in scale, but, as with some previous concepts around notions of social control (see Police and policing) and legitimacy in the use of force, some crimes are not crimes depending on who is committing the act/s of force or violence and whether or not those acts are perceived to be legitimate. Acts of genocide are only defined as such as long as the perpetrators are defined as illegitimate. These concepts consider formal definitions of Terrorism and War crime but also consider the frameworks of legitimacy that affect their usage.

The idea of Victimless crime is an important but contested issue. Is a 'crime' like drug use really a crime if you choose to do it to yourself? Is homosexuality really a crime if committed between two consenting adults? The issues are teased out and appraised. It might be assumed that a less contentious concept in that respect is Violence/interpersonal violence towards others. Yet, we find that definitions of violence vary across time and space and interpersonal relationships affect how 'violence' is both perceived and experienced.

In Section Three, we consider how crime has been responded to by the media and critically explore the much used notion of Moral panic. Each concept considers issues of 'social control' and the extent to which crimes are being constructed and for whom. Not unrelated to that theme, Police and policing is considered as an evolving and developing project that continuously struggles with tensions between upholding the law and doing so with proper authority and accountability, while deterence and prevention, Punishment, Rehabilitation and Alternatives to imprisonment look at how policy towards crime reduction is rationalised and implemented and why.

As with *Key Concepts in Drugs and Society*, the book can be both 'dipped' into for insight into specific topic areas or it can be read as a whole. In terms of the latter, the reader would gain cumulative knowledge about crime in society, as well as about how society has viewed and responded to crime historically and in the present day.

Ross Coomber
Joe Donnermeyer
Karen McElrath
John Scott

key concepts in
crime and society

acknowledgements

We are thankful for and would like to acknowledge the help and/or support of a number of people at different times in the course of this project, most notably: Leigh Booker, Margaret Pereira and Sandra Coe, Joan Gavin, RJ and ARM. In addition, we would also like to thank Chris Rojek, Martine Jonsrud and latterly Gemma Shields at SAGE for their support and patience.

acknowledgements

Section One

Understanding Crime and Criminality

> **Definition**: *Deviance can be defined as an attitude or action which violates the norms, values or beliefs of the mainstream. Crime is deviance which violates a law. Both deviance and crime represent expressions of how a society frames or constructs what is appropriate and what is inappropriate behaviour.*

All societies vary in their tolerance of deviant behaviours and attitudes of its members. Some kinds of deviance are labelled as bad, evil, immoral and criminal, while other differences are viewed as good, benign, harmless and even healthy.

FRAMING DEVIANCE AND CRIME

The way deviance is defined can change with time (see also *Deviance (definition of)*). For example, smoking tobacco, especially in public places, is less tolerated in many societies today than in the past, as information about its link to cancer, emphysema and other health issues becomes more widespread. In the 1960s, smoking in a college classroom by both the students and the professor was common. A considerate college would place small, aluminium ashtrays on every desk. Today, at most institutions of higher learning, smoking inside classrooms and administrative buildings is forbidden, and at some universities, smoking is prohibited anywhere on the campus grounds. Students seen smoking by the university police may be issued a fine or citation, much like violators of traffic laws.

Likewise, the field of criminology frames deviance and crime in differing ways, so that attention to some criminological phenomenon is prominent, while other areas are virtually ignored. For example, at one time, domestic violence and violence against women were not well examined, but this is no longer true with the emergence of feminist perspectives and the growth of divisions within criminological societies devoted to issues of women and crime (Renzetti 2012).

Sociologically speaking, deviance is an attitude or action that is considered a violation of the norms, beliefs and values of a society. A deviant action either violates what the majority of a society's members view as acceptable and/or is contrary to what the powerful in a society see as appropriate. All societies have subcultures where expressions of deviance among its members are what provide the group with its identity and cohesion. For example, in the USA, there is a religious group in the rural, Appalachian region of several southern states who throw poisonous rattlesnakes during their church service to prove they have been saved, based on an interpretation of New Testament passages from the Christian Bible (see also *Deviance (definition of)*). Mainstream US society defines their practices as deviant, and states have passed laws prohibiting the practice. These laws, however, are ignored by church members and function to reinforce the beliefs of those who have joined this small but unique religious subculture (Covington 1995).

The example of the snake handlers shows many of the complexities associated with the definition of crime. Some divide crimes into two primary types: those categorised as *mala in se* or inherently wrong, and those considered *mala prohibita* or wrong by legislation or because it has been prohibited in some form by a regulation issued by a governmental agency (see also *Social control, governance and governmentality*). Hence, nearly everyone in every society of the world would agree that sexual abuse of children by their parents is *mala in se*, but in only recent times has smoking on a college campus become *mala prohibita*.

Often, when mainstream society sees behaviour as repugnant or wrong, a law is passed to make that behaviour illegal, and there is enforcement of the law if an incident is known to authorities. As Durkheim (1965) reminds us, crime is a functional, normal part of every society, and provides opportunities for the reassertion of social order by those who have power, make the laws and believe the behaviour is illegal (see also *Social construction of crime and deviance*).

On the surface, a definition of crime seems quite elemental. For example, a simplistic definition defines crime as the violation of a law. The reality is more complex and derives from two fundamental questions. First, how is a law made? What are the cultural, economic, political and social dynamics within any society that form the way a certain action is defined as criminal? Second, how is behaviour determined to be in violation of a law such that others notify law enforcement or the police or someone else with legally established authority decides to make an arrest or issue a fine?

Both questions point to two fundamental dynamics of a society by which laws are established in order to increase conformity and reduce deviance. The first is based on the consensus of a society's members that something is wrong or immoral to the extent that a law should be enacted by a government to reduce the likelihood that it will happen again (see also *Deterrence and prevention*). The second is based on differences in a society, especially factors which consider the roles played by inequality and political power. This view sees crime and the enforcement of crime as a function of the powerful in a society who seek to advance their hegemonic interests and keep others in subordinate positions through laws passed by government and the differential enforcement of those laws. Both views have their strengths and their limitations but fall back on the same ideas that crime is a violation of the law and that laws require a government of some kind for their enactment.

TYPES OF CRIME

Crimes can be classified into various types. One group is the 'index' crimes, which are those where records of their occurrence are kept by the police and collected by justice agencies. They are offences which most individuals in the mainstream would regard as threats to the safety and security of property and persons (Welch et al. 1997). Perhaps the most famous index crime is the set of seven offences reported annually by the Federal Bureau of Investigation in the USA. These include four violent crimes, defined as such because they involve injury or the threat of injury to a person. They are: homicide or non-negligent manslaughter, forcible rape, aggravated assault (i.e. injuries that usually require medical attention) and robbery. Even though robbery is a theft, it is considered a violent crime because it entails direct contact between an offender and a victim, and a threat of force or the actual use of force by the offender. There are then three property crimes, which are larceny (i.e. theft), burglary (i.e. unlawful breaking and entering into a building) and motor vehicle theft.

A second set of crimes is considered 'organised crime'. Organised crime refers to crimes which resemble a normal business except that the product sold or distributed is in violation of the law. Some criminological theories, such as routine activities, situational crime prevention and social learning, among others, imply that all crimes are organised insofar as even criminals who act alone are rational decision makers and most things they steal are passed on to others for sale. However, some crimes are historically associated with organised crime groups, such as gambling, prostitution and trafficking/smuggling in drugs, humans, flora and fauna and anything else which is valuable and restricted by laws, tariffs and taxes.

A third class of criminal activities is known as 'white-collar' crimes because they are associated with business activities. Shoplifting by customers and theft of a business's assets by employees are certainly included here. However, far more serious and elusive to document are crimes committed by corporations, including land grabbing or land theft for ranching, mining and other forms of natural resource exploitation; exploitation of workers through violations of labour laws and workplace safety rules; and fraud associated with misrepresentation of profits and financial solvency with individual investors, other businesses and investment institutions (i.e. stock markets, financial institutions, stock holders) (Hartley 2008).

Crimes motivated by political, religious and other ideologies form a fourth class of crimes. Generally referred to as terrorism, these crimes are meant to protest about something or promote a cause through the threat of violence against individuals or specific targets (Harmon 2008). The July 2005 suicide attacks on buses and the London Underground subway system were committed by militant members of the Islamic faith. The ethnic cleansing perpetrated against the Islamic people of Bosnia by Christian Serbs (mostly Orthodox and Catholic) is an example of state-supported terrorism, based on both religious and ethnic tensions which were released by the break-up of Yugoslavia in the early 1990s. This 'ethnic cleansing' was also considered a war crime and some of those responsible were brought to trial and convicted before an international court of law. The religious cult known as Aum Shinrikyo released deadly saran nerve gas into the subway system of Tokyo, killing 13 people. The group's motivation was to hasten the time to the end of days, as described in the Christian Bible's 'Book of Revelations'.

There are thousands of examples of ideologically based crimes today. Each of these examples illustrates the complexity of defining terrorism as a crime. In fact, it could be claimed that these are acts of liberation and protest from the point of view of the terrorists. Sometimes the perpetrators are individuals or small groups acting on their own, and sometimes crimes known as terrorism are state-supported, such as the conflict in Bosnia. Sometimes the perpetrators are 'domestic', that is, they are people who grew up in the very society they target for a terrorist crime. Others are considered 'international' because they involve groups who are members of one country taking action against sites located in other countries. Regardless, the phrase 'homeland security' has become common parlance used by both criminologists and the public alike.

Homeland security also illustrates how actions come to be identified as criminal, how public funds spent on the construction of police apparatus and other criminal justice bureaucracies are justified, and how and what kinds of punishments are meted out to the guilty (see also *Deterrence and prevention*). Criminologists not only count up the prevalence and incidence of crime, and attempt to identify factors associated with people becoming involved in acts of terrorism, they also attempt to understand how actions are framed within societies as wrong and immoral. They use concepts related to governance and governmentality, such as 'moral panic' (Welch et al. 1997). Briefly, moral panic refers to the connection between the dominant ideologies of a society and how some actions come to be known as criminal (Cohen 1972). Moral panic can be described as a collective reaction to incidents which are perceived to threaten the social and moral order of the mainstream of a society, as framed by the media, law enforcement experts, politicians and others who hold power, especially political power (see also *Moral panics*).

The final definition of crime comes mostly from several interrelated communities of scholars in critical criminology and green criminology (see also *Environmental crime and green criminology*). It is how the concept of harm defines what actions by individuals, corporations and governments can be considered criminal. Its focus takes a more explicit view of crime as an expression of relationships of power associated with social class distinctions and inequalities, and of political authority and control. Harm is often used to frame the discussion based on the assumption that a definition of crime as the violation of a law is often too narrow because it fails to recognise that laws are often made by the powerful to maintain hegemonic control over those who are more subordinate. Also, a definition of crime as a harm informs efforts centred on restorative justice and peace making.

Crime can be defined in many ways. Each helps clarify the cultural, economic and political dynamics of a society, a society's definition of morality, and how a society maintains social order and exercises social control.

REFERENCES

Cohen, S. (1972) *Folk Devils and Moral Panics*. London: McGibbon & Kee.

Covington, D. (1995) *Salvation on Sand Mountain: Snake Handling and Redemption in Southern Appalachia*. Cambridge, MA: Da Capo Press.

Durkheim, E. (1965) *The Rules of the Sociological Method*. New York: Free Press.

Harmon, C. (2008) *Terrorism Today*. London: Routledge.

Hartley, R.D. (2008) *Corporate Crime: A Reference Handbook*. Santa Barbara, CA: ABC-CLIO.

Renzetti, C. (2012) 'Feminist perspectives in criminology', in W.S. DeKeseredy and M. Dragiewicz (eds) *Routledge Handbook of Critical Criminology*. London: Routledge, pp. 129–37.

Welch, M., Fenwick, M. and Roberts, M. (1997) 'Primary definitions of crime and moral panic: A content analysis of experts – Quotes in feature newspaper articles on crime', *Journal of Research in Crime and Delinquency*, 34(4): 474–94.

Definition: *The traditional (normative) definition of deviance focuses on violations of social norms that are widely shared in society. In contrast, the relativistic or reactivist definition of deviance emphasises the importance of the social audience and its reaction to deviance.*

The sociological study of deviance has focused largely on behaviours that violate legal norms (i.e. crime), as well as legal behaviours that are highly stigmatised or violate other social norms (e.g. eating disorders, self-harm, plagiarism, home schooling, exotic dancing). An insight into social norms is important for understanding the conceptual debates around deviance.

SOCIAL NORMS

Social norms are present in all societies and help to reinforce social order by shaping the boundaries for appropriate conduct. Social norms refer to formal or informal rules that attempt to guide and regulate people's behaviour in particular situations. In the early 1900s, William Sumner introduced a three-tier classification of social norms, i.e. folkways, mores and laws (Sumner 1994). Folkways refer to expected ways of behaving in routine social interactions, such as the style of dress that is appropriate at a funeral or holding a door open for an elderly person. Although folkways reflect societal norms, sanctions that are imposed for violating folkways are usually informal. Mores are a set of social norms that differ from folkways in that the former are influenced by strong moral values. Mores seek to constrain and regulate our behaviour, and several but not all mores violate the criminal law. Sumner argued that laws are mores that officially proscribe certain behaviours, and institutions that enforce laws are derived from strong societal mores. According to Sumner (1994), we learn about folkways, mores and laws through a process of repetition, i.e. we engage in certain behaviours and learn that certain behaviours result in informal or formal sanctions.

Social norms vary across cultures. Additionally, behaviour can be acceptable in one social setting and deemed to violate social norms in another. For example, dance styles, music genres and use of MDMA are appropriate behaviour in some club settings, yet would be considered to be inappropriate in other settings, including mainstream pubs. Social norms can also change over time. For example, tattoos were once socially restricted to the bodies of male members of particular subcultures, e.g. prisoners, gangs, military personnel (Kosut 2006). In some contemporary societies, tattoos have grown in popularity and have expanded to other social groups, including college athletes in the USA and women. This example demonstrates that some socially restricted behaviours can become more accepted and normalised over time.

DEBATING THE MEANING OF DEVIANCE

Negative deviance is generally considered to be behaviour that violates widely shared social norms and the criminal law. Other kinds of deviance violate social but not legal norms. Heckert and Heckert (2004) proposed a method to integrate different kinds of deviance, in relation to the nature of conformity and social reactions. Their typology included four categories: (1) negative deviance (nonconformity, negative social reaction, e.g. a number of crimes, extreme/unacceptable religious beliefs), (2) deviance admiration (nonconformity, positive reaction, e.g. the 'class clown'), (3) rate busting (over-conformity, negative social reaction, e.g. peer rejection of children who are exceptionally intelligent), and (4) positive deviance (over-conformity, positive social reaction, e.g. an individual who saves the life of another).

Social scientists have debated the conceptualisation of negative deviance, and definitions generally incorporate normative or relativistic/reactionist dimensions (Orcutt 2004). The traditional view of deviance reflects a normative perspective that assumes a general consensus about behaviours deemed to be right and wrong; deviance is behaviour that violates these norms. Durkheim (1982) argued that deviance exists in all societies and can be beneficial because it reinforces moral boundaries and strengthens societal bonds. The relativistic perspective challenges the assumption of public consensus regarding social norms. Normative views about deviance do not recognise power differentials in society, and how these might shape social and legal reactions to deviance. The relativistic perspective posits that consensus can vary across societal groups and subcultures, although some scholars have acknowledged strong consensus for some social norms – for example, we are expected to not commit murder (Schur 1974). The relativistic perspective departs from normative assumptions in that it emphasises the importance of the social audience and how it responds or reacts to deviance (Orcutt 2004). In other words, an act is only deviant because others define or label it as such (Becker 1963). The social audience includes individuals, groups or societal institutions that have the power to define and exert control over deviance. According to Becker (1963), the audience reaction is influenced greatly by moral entrepreneurs who invoke the behavioural standards of the ruling class on people or groups with less power in society. The nature and extent of social reaction varies, thus relativistic arguments suggest that deviance is socially constructed (see also *Social construction of crime and deviance*). In contrast, the normative view of deviance is grounded in positivism. Scholars' conceptual perspectives of deviance generally influence their methodological preferences for studying it (see also *Researching crime*).

DEVIANT LABELS

The relativistic view of deviance is closely tied to the labelling perspective, which assumes that individuals who are labelled deviant (e.g. 'criminal', 'delinquent', 'hood', 'felon', 'addict', 'junkie') can internalise the label and subsequently act in a manner that is consistent with the label (secondary deviance). The negative label becomes the 'master status' for the individual, i.e. the most salient characteristic that defines an individual's identity. This status makes it difficult to transform the identity even when individuals are no longer involved in the behaviour. The label-ling process was highlighted in a covert observational study by David Rosenhan (1973) . Eight individuals, including the author, were admitted to psychiatric hos-pitals after pretending to experience symptoms that were consistent with schizophrenia (e.g. hearing voices). Following admittance, the 'pseudopatients' desisted from abnormal behaviours although hospital staff continued to view them as mentally ill. Hospital stays ranged from 7 to 52 days, during which the pseudo-patients received daily medications that were designed to control their thoughts and behaviours (only two of approximately 2100 tablets were consumed). Pseudopatients were released from hospital with a diagnosis of schizophrenia in remission. Rosenhan concluded that the power of the deviant label makes it dif-ficult to differentiate between the 'sane' and 'insane' in psychiatric hospitals.

CRITIQUE OF THE LABELLING PERSPECTIVE

In the 1960s and 1970s, scholars engaged in considerable debate over the label-ling perspective. Critics argued that the perspective ignores other motivations for engaging in secondary deviance, such as profit or pleasure from engaging in rule breaking. Others have suggested that the labelling perspective neglects the inter-action between the deviant so labelled and the social audience which reacts to the deviance (Hagan 1973). Additionally, scholars noted that some individuals do not passively accept the deviant label; rather, individuals who are labelled deviant can respond in various ways, including modifying their behaviour or rejecting the deviant label (Rogers and Buffalo 1974). Despite these criticisms, the implications of labelling have to some extent contributed to changes in criminal justice and mental health practices. For example, diversion and de-institutionalisation are initiatives that are consistent with the principles of the labelling perspective.

THE DECLINE OF THE SOCIOLOGY OF DEVIANCE?

Sociological scholarship in the field of deviance flourished in the 1960s and early 1970s, with major contributions from writers in the USA such as Howard Becker and Edwin Schur. The field also benefitted from scholars in Britain, including Jock Young, Stanley Cohen and faculty affiliated with the Centre for Contemporary Cultural Studies at Birmingham University. Much of the Centre's work focused on 'deviant subcultures' within a Marxist context. Diverse societal reaction to 'deviant subcultures' was highlighted by William Chambliss (1973) in his study of the 'saints' and the 'roughnecks'. Chambliss demonstrated the importance of institutional and community power that affected the ability to apply deviant labels and resist the same. Still, Sumner (1994) argued that the major scholarly contributions from the sociology of deviance had peaked by 1975, with considerably less scholarly interest in deviance after that time. The diminishing interest in deviance has been attributed to several factors, including the rise of criminology as a discipline with a focus on behaviours that violate legal norms (i.e. crime) and the theoretical difficulties involved in attempting to explain legal and illegal behaviours. Although scholars have found some support for Sumner's claims, some researchers continue to focus on the sociology of deviance, and a leading journal (*Deviant Behavior*) has published articles from the field since 1979.

REFERENCES

Becker, H.S. (1963) *Outsiders: Studies in the Sociology of Deviance*. New York: Free Press.

Chambliss, W. J. (1973) 'The Saints and the Roughnecks', *Society*, 11: 24–31.

Durkheim, E. (1982) *The Rules of Sociological Method*. New York: Free Press.

Hagen, J. (1973) 'Labeling and deviance: A case study in the sociology of the interesting.' *Social Problems*, 20 (Spring): 447–58.

Heckert, A. and Heckert, D. (2004) 'Using an integrated typology of deviance to analyze ten common norms of the US middle class', *Sociological Quarterly*, 45: 209–28.

Kosut, M. (2006) 'Mad artists and tattooed perverts: Deviant discourse and the social construction of cultural categories', *Deviant Behavior*, 27: 73–95.

Orcutt, J.D. (2004) Sociological Viewpoints on Deviance and Social Control, Part 1: Sociological Definitions of Deviance. Available at: http://deviance.socprobs.net/Unit_1/Page_1.htm (accessed 15/07/14).

Rogers, J.W. and Buffalo, M.D. (1974) 'Fighting back: Nine modes of adaptation to a deviant label', *Social Problems*, 22: 101–18.

Rosenhan, D.L. (1973) 'On being sane in insane places', *Science*, 179: 250–8.

Schur, E.M. (1974) *Radical Non Intervention: Rethinking the Delinquency Problem*. Englewood Cliffs, NJ: Prentice-Hall.

Sumner, C. (1994) *The Sociology of Deviance: An Obituary*. New York: Continuum.

3 Crime in Pre-industrial, Pre-modern and Post-modern Societies

Definition: *Actions that violate social norms, with such violations attracting state sanctions or punishments (see* Crime *and* Deviance *and also* Punishment*), are referred to as crimes. Exactly what constitutes a crime is difficult to define and quantify, as criminal actions vary within societies, across societies and across time. Thus, it is important to view crime in specific socio-historical periods. The three main periods examined by historical criminologists are termed pre-industrial, pre-modern and post-modern.* **Pre-industrial** *generally refers to the time period before 1750 where crime and punishment were predominantly situated within communities.*

> *Following industrialisation and the Enlightenment period, crime and punishment became more centralised with states taking on stronger roles in this regard. This time period is generally referred to as **pre-modern**, with the prevailing beliefs at the time being those of progression and rationality. Thus, this period saw the development of codified laws and theories of crime and punishment. **Post-modern** thought questions the rationalities of pre-modern proponents, challenging the claims of progression and the development of more humane mechanisms for crime control.*

With crime being a slippery concept, criminology has largely attempted to understand the nexus between crime, society and punishment with historical criminology exploring the transitions that occur between the three. Much attention in this field has been paid to how changes in law, crime and punishment relate to the socio-economic transition from feudalism to capitalism (Herrup 1985). The general consensus is that the Industrial Revolution produced significant changes to how crime was understood, practised and governed. From 1750 onwards, new institutions developed to manage law and order. With the expanding capitalist market requiring a legal system that was predictable, systematic and regular, abstract scales of justice were replaced by codified systems, offering more precise correspondence between crime and punishment (O'Brien 1978).

PRE-MODERN CRIME

Two schools of thought emerged regarding modern crime and criminal justice. Enlightenment or Whiggish histories presented change as 'reform' motivated by humanitarian concerns and read as a story of incremental progress and scientific knowledge succeeding over barbarity and irrationality (Cohen 1985). In early histories, the industrial age was considered to have initiated dramatic social progress along moral and behavioural lines. The Enlightenment represented a source of civilisation and escape from an oppressive rural order (Lane 1974).

Pre-modern criminal justice was characterised as retributive, with visible and enduring deterrents to crime. Proportionality to crime was ignored with practices reliant on capital and corporal punishment. Justice was often haphazard, local, irregular and unsystematic. There was also an absence of formal legal status for individuals during this period. Rights were not recognised as universal, with any that did exist linked to individual station and class. Power was typically in the hands of elite interests and maintained through repression, tradition and custom.

Pre-modern systems were largely encountered in the rural societies of medieval Europe. They are described as 'community law' systems and contrasted with 'state law'. Common criminal acts were minor acts of theft or violence, typically against social equals. Under community law, the aggrieved victim retained control of the prosecution process with formal court action avoided through extrajudicial settlements and compensation. The objective of the process was restoration of local peace.

The other emphasis of early histories of criminal justice was on the idea that pre-modern systems lacked rationality, with the religious character of criminal law in pre-industrial societies highlighted. In Europe during the medieval period, it was difficult to distinguish between religious and secular regulation with the church heavily influencing state affairs. Crime was often defined in terms of spiritual harm and a transgression against God and Christian society.

CRITICAL PERSPECTIVES

In contrast with pre-modern accounts of criminal justice, socialist or left-leaning writers were more critical of the outcomes of this historical transition. Adopting a more romantic view of the pre-modern period, the transition from rural village or farm to city was regarded as a descent into violence, uncivil behaviour and crime. Early criminologists linked crime and social disorder to population increases, poverty, urbanisation and lack of education. Crime was localised by both left- and right-wing commentators to one class – the working class. The criminal was a worker without religion, morals or job (O'Brien 1978).

Under the new class structure, brought about through industrialisation, crime changed, becoming more random, entrepreneurial and premeditated. Fear of crime among the middle and upper classes produced further extensions to the state's control of justice, with the creation of prisons and the police (Herrup 1985: 160). This fear grew with the increase of the working class. Often, it was the activities of the working class that became criminal. The historian E.P. Thompson's classic *Whigs and Hunters* (1975) and *Albion's Fatal Tree* (Hay et al. 1975) showed that 'social' activities constituted as criminal by authorities were often considered legal or justifiable by some sections of the populace during the eighteenth and nineteenth centuries.

MODERN EUROPE

The nation states that emerged in modern Europe laid claim to a monopoly of legitimate, organised violence in their borders and over time most achieved levels of pacification and authority which gave substance to this claim. The new forms of criminal justice that emerged were bureaucratic, providing a more systematic method of judicial administration. The French police emerged in 1800 and the British Metropolitan Police in 1829. Both became models for the creation of police systems throughout the world.

The shift in power from monarch to the middle classes in the Early Modern period also saw the development of new institutions such as parliaments. The shift away from ecclesiastical authority served to reinforce the state's public authority. Eventually, the state became the only agency which could legitimately punish offenders. Crime was conceptualised as an offence against the state and therefore society. All crimes were deemed antisocial rather than personal, with the uniformity of process emphasised. Because crime was a public event, private compensation became a secondary consideration.

In the modern world, crime became a matter for public agencies and states. Justice was based on the 'social contract', where individuals gave up certain rights in return for state protection of their persons and property (known as the 'rule of law'). The ideals of universal and individual rights, rather than customary and traditional bonds and hereditary privilege, were central to the new bourgeois order. Justice was understood in terms of relationships between states and offenders (Herrup 1985: 160). The modern system of corrections became a specialised and differentiated one – formally independent of other normative systems and increasingly distinct from other systems of legal regulation (see also *The criminal justice system*). It was largely state controlled and administered by professional bureaucracies exercising legally sanctioned powers over individual offenders (Garland 1995: 184).

POSTMODERN

Post-modern accounts of the history of the criminal justice system and crime have continued to hold a negative or ambivalent attitude towards the Enlightenment tradition. The post-modern argument can be seen in Malcolm Feeley and Jonathan Simon's work *The New Penology* (1992), which documents the collapse of grand narratives of penal reform and progress. As with earlier leftist criticism, post-modernists see a darker side to the supposed advance of humanity and reason. The French philosopher Michel Foucault (1975), in documenting the shift from retribution to rehabilitation, argued that power merely ceased to be directed at the body of the criminal and instead targeted the mind and spirit (see also *Social control, governance and governmentality*). According to these accounts, the modernist project was a failure, which was intrusive and authoritarian.

In contrast to traditional criminology, this approach no longer takes the state and its agencies to be primary or proximate actors in the business of crime control. The criminal subject it depicts is not the poorly socialised misfit in need of assistance, but instead an illicit, opportunistic consumer, whose access to social goods must be barred. This criminal figure – described as the situational man – lacks a strong moral compass or effective internal controls, aside from the capacity for rationale calculation and a will to pleasure (see also *Crime and theory*).

Post-modern accounts have their origins in 1970s disillusionment with state-central criminal justice systems and advocacy for liberal reform. For a time, the new state forces, along with the institutions of civil society, succeeded in reducing crime and maintaining a high degree of order. But having taken over the functions and responsibilities that had once belonged to civil society, in the mid-twentieth century the state was faced with immobility to deliver the expected levels of control of criminal conduct. The idea that the west was experiencing unprecedented high rates of property and violent crime, along with the widespread fear of crime, was pervasive in political, media and cultural presentation of crime. Crime was no longer considered to be an unexpected aberration, but its threat had become a routine part of modern consciousness, an everyday risk to be assessed and another modern-day danger to be normalised and routinised over time (see also *Normalisation*).

JUSTICE REFORM

The early justice reform movement was a reaction to the 'crisis of penal modernism', captured in nihilistic slogans like 'nothing works', indicating the erosion of the myth that the sovereign state is capable of providing security, law and order within its territorial boundaries.

By the 1980s, and for the first time in 200 years, no guiding vision or coherent philosophy was steering penal policy in most western nations. Local initiatives dominated, characterised by low-level ambitions. There was less interest in criminological depth and criminological truth, such as traits of an offender's psychology and biography, and more concern with surface phenomena, such as choices, opportunities and rational calculations. Offenders were conceived of as being free, rational and responsible individuals. Genetic, neurological and biological perspectives, once considered archaic, made ground (Garland 1995: 195).

CONCLUSION

The notion of a shift from modernist to post-modern criminal justice has been debated by criminologists. David Garland (1995) has argued that post-modernism has not been well defined in criminology, claiming the term to be misleading if it involves some distinct break from modernism. Rather, it is better to consider recent changes in terms of shifting emphasis and mutations of modernism. For Garland, many enlightenment or modern ideals remain central considerations of contemporary criminal justice systems. For example, much current criminal justice thought draws on utilitarian and neoclassical economics. Modernity may be best considered a dynamic historical process, rather than a static stage of development.

Garland argues that the normalising apparatus of modernity grows more extensive and diffuse, even if what guides it is now different. He sees more a shift in modernist ideals rather than an end to the modernist project, with a managerialist ethos influencing contemporary criminal justice projects (Garland 1995). The move has been from a naive project of enthusiasm and optimism to more mature, informed and ambivalent understandings of criminal justice practices, with the modernist project having come to understand itself better through a process of disillusionment and adjustment.

Table 3.1 (adapted from Cohen 1985) provides a useful summary of key shifts in social control.

Table 3.1 Key shifts in social control

	Pre-modern	Modern	Post-modern
Role of state	Weak, decentralised, arbitrary	Strong, centralised, rationalised	Minimalist state, but often with greater reach and controls
Space of control	Community	Closed institutions	Partial decarceration: old institutions with new forms of community control
Focus of control	Undifferentiated	Concentrated	Dispersed and diffuse
Target of control	External: the body	Internal: the mind	Body and mind

	Pre-modern	Modern	Post-modern
Status of criminal justice system	Not established or criminal law only one form of social control	Monopoly, but supplemented by new systems	Questioned but not weakened and alternative systems expanded
Role of professionals	Not present	Established and strengthened	Questioned but often further extended
Framework of punishment	Moralistic	Classical and positivist	Classical and positivist aspects remain, but are revised
Mode of control	Inclusive	Exclusive and stigmatising	Mixed: retributive aspect remains, but with an emphasis on restorative justice

REFERENCES

Cohen, S. (1985) *Visions of Social Control: Crime, Punishment and Classification*. Cambridge: Polity Press.

Feeley, M.M. and Simon, J. (1992) The New Penology: Notes on the Emerging Strategy of Corrections and its Implications. Available at: http://scholarship.law.berkeley.edu/facpubs/718 (date accessed 17/02/12).

Foucault, M. (1977) *Discipline and Punish: the Birth of the Prison*. London: Allen Lane.

Garland, D. (1995) 'Penal modernism and postmodernism', in T. Blomberg and S. Cohen (eds) *Punishment and Social Control: Essays in Honour of Sheldon L. Messinger*. New York: De Gruyter.

Hay, D., Linebaugh, P. and Thompson, E.P. (eds) (1975) *Albion's Fatal Tree: Crime and Society in Eighteenth Century England*. New York: Pantheon Books.

Herrup, C. (1985) 'Crime, law and society: A review article', *Comparative Studies in Society and History*, 27(1): 159–70.

Lane, R. (1974) 'Crime and the Industrial Revolution: British and American views', *Journal of Social History*, 7(3): 287–303.

O'Brien, P. (1978) 'Crime and punishment as historical problem', *Journal of Social History*, 11: 508–20. Reproduced in R. Weiss (ed) (1999) *Social History of Crime, Policing and Punishment*, Aldershot/Brookfield/Singapore/Sydney: Ashgate, pp. 403–16.

Thompson, E.P. (1975) *Whigs and Hunters: The Origin of the Black Act*. New York: Pantheon Books.

4 The Criminal Justice System

Definition: The **criminal justice system** in common law countries has two key purposes. The first is to prevent and reduce crime for the protection of the community

(Continued)

(Continued)

and includes policies and practices to deter and reform offenders. The second is symbolic and based on moral principles and aims to set an example of those who break the law and subsequently offend against commonly accepted social and cultural codes of right and wrong behaviour (Daly 2012: 390). Ideologically, laws serve as part of the normative context within which individuals' personal values and beliefs take shape and law enforcement is seen to operate (Tonry and Farrington 1995: 3–5). Criminal justice systems in western jurisdictions are generally composed of three elements – police, courts and corrections.

COMPARATIVE CRIMINAL JUSTICE

Historically and cross-culturally, there is significant variation in the structure, organisation and goals of criminal justice systems. Differences are typically grounded in social context. For example, folk or communal societies are likely to differ significantly from urbanised, industrial or bureaucratic societies. One tendency in later societies is that towards a specialisation and rationalisation of criminal justice. Despite differences, it is common to categorise criminal justice systems in terms of policing, adjudication and corrections. Legal traditions also differ internationally, with common law prevailing in jurisdictions which were once part of the British Empire, civil law prevalent in Continental Europe and its former colonies, Islamic law practised to various extents in Muslim countries, and socialist law influential and current in former Marxist-Leninist states.

THE ROLE OF POLICE

Morally, crime is often seen as a failure on the part of wrongdoers and law enforcement, and the imposition of sanctions expressing condemnation of offenders is seen as the only morally appropriate policy for crime prevention. The process of criminal justice typically begins with a report to police whose role it is to prevent crime, investigate, detect, maintain public order, make arrests and initiate prosecutions (Prenzler and Sarre 2009). After the initial reporting to police, there is a 'funnelling' or narrowing process through criminal justice systems and only a minority of cases continue through all stages to incarceration or other punishments.

Those problems which attract most police attention are usually those perceived as interfering with public order, or those which are disruptive to the peace of the community. Police practices attract criticism because, intentionally or not, they target those groups which are the most likely to spend their leisure time occupying public spaces, such as young people and the unemployed. Some ethnic or Indigenous groups may also attract unwarranted police attention due to public perceptions that they are more likely to commit crime (Hogg and Carrington 2006).

Police are the primary point of contact between citizens and the law and have an enormous impact on the lives of those in the community (McCulloch 2008: 206). The role of police is often contextual, changeable and situational, and is sometimes quite ambiguous. Consequently, police are not always able to simply 'follow the rules', but sometimes need to exercise discretion in their decision making of what course of action to take to achieve the goals of law and order (Findlay 2003).

POLICE DISCRETION

Police discretion is accepted as an essential part of organisational police practice to balance the constraints of legal regulation with the imperatives of crime control. Discretion allows police some limited decision-making powers regarding how to respond to a range of suspicious, observed or reported events. The scope police have for discretion includes ignoring the complaint or offence, issuing a warning or caution or proceeding with arrest, or stepping outside of the normal boundaries of law in order to successfully carry out their work. To some extent, discretion gives police the power to interpret justice as they see fit and this may sometimes include selectiveness in decision making, discrimination and even an abuse of power (Findlay 2003: 70–3). This can occur if law enforcement is used selectively for the surveillance of and intervention in particular groups, especially those who are most visible (McCulloch 2008: 206–7).

When police discretion is used in discriminatory ways, there are risks of abuse of power and corruption. Police corruption tends to be fostered within a police culture of cynical, suspicious attitudes, masculinity and sexism, and a strong sense of solidarity with other police officers (Chan 2008: 221). Police abuse of power can take a number of different forms, including verbal abuse, racist comments, sexist remarks to women, physical and sexual intimidation, fabrication of evidence, inventing charges, brutality and physical violence to obtain 'admissions' from those accused. Corruption generally involves taking advantage of opportunities for personal gain, for example from seized stolen property, drugs and drug money, and accepting bribes. Police abuses can be sanctioned through criminal laws, although these are not always applied (McCulloch 2008: 207–11).

COURTS AND SENTENCING

In western jurisdictions, common law criminal justice systems are based on an adversarial approach where the state is in contest with accused persons who are presumed innocent until proven guilty. Systems are underpinned by the 'rule of law', which assumes all people are equal in the eyes of the law, including those who make the laws. In countries like Australia, a key principle of the rule of law is a 'separation of powers', which refers to a separation between parliament as the authority that enacts the law, the judiciary as the authority that interprets the law, and the executive which administers the law (White and Perrone 1996: 76). This separation prevents a conflict of interest between powers that make laws, interpret laws and administer laws, and helps ensure the partiality of evidence presented by police to the courts (Prenzler and Sarre 2009: 262).

When a suspect is charged, the courts decide whether they should be released on bail or detained in custody. Factors influencing these decisions are whether or not the person is a danger to the community and/or whether they are likely to abscond. Once the matter proceeds to a court, police collect evidence such as exhibits and witness statements and submit them to the court in presentation of a case against the alleged offender. If the defendant pleads not guilty, the case against them will proceed to trial and the onus will be on the prosecution to prove the defendant's guilt beyond reasonable doubt. After admitting guilt or being found guilty by a court, a magistrate or judge will impose a sentence as penalty for the wrongdoing. Generally, there are prescribed sentences for offences with punishment within a range between minimum and maximum. The circumstances and seriousness of offences are crucial elements when deciding appropriate sentences.

PUNISHMENT

Since the 1970s, there has been a growth in more punitive approaches to law and order, such as mandatory sentencing, and an increasing reliance on incarceration as a form of punishment (see also *Punishment*). Comparative criminology has noted that developing countries often have harsher sentencing, and even when it comes to capital punishment resort to more violent modes of execution than developed countries. The recent shift in the west towards harsher prison penalties tends to impact on profoundly on poor and socially marginalised offenders, including some racial and ethnic groups who are more likely to commit the sorts of offences covered by tighter regulations and punitive sentencing practices such as mandatory sentencing (Tonry 1994). Increases in prisoner numbers globally are not simply the result of more crime being committed, but can be attributed to combined factors including legislative and policy changes. These changes include trends towards holding people in custody while awaiting trial, an expanded use of imprisonment for those who breach community-based orders, more offenders with no previous custodial history being jailed for first offences, and increases in the average length of prison sentences (Garland 2001).

DECARCERATION AND DIVERSION

While there has been an emphasis on harsher forms of punishment in the past three decades or so, there have also been calls to reduce the impact of criminal justice systems on offenders, particularly young people. With growing recognition of the harm caused by stigmatisation for young people who come into contact with criminal justice interventions, there has been an increased use of decarceration and diversion in western nations and some Asian countries (Wing et al. 2006). Governments choosing to adopt a policy of reducing prison numbers do so for a variety of reasons, including cost savings, a belief that prison creates criminality, public opinion, and to relieve over-burdened criminal justice systems (Heseltine 2012: 508).

Decarceration includes, but is not limited to, community-based and non-custodial sentencing options, such as probation, community work, parole, periodic detention, good behaviour bonds, suspended sentences and home detention. Some of these approaches are more effective than others and are implemented due to the advantages they have over imprisonment. Offenders can undertake rehabilitation programmes aimed at reducing offending without the stigmatising and labelling effects of prison (see also *Rehabilitation*); this strategy may prove more effective in deterring crime in the long term, particularly for young people (Bargen 2001).

Diversion can include police cautioning, warnings and justice conferencing which is based on the philosophy and principles of restorative justice. The restorative model encourages community participation, limiting the involvement of professionals and maintaining offender responsibility for the harms caused to victims. While sentencing within the criminal justice system excludes offenders from society, restorative models aim to ensure offenders remain part of their community (Hudson 2002) and maintain family, social and employment relationships, rather than breaking these ties through imprisonment.

REFERENCES

Bargen, J. (2001) 'Diverting ATSI young offenders from court and custody in New South Wales: Practices, perspectives and possibilities under the Young Offenders Act 1997.' Paper presented at the Best Practice Interventions in Corrections for Indigenous People conference convened by the Australian Institute of Criminology, Sydney, 8–9 October.

Chan, J. (2008) 'Police culture: A brief history of a concept', in T. Anthony and C. Cunneen (eds) *The Critical Criminology Companion*. Sydney: Hawkins Press, pp. 218–27.

Daly, K. (2012) 'Aims of the criminal justice system', in M. Marmo, W. de Lint and D. Palmer (eds) *Crime and Justice: A Guide to Criminology*, 4th edn. Sydney: Thomson Reuters, pp. 389–406.

Findlay, M. (2003) *Introducing Policing*. Melbourne: Oxford University Press.

Garland, D. (2001) *The Culture of Control: Crime and Social Order in Contemporary Society*. Chicago: University of Chicago Press.

Heseltine, K. (2012) 'Community-based corrections', in M. Marmo, W. de Lint and D. Palmer (eds) *Crime and Justice: A Guide to Criminology*, 4th edn. Sydney: Thomson Reuters, pp. 507–26.

Hogg, R. and Carrington, K. (2006) *Policing the Rural Crisis*. Sydney: Federation Press.

Hudson, B. (2002) 'Restorative justice and gendered violence', *British Journal of Criminology*, 42: 616–34.

McCulloch, J. (2008) 'Key issues in a critical approach to policing', in T. Anthony and C. Cunneen (eds) *The Critical Companion*. Sydney: Hawkins Press, pp. 206–17.

Prenzler, T. and Sarre, R. (2009) 'The criminal justice system', in H. Hayes and T. Prenzler (eds) *Introduction to Crime and Criminology*. Sydney: Pearson Education Australia, pp. 259–73.

Tonry, M. (1994) 'Racial disproportions in US prisons', *British Journal of Criminology*, 34: 97–115.

Tonry, M. and Farrington, D.P. (1995) 'Strategic approaches to crime prevention', in M. Tonry and D.P. Farrington (eds) *Building a Safer Society: Strategic Approaches to Crime Prevention*. Chicago: University of Chicago Press, pp. 1–20.

White, R. and Perrone, S. (1996) 'Law, courts and the legal profession', in *Crime and Social Control*. Melbourne: Oxford University Press, pp. 64–80.

Wing, T., Maxwell, G. and Wong, D. (2006) 'Diversion from youth courts in five Asia Pacific jurisdictions: Welfare or restorative solutions', *International Journal of Offender Therapy and Comparative Criminology*, 50(1): 5–20.

> **Definition**: In order for any group, regardless of how large it is, to live together, a set of rules or 'norms' is required to maintain relative peace and harmony. Norms can be explicit (in the form of rules and laws) or implicit (through beliefs, shared meanings and understandings of how things are). Social order is maintained when individuals conform to these shared norms. **Deviancy** occurs when people step outside these rules or norms. In some cases, when the deviancy is considered serious enough, it will be constituted as a **crime**. Actions that are viewed as crimes attract state sanctions such as fines, incarceration and, in some cases, corporal punishments like execution.

Everyone commits crime, but only some people come to be known as 'criminals'. This is because reactions to crime are highly variable. Two people can commit an identical criminal act, but the social reactions to the act are likely to vary. For example, one person may be imprisoned for the act, while the other person may suffer a lesser penalty or no penalty at all. Activities considered deviant or criminal in some contexts are even rewarded in other contexts. Take, for example, terrorism. It has been noted that 'one person's terrorist is another person's freedom fighter'.

We can use the death of another as an excellent example to demonstrate this paradox. In some cases, it might be viewed as murder, homicide or accidental death. Moreover, not all actions resulting in the death of another are even criminalised. Take, for example, deaths that occur due to medical, workplace and road accidents. Then we must add to this those actions that are authorised, excused and sanctioned. Soldiers operating during times of war are authorised to take the lives of others. Some states sanction the killing of their citizens for crimes considered so serious that offenders forfeit their lives as punishment for these acts. And some actions are often excused, such as self-defence.

SOCIAL CONSTRUCTIONISM

In order to understand crime and deviance, we need to focus our attention on how actions are defined. Social constructionism can explain why some potentially harmful acts are prohibited by criminal law while others are not. In the same instance, some behaviour may be relatively inoffensive or harmless, but is illegal.

Social constructionism begins with the simple premise that what is considered criminal is historically and culturally variable. Therefore, what is criminologically significant need not be the criminal act or even the behaviour of the actor, but the social reaction to that act and actor. Reactions to deviance and crime depend not only on the violation of a rule or law, but on who breaks it, the time and place at which it is broken and the degree to which others are motivated or have the authority to make sanctions. This helps to explain why two people might commit the same offence, but the responses to that offence may vary.

The development of social constructionism

Early criminology was reluctant to question definitions of crime and criminals. There was a broad consensus that behaviours, groups and individuals legally defined as criminal were, indeed, socially problematic. Social constructionist perspectives on crime largely emerged within sociological traditions, especially those pertaining to the sociology of deviance or law. In various works the French sociologist Emile Durkheim (1958–1917) famously questioned the notion that crime was necessarily problematic by arguing that crime could be socially 'functional' (see also *Crime and theory*). Durkheim argued that collective sentiments of crime and deviance were open to change and variation, so that 'nothing is good infinitely and without limits'. As such, Durkheim was one of the first social theorists to focus attention on crime as a product of diverse social conditions. Extreme and exaggerated responses to crime can be explained in this context.

While Durkheim's work may have opened a space for consideration of social constructionist ideas, by showing that crime was not pre-social, it was not until the 1960s and 1970s that constructionist ideas were widely deployed in studies of deviance and crime. In terms of its philosophical underpinnings, Edmund Husserl's (1859–1838) transcendental phenomenology is important to the development of social constructionism, as he argued that in acting towards objects as though they are real, we constitute them as real.

Following this tradition, Alfred Shutz (1899–1959) showed reality to be collectively interpreted, producing multiple interpretations. These ideas were popularised in sociology through the work of Berger and Luckmann (1966), who examined how reality was at once objective and external to the individual, while also a product of social interaction. Erving Goffman's (1922–82) works, such as *The Presentation of Self in Everyday Life* (1959) and *Stigma* (1963), helped to popularise this approach to the study of deviance and examined how a sense of self arises through social interaction.

DEVIANCE

Two areas of deviance which have attracted sustained interest from social constructionists are mental health and human sexuality. Work in these areas has focused on how various forms of social deviance were increasingly subject to medical definitions and formal social controls, including criminal regulation, during modernity (Conrad and Schneider 1992).

A branch of social constructionism that has held considerable influence within criminology has been referred to as 'labelling theories'. Howard Becker (1964) argued that social groups define problems and organise specific responses to problems. The deviant or criminal is someone to whom a label has successfully been applied, marking them as socially problematic. Labelling theories are also concerned with what happens to people after they are defined as deviant.

Drawing on labelling perspectives, Edwin Lemert (1967) distinguished between primary and secondary deviation. He argued that most people engage in primary deviation which is situational and rationalised and which usually does not alter their identity. However, secondary deviation occurs in response to the sanctions applied from primary deviations, escalating the individual's deviant or criminal behaviour. The offender starts to identify with the label. Thus, labelling may have a range of consequences on those labelled, which may affect their life chances and access to legitimate activities and social resources. In recent times, the social constructionist perspective provided renewed impetus through post-structuralism, especially through the writings of Michel Foucault (1926–84).

PROBLEM SOLVING OR ANALYSIS

A useful distinction might be between problem 'solving' (realists) and problem 'analysis' (constructionists). Problem analysis is concerned with providing an account of the definitional activities of people. Social problem analysis therefore accounts for the emergence and maintenance of claim making about such things as crime and deviance. The issue here is the viability of claims, rather than assessing the validity of claims, such as why some conditions are deemed problematic and others are not. Although harmful conditions exist, they will not be constituted as social problems until collectively defined as such. Thus, interests, resources and legitimacy have a role in the constitution of social problems.

For social constructions, so-called 'facts' about crime, including statistics, are deemed 'truth claims' because they purport to represent the truth of something, rendering invisible their constructed nature (Schneider 1985). When it comes to defining crime, some individuals or groups have more ability (power and/or authority) to create laws than others, such as the criminologist over the criminal. Therefore, even though there is some social consensus on what activities represent deviancy and criminality, definitional practices are the products of power relations, with some groups having a greater ability to define reality according to their own interests.

In contrast to problem analysis, problem solvers (realists) argue 'that crime is unproblematically a "problem" and that people's perceptions are unproblematically "real"' (Holloway and Jefferson 1997: 257). The fear of crime is a phenomenon that has developed in modern societies with widespread public concern over crime, even when rates indicate it to be on the decline. The social reaction to crime amplifies the significance of original violations A significant body of literature has developed around the fear of crime, much of which is devoted to the causes of crime, vulnerability and victimisation, measurement of fear, and policies to reduce fear (see also *Fear and the fear of crime*). The bulk of this work has been firmly entrenched in 'problem-solving' traditions in sociology and criminology.

In contrast, constructionists would investigate fear of crime as a comparative analysis of perceptions of disorganisation and dangerousness. Worries and talk about crime are rarely a reflection of objective risks or behavioural changes, but are bound up in wider contexts of meaning and significance, usually around questions of order and control. Constructionists avoid reifying fear of crime as though it were manifestly separate to the social context in which it is expressed. Although most social constructionists hold that some reality exists, some, labelled 'hard', hold a more relativistic position, subjecting their own analysis to constructionist critiques. They argue that reality (acts, behaviours, events) has no existence beyond the human mind.

REFERENCES

Becker, H. (ed.) (1964) *The Other Side: Perspectives on Deviance*. London: Collier-Macmillan.

Berger, P. and Luckmann, T. (1966) *The Social Construction of Reality: A Treatise on the Sociology of Knowledge*. London: Allen Lane.

Conrad, P. and Schneider, J.W. (1992) *Deviance and Medicalization: From Badness to Sickness*. Philadelphia, PA: Temple University Press.

Goffman, E. (1959) *The Presentation of Self in Everyday Life*. New York: Doubleday Anchor.

Goffman, E. (1963) *Stigma: Notes on the Management of Spoiled Identity*. London: Penguin.

Holloway, W. and Jefferson, T. (1997) 'The risk society in an age of anxiety: Situating fear of crime', *British Journal of Sociology*, 48(2): 255–66.

Lemert, E. (1967) *Human Deviance, Social Problems and Social Control*. Englewood Cliffs, NJ: Prentice-Hall.

Schneider, J.W. (1985) 'Social problems theory: The constructionist view', *Annual Review of Sociology*, 11: 209–29.

.... 6 Crime and Theory ....

> **Definition**: *Criminological theories seek to explain criminal behaviour and crime or the response to these phenomena.*

Theories attempt to explain the relationship between two or more phenomena. Similar to other social sciences, causation is interpreted in terms of likelihood, i.e. A *generally* leads to B. Theories must be stated in a way that allows them to be tested by research conducted in different settings. Understanding the cultural reach of criminological theory is important; factors contributing to crime in one culture can differ from those that explain crime in another. The benefits of theory are that it can increase our understanding of crime and, in some instances, can inform public policy.

Most criminological theories attempt to explain street crime (see also *State crime; White-collar/middle-class and corporate-class crime*); however, the diversity of criminal behaviour means that one single theory is unlikely to explain all criminal acts. Dozens of criminological theories have been proposed and there are different ways to classify theories, such as by paradigms (e.g. positivism versus classical; social consensus or conflict), levels of analysis (e.g. macro and micro), chronologically and by disciplinary focus. In this section, we draw on a selection of historical and contemporary theories that have shaped the discipline of criminology.

INDIVIDUALS AS RATIONAL ACTORS

The Classical School of Criminology emerged in the 1700s and constituted a shift in criminological thought (see also *Crime in pre-industrial, pre-modern and post-modern societies*). The School's basic premise was that human behaviour derives from free will, i.e. individuals were assumed to be rational thinkers and motivated by hedonism. Jeremy Bentham and Cesare Beccaria were particularly influential in their critique of laws and barbaric punishments. Influenced by social contract philosophers, Bentham and Beccaria encouraged legal and penal reform and viewed deterrence rather than vengeance as the purpose of punishment. The ideology of the Classical School is reflected in contemporary criminal justice with its emphasis on general and specific deterrence (see also *Deterrence and prevention*), and the assumption that offenders are rational actors.

Rational choice theory

This classicist perspective is generally not concerned with the causes of criminal behaviour because it assumes that individuals freely and wilfully engage in crime. The major premise of rational choice theory is that individuals engage in a complex cost–benefit analysis that guides their decisions about specific types of offending. Crime occurs when it is deemed to be beneficial and the negative implications for the offender are perceived to be low. Rational choice theorists have argued that the likelihood of punishment is one factor that influences offender decision making, hence rational choice theorists generally advocate deterrence and focus their efforts on situational crime prevention (e.g. closed-circuit television) that restricts the opportunity for crime.

Routine activity theory

Lawrence Cohen and Marcus Felson (1979) argued that three criteria must converge for crime to occur: motivated offenders, suitable targets and lack of capable guardians. The last two criteria reflect *opportunity* – one of the most important concepts in this theoretical approach. Routine activity theory assumes that life activities or *routines* (e.g. travelling to school or work, engaging in leisure activities) create targets for crime, particularly in the absence of capable guardians (other individuals who are in or near the setting whose presence has the potential to deter potential offenders). The premise here is that crime can be reduced by restricting opportunities for crime.

INDIVIDUALS AS PASSIVE ACTORS

The Positivist School developed in the nineteenth century and challenged the basic premise of the Classical School by rejecting the concept of free will, and asserting that criminal behaviour is pathological and caused by internal (biological) or external (i.e. environmental) factors over which the individual has little control. Positivists also argued that the scientific method (see *Researching crime*) was the most appropriate way to study criminality.

BIOLOGICAL POSITIVISM

Phrenological and evolutionary perspectives are believed to have influenced Cesare Lombroso, an Italian physician whose work focused on 'born criminals'. His classic yet misinformed treatise *Criminal Man* (2006) was first published in 1876 and illustrated the concept of atavism, i.e. that 'born criminals' were less evolved and could be identified through physical attributes. He later conceded that born criminals comprise approximately one-third of all criminals. Lombroso neglected the role of political and socio-economic conditions (e.g. he focused largely on Sicilian prisoners from impoverished backgrounds) that might explain criminality or the response to it. Still, he has been credited for his careful analysis of data over time, which contributed to the growth of positivistic inquiry in criminology for over 100 years (Rafter 2005).

Biological positivism continued into the twentieth century with work by William Sheldon (on somatotypes; body type and physique). *Biosocial* perspectives were proposed by Eleanor and Sheldon Glueck (1940) who compared non-delinquents with officially designated delinquents. Their multiple-factor approach was not received well by sociologists who tended to reject suggestions of a biological basis for criminal behaviour. Contemporary approaches have utilised biosocial and biopsychological frameworks; i.e. biological conditions can predispose people to criminality but internal or external environments also shape behaviour. For example, genetics or neurochemistry has been linked with aggression among males.

PSYCHOLOGICAL POSITIVISM

Both psychological and biological theories seek to explain crime at the level of the individual. That is, they focus on individual differences in criminality. Early theories suggested that low intelligence was a leading cause of crime, and social control mechanisms were imposed to incapacitate people who were labelled as 'feeble-minded'. Sigmund Freud suggested that criminality resulted from an underdeveloped superego that produces psychological conflict (Dixon 1986). Several contemporary psychological theorists prefer the term antisocial (i.e. rewarding outcomes for the offender; loss or harm to others) to that of deviant behaviour. Various strands of psychological theory have sought to explain crime through personality (e.g. antisocial, psychopathic), human development (e.g. unmet needs during childhood), cognitive difficulties (e.g. faulty processing of information), traits (e.g. impulsivity) and mental illness. Some contemporary theories that have strong psychological roots have incorporated biological or sociological concepts. For example, social psychological theories have made important contributions to the study of crime, e.g. social learning theory developed by Ronald Akers (discussed below).

SOCIOLOGICAL POSITIVISM: SOCIAL STRUCTURAL THEORIES

Social structural perspectives assume that individuals are passive actors who engage in crime because of structural factors that shape their lives. Early structural theories of crime focused exclusively on the rates of crime among individuals from working-class or impoverished backgrounds.

Social disorganisation

Industrialisation and massive immigration altered the social landscape of several US cities in the early twentieth century. In their book *The City* (1976) Robert Park, Ernest Burgess and Roderick McKenzie used an ecological view of Chicago that led to their theory of concentric zones – multiple rings that surrounded the central business district. Their primary concern was Zone II, a densely populated area where residents were impoverished or were recent immigrants to the USA. Zone II was also characterised by in/out migration ('transition'). According to the model, rapid social change was accompanied by residential mobility as immigrant groups migrated out of Zone II, following economic gain. New immigrant groups replaced them in this zone of transition. This in/out migration 'upset' the social order and social rules in the zone of transition, a condition referred to as *social disorganisation*.

Clifford Shaw and Henry McKay (1969) found that rates of delinquency were highest in the zone of transition. Moreover, they argued that this pattern held over time, despite changes in the ethnic composition of the zone of transition. They found that this zone was characterised by high rates of racial heterogeneity (which they often confused with ethnic heterogeneity), of in/out residential mobility and poverty. These three *structural* variables created the conditions for social disorganisation, i.e. limited or lack of common values among neighbourhood residents that made it difficult for residents to regulate criminal behaviour in their areas. Over time, social disorganisation theory lost its appeal but re-emerged in the 1980s. Since then, criminologists have expanded on the theory by focusing on collective efficacy or social capital, testing the theory in areas other than cities, and in areas outside the USA, including South Africa (Breetzke 2010) and Estonia (Ceccato 2009).

Strain theory

Strain theory was developed by Robert Merton (1957) whose work drew on Émile Durkheim's idea of anomie (i.e. the breakdown of social norms and the inability to regulate norm violations following rapid social change). Merton suggested that 'success' was defined in terms of material wealth (i.e. a culturally defined goal in the USA) and that hard work was the legitimate way to achieve it. According to Merton, individuals respond to culturally defined goals in one of five ways (*modes of adaptation*), with *conformity* being the most common (accepting and pursuing a goal through legitimate means). In contrast, innovation occurs when people accept the cultural goals but have little or no access to legitimate means to achieve these goals. Robert Agnew (1992) expanded on the concept of strain by considering other sources of strain, such as serious stressors like adverse life events or destructive relationships. Agnew suggested that different kinds of strain can produce anger or distress and that some individuals engage in crime as a way of addressing these feelings.

Cultural deviance and subcultures

Cultural deviance theorists focused on explaining crime among individuals from working-class or impoverished backgrounds (they used the more negative label 'lower class'). Theoretical positions here have focused on the rejection of middle-class values (Albert Cohen), alternative value systems (Walter Miller) and the unequal distribution of illegitimate means to achieve cultural goals (Cloward and Ohlin). In *Delinquency and Drift* (1964), David Matza rejected the idea of subcultural deviance and argued that most delinquents accept the dominant values in society, and intermittently engage in delinquency. Matza acknowledged that external forces shape behaviour but also believed that individuals exercise some degree of free will. A contemporary example of cultural deviance lies in the work of Elijah Anderson (*Code of the Street*), who described focal concerns (i.e. codes of behaviour associated with street culture) among young African American males residing in urban areas (Anderson 1994).

SOCIOLOGICAL POSITIVISM: SOCIAL PROCESS THEORIES

Social learning

Edwin Sutherland (1924) proposed the theory of differential association as an explanation of crime. The theory comprises nine principles that suggest that crime is learned through interactions with significant others who view crime as acceptable behaviour and who 'teach' individuals the techniques and justifications for committing crime. Sutherland's work led other scholars to explore the extent to which 'deviant peers' contributed to delinquency. Ronald Akers (1973) advanced the work of Sutherland by incorporating operant conditioning (reinforcement and punishment) and social structure. Akers' social learning theory has been applied to various types of criminality, including street and white-collar crime.

Social bonds

Travis Hirschi (1969) proposed that delinquency results from weakened social bonds between individuals and society. The premise is that most people conform and engage in law-abiding behaviour because deviations have the potential to risk relationships with significant others and with social institutions (e.g. school, work).

Hirschi suggested that conformity is more likely when strong social bonds are in place. Elements of the social bond include: commitment (i.e. a stake in society), involvement (in conventional activity), attachment (to significant others and social institutions) and belief (in social values and laws).

INDIVIDUALS AS LACKING POWER

Labelling, critical and radical theories

Power – or power imbalance – is central to the theories described in this section. This body of theory asserts that power manifests in different ways but is disseminated through elites and agents of social control. In the 1960s, labelling theory challenged mainstream criminological thought through its emphasis on the social construction of deviance (see also *Social construction of crime and deviance; Deviance (definition of)*) and the importance of the social audience and its reaction to deviance. Labelling theorists such as Howard Becker (1963) were influenced by symbolic interactionists and Frank Tannenbaum, who, in the 1930s, described the 'dramatisation of evil' that affects certain youth who are 'tagged' with deviant labels. They were also influenced by sociologist Edwin Lemert whose work in 1951 distinguished between primary and secondary deviance (Lemert 1967). In the 1970s, British scholars Jock Young (1971) and Stan Cohen (1973) were instrumental in highlighting the role of moral crusaders, entrepreneurs and panics in the construction of deviance.

Critical criminology focuses on a wide range of topics that have in common a 'critique of domination' (Michalowski 2010: 4) that has addressed social injustices, including the criminalisation of the poor and repressive criminal justice systems. Critical criminologists have dismissed individual and community pathologies as causes of crime, have rejected positivistic inquiry and have critiqued mainstream criminology. Much of their work has been marginalised from mainstream journals, university curricula and research funding because their research interests serve to critique rather than support contemporary crime-control policies. Still, as a disciplinary genre, critical criminology has grown considerably in the last four decades. Cultural criminology focuses on the cultural processes of crime and the social control of crime. Cultural criminologists have been critical of the discipline of criminology and its role in constructing crime. This theoretical approach is multidisciplinary, with roots in cultural studies from the UK and interactionist approaches from the USA.

Radical theories have also critiqued mainstream criminology for its narrow focus on street crime. Radical theories include various strands of Marxism that emphasise social and economic inequalities that derive from capitalism and its exploitation of labour that profits the capitalist class. Criminal behaviour among the working class towards their peers is viewed as 'disorganized forms of protest, being an expression of their anger and disillusionment at the system' (Henry and Lukas 2009: xxx). New theoretical directions have included *cultural criminology* that emphasises the cultural meaning of crime. *Feminist approaches* in criminology have developed since the 1970s and have critiqued mainstream criminological theories for their focus on male offenders and the inappropriate way that they conceptualise gender and gender relations (see also *Gender and crime*).

EVALUATING CRIMINOLOGICAL THEORIES

Criminological theories have strengths as well as limitations and are assessed through critical discussions of theoretical concepts and primary assumptions and through the culmination of research evidence. Criminal behaviour is multidimensional and theoretical integration may be best suited for explaining criminal behaviour. Integration means two things: (1) combining concepts from different theories within the same discipline, and (2) integrating concepts from different disciplines. The latter is particularly challenging because of disciplinary ethnocentrism.

REFERENCES

Agnew, R. (1992) 'Foundation for a general strain theory', *Criminology*, 30(1): 47–87.
Akers, Ronald L. (1973) *Deviant Behavior: A Social Learning Approach*. Belmont, CA: Wadsworth.
Anderson, E. (1994) 'The code of the streets', *The Atlantic Monthly*, 273(5): 81–49.
Becker, H.S. (1963) *Outsiders: Studies in the Sociology of Deviance*. New York: Macmillan.
Breetzke, G.D. (2010) 'Modeling violent crime rates: A test of social disorganization in the city of Tshwane, South Africa', *Journal of Criminal Justice*, 38: 446–52.
Ceccato, V. (2009) 'Crime in a city in transition: The case of Tallinn, Estonia', *Urban Studies*, 46: 1611–38.
Cohen, S. (1973) *Folk Devils and Moral Panics*. St Albans: Paladin
Cohen, l. and Felson, M. (1979) 'Social change and crime rate trends : A routine activity approach', *American Sociological Review*, 44(4): 588–608.
Dixon, D.J. (1986) 'On the criminal mind: An imaginary lecture by Sigmund Freud', *International Journal of Offender Therapy and Comparative Criminology*, 30(2): 101–9.
Glueck, S. and Glueck, E. (1940) *Juvenile Delinquents Grown Up*. New York: Commonwealth Fund.
Henry, S. and Lukas, S.A. (eds) (2009) *Recent Developments in Criminological Theory: Toward Disciplinary Diversity and Theoretical Integration*. Farnham: Ashgate.
Hirschi, T. (1969) *Causes and Delinquency*. Berkeley: University of California Press.
Lemert, E. (1967) *Human Deviance, Social Problems and Social Control*. Englewood Cliffs, NJ: Prentice-Hall.
Lombroso, C. (2006) *Criminal Man*. Durham, NC: Duke University Press. (First published 1876.)
Matza, D. (1964) *Delinquency and Drift*. New Jersey: Transaction Publishers
Merton, R.K. (1957) *Social Theory and Social Structure* (rev. edn). New York: Free Press.
Michalowski, R. (2010) 'Keynote address: Critical criminology for a global age', *Western Criminology Review*, 11(1): 3–10.
Park, R.E., Burgess, E.W. and McKenzie, R.D. (1925) *The City*. Chicago: University of Chicago Press.
Rafter, N.H. (2005) 'Cesare Lombroso and the origins of criminology: Rethinking criminological tradition', in S. Henry and M. Lanier (eds) *The Essential Criminology Reader*. Boulder, CO: Westview/Basic Books, pp. 33–42.
Shaw, Clifford R. and McKay, Henry D. (1969) *Juvenile Delinquency and Urban Areas*. Chicago: University of Chicago Press.
Sutherland, E. H. (1924) *Principles of Criminology*. Chicago: University of Chicago Press.
Young. J (1971) 'The role of thepolice as amplifiers of deviance' in *Images of Deviance*; Young, J. (1971) *The Drugtakers: The Social Meaning of Drug Use*. London: Paladin.

> **Definition**: *Social control is defined as the various processes by which groups within a society attempt to regulate the behaviour of its members, thereby reducing deviance and enhancing conformity. Governance is the practice of governing through formal institutions within a society based on political, religious and other forms of authority. Governmentality refers to both external and internal processes by which individuals learn to control their own behaviours through various sanctions and socialisation strategies used by groups and institutions within a society.*

Open up any 'introduction to sociology' textbook, and most criminology and criminal justice textbooks as well, and one can readily find a definition of 'social control'. Generally, the definition will say something like: social control is a society's way of reducing deviance and encouraging conformity of its members. Social control is an essential function or consequence of any society, and every human group has techniques or practices which reduce diversity and dysfunctional conflict, and enhance cohesion, conformity and coordination, among its members. Related to social control are the concepts of governance and governmentality, both of which seek to understand the wider context in which societies, institutions and individuals engage in both conforming and deviant actions.

SOCIAL CONTROL

Social control has deep roots in western philosophy, from Plato to Hobbes to the classic sociological theories of Durkheim, Marx and Weber. Their expressions in classic theories of criminology include the social control theories of Albert Reiss (1951), Travis Hirschi and Michael Gottfredson, and David Matza (Gottfredson and Hirschi 1990; Matza 1964) (see also *Crime and theory*).

On a fundamental level, social control is broken down into two kinds. The first is called internal social control. It includes controls which are the product of socialisation of the values, beliefs and norms of a society, or of groups within it, by its members. It creates self-restraint within individuals through conscience and self-awareness of what is right and wrong. Even though socially derived definitions of basic morality and ethics – what is right and what is wrong – vary from society to society, all societies have ways of socialising their members so that they voluntarily select certain options from an array of alternatives as defined by the mainstream of a society and by those who hold power within society. For example, there are many opportunities to steal, but since stealing is defined by society as a crime, with associated punishments, most individuals do not consider this option for getting what they want. Further, even if they consciously consider stealing something, they constrain or control their own behaviours when such opportunities present themselves because they have been taught to believe it is wrong.

There is a second form of social control, which is external. External forms of social control include groups and organisations within a society who enforce conformity and reduce deviance through various rules and regulations. For example, regulatory agencies at the local, national and even international level function to externally enforce conformity and reduce violations of rules.

In general, both internal and external forms of control interact to create varying levels of conformity and deviance. Social groups also simultaneously impose both internal and external control on their members, such as schools, who seek to socialise students to willingly conform to their own rules and regulations (e.g. internal social control) while, at the same time, they use schedules and school bells, supervised exams, detention and other actions as external means of control.

GOVERNANCE AND GOVERNMENTALITY

Related to social control are the concepts of governance and governmentality. In its most simplistic form, governance is the practice of governing. Hence, it includes government and its associated agencies, as well as the political, administrative and other forms of authority within a society that may contribute to its operation (United Nations Development Programme 1997).

Governance is different from but related to, and often conflated with, the concept of governmentality. Governmentality derives from the work of Michael Foucault, including his oft-cited *Discipline and Punish* (1977). In this classic work of criminology, Foucault focused on the micro processes of power and strategies related to social control within prison settings, and by doing so, had much to say about the larger society and all societal institutions which seek to control their members or participants, from schools to religious entities (Lemke 2000). Hence, governance refers to the more general processes and related organisational features of a society that regulate or bring order and control to the behaviours and attitudes of individuals and groups within it. Governmentality, on the other hand, generally refers to more specific or micro-level features of groups/institutions and how they apply mechanisms for controlling or managing individuals within them, both enhancing desired forms of conformity and reducing undesirable types of deviance (Bevir 2010).

Beyond this distinction, however, even though governance and governmentality are both frequently cited with less than rigorous conceptual clarity, they have proven to be increasingly useful concepts in criminology to examine the processes by which various criminal justice agencies, governments, regulatory agencies, organisations and societal institutions contribute to the development of strategies and techniques of social control.

Criminologists who apply the concept of governmentality in their scholarly work often begin by breaking down the word into its constituent parts – government and mentality – and then focus more narrowly on either internal or external forms of social control. Within the concept of governmentality, there are numerous kinds of techniques or 'technologies of power', that is, forms of control whose main function is to produce desired outcomes and avoid undesirable outcomes in the behaviours and attitudes of people. Variants on technologies of power include technologies of self, healthism, normalisation and self-esteem.

Technologies of self are similar to the sociological definition of internal social control, representing ways that individuals acquire capacities for governing themselves so that they abide by the law and restrict their own expressions of anti-social behaviour. These include 'responsibilisation', that is, techniques which socialise individuals to see behaviours as the responsibility of the self. Hence, television ads in the USA, featuring the fictional 'McGruff the Crime Dog', encourage citizens to 'take a bite out of crime', by calling law enforcement if suspicious activity is observed and reminding citizens that they are in a partnership with the police to build safe neighbourhoods.

Another set of techniques is called 'healthism'. These techniques are represented by strategies seeking to associate healthy choices with the public good. Hence, public relations campaigns against drug abuse, smoking and other risky behaviours are aimed at teaching so-called 'responsible' behaviours, whereby citizens constrain themselves and believe their self-regulation to be both socially and morally responsible.

'Normalisation' is a set of techniques of self by which individuals are taught to exhibit appropriate behaviours and attitudes that meet idealised goals of a society or groups within it, and avoid inappropriate behaviours and attitudes. For example, religions classify 'sin' variably, from less serious to more serious in the same way crimes are classified as misdemeanours and felonies. People learn that more serious sins and felonies are farther away from the ideal, and by implication, closer to evil, sociopathic behaviour and other adjectives/phrases which justify harsher punishments (see also *Normalisation*).

Techniques of self-esteem are another way that technologies of power can be expressed. They represent the ways that individuals learn to associate conformity with notions of self-respect and feeling good about oneself, while deviance or doing bad is connected to low self-esteem (see also *Why people commit crime*).

A second set of technologies under the concept of governmentality is 'technologies of the market'. Specifically, these kinds of social control refer to the ways that individuals who seek to fulfil needs created through socialisation are taught desired behaviours and attitudes. Within market-based forms of governmentality are techniques of desire which induce individuals to work towards satisfying socially learned needs. Also, 'technologies of identity' are intended to induce individuals to associate their status or social standing within a society or group to which they belong with striving towards desired goals, which, in turn, have been created by government, religion institutions and other groups within a society.

FINAL THOUGHTS

Altogether, both sets of technologies – power and the market – can work simultaneously to establish socially defined sets of appropriate behaviours and attitudes that govern and socially control individual members. In criminology, these concepts are used to deconstruct the ways in which society attempts to establish controls and define what is criminal, and how these change with a shifting political economy. Hence, governmentality dovetails into forms of scholarship in criminology which emphasise the concept of governance. For example, crime prevention – which can include a full range of specific actions, such as neighbourhood or crime watch, street lighting and crime prevention through environmental design – can be seen as a form of governance which shifts the responsibility of safety and security in a neighbourhood to include local community or civic groups as a form of co-production with law enforcement. What lies behind this form of political economy is the shifting nature of conservative and liberal forms of government and the extent to which governmental agencies are responsible for the governance or social control of crime in a society.

Likewise, governance is a useful concept for understanding the wider context in which certain behaviours are criminalised and de-criminalised, such as changes in laws about growing, selling and consuming marijuana. Social movements and non-governmental groups (from churches to political parties), the electronic media, shifting public opinion and other factors converge to create the context in which certain behaviours are defined as legal or illegal at particular points in time. Hence, in the USA during the twenty-first century, regulations against the consumption of tobacco have become increasingly harsh, while rules prohibiting marijuana have simultaneously become more relaxed (see also *Social construction of crime and deviance*).

Not only at a national level, but at the local level as well, definitions of criminal behaviour can be 'contested' by understanding how social control is linked to both governance and governmentality. An issue like intimate partner violence can be examined and understood in terms of localised forms of community norms, representing both techniques of power and the market as expressed through local institutions and civic groups, such as law enforcement, government, schools and churches. For example, a gendered social order and forms of violence against women vary across space and time (Carrington et al. 2013). Hence, the dynamics of social control within a localised context determine the extent to which certain crimes are tolerated or not, and what actions may be taken by both formal authorities and groups therein. In turn, this understanding informs strategies and actions which could be undertaken to challenge and contest an established patriarchal social order and to redefine appropriate behaviours. For example, there is a variation on crime prevention to reduce violence against women called 'Second Generation' CPTED (DeKeseredy et al. 2009), which is concerned with changing the normative environment of a community through advertising campaigns and demonstrations and using social media to focus attention on local officials who fail to take action against men who are the perpetrators on behalf of women who are the victims. Similarly, other forms of crime prevention can be built from a clear understanding of social control, governance and governmentality.

REFERENCES

Bevir, M. (2010) 'Rethinking governmentality: Towards genealogies of governance', *European Journal of Social Theory*, 13(4): 423–41.

Carrington, K., McIntosh, A., Hogg, R. and Scott, J. (2013) 'Rural masculinities and the internalization of violence in agricultural communities', *International Journal of Rural Criminology*, 2(1): 43–71.

DeKeseredy, W.S., Donnermeyer, J.F. and Schwartz, M.D. (2009) 'Toward a gendered second genera-tion CPTED for preventing woman abuse in rural communities', *Security Journal*, 22 (July): 178–89.

Foucalt, M. (1977) *Discipline and Punish: The Birth of the Prison*. London: Allen Lane.

Gottfredson, M.R., and Hirschi, T. (1990) *A General Theory of Crime*. Stanford, CA: Stanford University Press.

Lemke, T. (2000) 'Foucault, governmentality, and critique.' Paper presented at the Rethinking Marxism conference, Amherst, MA, September.

Matza, D. (1964) *Delinquency and Drift*. New Jersey: Transaction Publishers.

Reiss, A. (1951) 'Delinquency as the failure of personal and social controls', *American Socialogical Review*, 16(2): 1961–207.

United Nations Development Programme (1997) *Reconceptualizing Governance*. Discussion Paper 2. New York: United Nations.

8 Researching Crime

> **Definition**: *Research involves the systematic inquiry of social phenomena that aims to develop new knowledge or contribute to existing knowledge. Much crime research focuses on individuals (victims, offenders), communities, institutions (such as pris-ons) or processes (law, criminal justice decision making). However, researching crime is not bound by particular topics. New crime topics and innovative approaches to studying them continue to shape the fields of criminology and criminal justice.*

The purposes of research include exploration (e.g. crimes that emerge after civil war), description (e.g. the prevalence of cybercrime), comparison (e.g. motives for murder among men and women), explanation (e.g. social factors that contribute to theft) and/or evaluation (e.g. outcomes for ex-offenders who participated in an employ-ment scheme). Research has several advantages. Studies can test or build theories about crime and the response to it. Findings can assist individuals, organisations, processes (e.g. criminal justice decision making) and policy makers. Research that investigates crime problems has the potential to identify solutions to those problems.

QUANTITATIVE AND QUALITATIVE APPROACHES

Quantitative and qualitative methods are distinct methodological approaches that view the social world very differently. Quantitative methods assume that social reality (such as crime) can be defined and measured in an objective manner. However, human behaviour and life events cannot be measured with absolute precision. For example, robbery in a given locale might be measured by the num-ber of times that individuals and businesses have reported robberies to the police. Or it might be measured through a survey that asks people about the number of times that they have been victimised by robberies. Neither of these measures will produce completely accurate data so we consider them to be indicators of crime, rather than exact measures of crime.

Research based on quantitative methods is guided by the scientific method, a set of procedures that allow for replication, measurement, hypothesis testing and prediction. In contrast, qualitative methods are based on the principle of interpretivism and assume that reality is socially constructed and best understood in the culture, context and era in which it occurs. Considerable debate has focused on the merits of quantitative and qualitative methods. The debate was fuelled by some scholars who argued that 'real science' required data collected from quantitative methods, because it utilised scientific principles similar to those of the natural sciences. Alternatively, qualitative researchers have questioned whether the complexity of human behaviour can be measured and counted.

The choice of methodology is supposed to be determined largely by the nature of the research question. In practice, a number of researchers choose methods with which they are comfortable, although the choice might also be influenced by policy makers' mistaken beliefs that 'real research' is based on quantitative methods. Scholarly journals in the field have published considerably more articles that draw on quantitative methods, however these journals also receive fewer submissions from authors who have used qualitative methods (Tewksbury 2009). Miller (2005) suggested that contemporary criminology has been relatively isolated from other social sciences, a factor that has contributed to a quantitative dominance in the field. This dominance has shaped the direction of criminology (particularly in the USA) which has implications for criminal justice policy.

RESEARCH STRATEGY

Research is a process that consists of a series of stages, which collectively reflect the overall strategy that guides the research. Specifying the research question or problem is the first stage of the research strategy. Some research questions focus on criminal justice processes – for example, how do arrestees' race and ethnic backgrounds influence jury decision making? How does the criminal justice system respond to corporate crime? Other research questions might address the impact of societal institutions on individual behaviour, such as: To what extent does community-based stigma contribute to recidivism? How do students' experiences in schools contribute to delinquency? When developing the research question, investigators consider their *ontological* (i.e. the nature of reality) and *epistemological* (i.e. the nature of knowledge) positions, hence how they view the social reality under study. Some positions assume that researchers can influence the social phenomena that they study and that social reality is subjective (constructionism, interpretivism). Other positions assume that social worlds operate independently of researchers and are generally not influenced by the researchers who study them. This position assumes that social reality is objective and can be measured (positivism). A researcher's ontological and epistemological positions are important because they guide the overall research strategy, including the choice of research design and method.

CRITICALLY REVIEWING THE SCHOLARLY LITERATURE

The next stage of the research strategy involves a review of the scholarly literature that relates to the research question or topic. This review generally focuses on previous research that has addressed the same or a similar topic. A thorough literature review will identify what is already known about the topic, what other researchers have found, and gaps in the literature. Describing the gaps is important because new research should further our understanding of a research topic. It is important to review the previous studies with a critical eye. For example, does the evidence support the conclusions drawn by researchers in earlier studies? What are the strengths and weaknesses of the previous studies? What kinds of people or events were excluded from the samples used in the previous research, and to what extent could these omissions have biased the results? At times, the original research question is revised or refined following a thorough review of the literature. The review also helps researchers clarify the main concepts in the research question.

RESEARCH METHOD AND DESIGN

The choice of research *method* should depend on the research question. That is, some methods are more suitable than others for addressing a particular research topic. Researchers might choose qualitative, quantitative or a combination of these methods (i.e. a mixed-methods approach). The choice of method is linked to the kinds of data that will be gathered. Quantitative approaches will produce data in the form of numbers, whereas qualitative methods will yield observations, narrative or visual data (i.e. collections of words or images).

The investigator also decides on the research *design*. The majority of studies on crime rely on cross-sectional designs, whereby data are collected at one point in time. These designs are advantageous because they often consume less time and fewer resources than other designs. However, cross-sectional designs make it difficult to ascertain causal links between two events because the ordering of events often cannot be established. Cross-sectional designs produce data that reflect a 'snapshot' of social reality at a particular time and place, thus they cannot be used to examine changes or trends over time.

Longitudinal designs are used to examine data that are collected at two or more points in time. For example, surveys can ask the same questions to the same group of people on an annual basis, so that researchers can analyse behavioural or attitudinal changes over time. These designs are best suited for establishing causal links between two or more variables, such as acquisitive/property crime and drug use (see also *Drug-related crime*), and for monitoring changes over time. Both quantitative and qualitative methods can incorporate longitudinal designs. For example, ethnography is a qualitative method whereby the researcher observes and collects other data on social behaviour in a natural setting. Some ethnographers collect data from the same individuals at different times, and revisit the field on several occasions, hence the longitudinal nature of ethnography. Longitudinal designs are expensive and time-consuming. There are also challenges with locating people for follow-up collection of data. Finally, anonymity is not usually possible with longitudinal designs; researchers generally need to know the names of people so subsequent contacts can be made.

SAMPLING DECISIONS

The research plan or strategy also requires investigators to make important decisions about the choice of sample, the criteria for inclusion in the study, and, depending on the research question, the recruitment of study participants. Random samples (including stratified random samples) are important if the researcher wishes to use the findings to generalise to some wider population. Random samples comprise study participants or events which are selected randomly from some population list. For example, obtaining a random sample of reported burglaries during 2013 requires a researcher to first obtain the full list of reported burglaries during the 12-month period, and then to select a sample of cases randomly. It is not always possible to obtain a full list of the population, thus some research relies on non-random samples. Criminal behaviour is a sensitive research topic in that it violates the criminal law, which can deter people from participating in research on crime. Some individuals are members of hidden or hard-to-reach populations (e.g. active offenders, people who use illicit drugs), whereby it is impossible to generate a full and accurate list of these populations. In these instances, non-random samples are used that might include chain referral (i.e. snowball) or respondent-driven sampling.

Investigators need to clearly specify the sample criteria, i.e. the types of events or people that the researcher hopes to include in the study in order to address the research question. When samples comprise people, researchers attempt to develop effective recruitment strategies in hopes of boosting study participation. Low response rates can bias the results, particularly when non-response is linked to the social phenomenon that is being studied. Recruitment can be bolstered by privileged-access interviewers, gatekeepers and sponsors, although each of these strategies has limitations. Collectively, sampling decisions are very important because people or events that comprise the final sample can affect the research findings.

MEASUREMENT

In the social sciences, direct measures of theoretical concepts are rare, so we use proxy variables or indicators that reflect the concepts. For example, crime is a theoretical concept and researchers often measure crime with data recorded by police or collected via victim or self-report surveys. These measures have strengths as well as weaknesses but none of them can directly measure the concept of crime (see also *Crime statistics*). The goal is to use indicators that most closely 'match' the theoretical concept. Using good indicators is likely to improve measurement validity, i.e. the extent to which our indicators reflect what we intend.

COLLECTING AND ANALYSING DATA

The method by which data are collected is likely to influence the research findings. Qualitative data are collected through methods such as focus groups, face-to-face interviews (e.g. semi-structured, in-depth, narrative or life history interviews), participant observation (i.e. observing people or events in a natural setting), ethnography and visual representations (e.g. photographs). These data often focus on the social meaning of phenomena from the perspective of individuals who experience it.

Quantitative data collection is generally produced from surveys or questionnaires and focuses on counts or numbers. Secondary data are those that have been collected or recorded by organisations (e.g. arrest data) or other researchers. These data can be qualitative (e.g. narrative accounts of prison visits by inspectors) or quantitative. The use of the mixed-methods approach is also a growing trend. This involves the combined use of qualitative and quantitative data to investigate a research question or problem. Finally, each method of collecting data has strengths as well as limitations.

Data analysis is a systematic process of 'making sense' of the data that are collected. Although this stage follows the collection of quantitative data, qualitative methods rely on an iterative process that involves an interplay between data collection and analysis. Indeed, analysis of qualitative data often begins with the first case. A number of analytical strategies (quantitative and qualitative) are available and these are characterised by intricate procedures that often focus on the relationships between variables (e.g. gender and crime victimisation, corporate crime across regions). Interpretation focuses on the meaning and implications of the results of analysis.

RESEARCH ETHICS

Researchers must follow strict ethical protocols developed by the institutions with which they are affiliated or the professional associations that relate to their disciplines. Informed consent is required in studies that collect data from people. Additionally, investigators must ensure that the research does not physically or emotionally harm those people who participate. Confidentiality and anonymity are also important.

REFERENCES

Miller, J. (2005) 'The status of qualitative research in criminology', in M. Lamont and P. White (eds) *Workshop on Interdisciplinary Standards for Systematic Qualitative Research*. Arlington, VA: National Science Foundation, pp. 69–75.

Tewksbury, R. (2009) 'Qualitative versus quantitative methods: Understanding why qualitative methods are superior for criminology and criminal justice', *Journal of Theoretical and Philosophical Criminology*, 1: 38–58.

9 Crime Statistics

Definition: *In general, statistics is the applied side of mathematics and refers to the analysis and interpretation of data. Crime statistics is the analysis and interpretation of data derived both from the police and the criminal justice system, and criminologists who conduct their own research.*

Statistics helps criminologists organise data and answer research questions about all aspects of crime and the performance of criminal justice agencies (see also *Researching crime*). Statistics is a tool for ensuring that criminologists abide by standards which are common to all sciences, namely a quest for objectivity. Statistical results tell criminologists who conduct research that their hypotheses can be accepted or rejected. Statistics is also useful for criminologists who seek to describe the extent and pattern of various criminological phenomena (see also *Prevalence, incidence and incident of crime*). And, most importantly, statistics is vital to the scientific standard of 'peer review', which means that researchers who seek to publish their results in a journal must report the statistical results of their tests. Those who review the articles judge whether or not the statistical procedures (plus other methodological issues associated with the research process, such as data collection) were appropriate, and interpretations of the statistical results were accurate.

SOURCES OF CRIMINAL JUSTICE STATISTICS

Criminal justice agencies generate a great deal of information which can be organised into a database from which statistics can be applied. The number of crimes in a neighbourhood, the number of arrests by a law enforcement agency, the number of cases before a court of law, the number of prisoners who enter or who are released from a correctional facility, etc. – the variety of examples of areas where numbers describe the criminal justice system is nearly infinite. Many of these statistics, especially descriptive statistics (i.e. those that use a frequency, a percentage and other easy to understand numerical indicators), are presented in 'Sourcebooks'. For example, both the *European Sourcebook of Crime and Criminal Justice Statistics* and its US counterpart, the *Sourcebook of Criminal Justice Statistics*, are invaluable for understanding crime and society. Both are now available online and specific tables can be downloaded as pdf files. Further, both are good places to start a research project because they identify the sources of their information, hence criminology researchers can use the sourcebooks to find the original databases and explore them for additional information (see also *The criminal justice system*).

The fourth edition of the *European Sourcebook* (2010) includes an extensive introduction discussing issues related to the compatibility of various forms of data across the countries for which information is available. As an example of what the *Sourcebook* contains, Table 1.2.1.1 reports 'Offences per 100,000 population – all offences' for 42 countries, from Albania to the UK: Scotland. These offences include homicide, bodily injury (assault), other forms of violence, rape, robbery, theft (i.e. larceny), motor vehicle theft, burglary, drug offences and other crimes such as internet fraud. Even though there is great variation in the overall rates (from 14,014 in Sweden to 187 in Albania), it would be inappropriate to conclude that Sweden is much more crime-ridden than other countries. These statistics, instead, indicate the extent to which crimes are known to law enforcement or a criminal justice agency. So too, the US *Sourcebook of Criminal Justice Statistics* (Hindelang Criminal Justice Research Center 2011) includes an extensive section entitled 'Nature and distribution of known offenses' that contains statistics from the Federal Bureau of Investigation's *Uniform Crime Report* (which can also be accessed independently of the *Sourcebook* at the FBI's website).

Both sourcebooks are organised by major parts of the criminal justice system. The first are statistics about the characteristics of police agencies. This can include: the number of personnel, broken down by type of agency or the population size of the jurisdiction; gender and race/ethnicity of law enforcement personnel, both sworn and civilian; educational requirements for various positions in a police agency; and complaints about police conduct, including the unnecessary use of force.

A second class of statistical data available is information about personnel who administer and manage correctional facilities, criminal courts and other criminal justice agencies. This can include the number of personnel and their specialisations, demographic characteristics and educational levels of these personnel, and expenditures for personnel.

A third set of statistics available from a sourcebook, or, alternatively, through the appropriate governmental agencies of many countries, is about arrests and convictions. This can include information such as: arrest and conviction rates by type of crime; the characteristics of arrestees and people serving time in prison (e.g. by gender, age and race/ethnicity); and crime-specific variations in arrests, convictions and the characteristics of arrestees.

The final and perhaps most extensive set of statistics ready-made for research about crime and society are self-report studies. Examples include the International Crime Victims' Survey or the National Crime Victimization Survey (USA) (see also *Victims of crime*), and Monitoring the Future Study out of the University of Michigan on self-reported substance use and delinquency (see also *Prevalence, incidence and incident of crime*). The British Crime Survey is very influential in helping criminologists to test theory; and for law enforcement, other criminal justice agencies and government leaders to formulate policies and devise strategies for preventing crime. There are also numerous regional and local data sets covering the full gamut of criminological topics which are based on survey data of one type or another.

Information for the statistical study of crime can often be found in places not directly associated with a governmental agency dedicated to crime and justice. For example, in the USA, the National Longitudinal Survey of Youth (e.g. Bureau of Labor Statistics 2013) includes nearly 9,000 respondents surveyed periodically on a large range of issues, including health and risk behaviours. Hence, an article on the 'Cumulative prevalence of arrest from ages 8 to 23 in a national sample' by Brame, Turner, Paternoster and Bushway can be found in the first issue of the 2012 edition of *Pediatrics*. Excluding arrests for minor violations (such traffic violations), the authors examine the cumulative percentage of self-reported arrests, beginning with the first wave of the National Longitudinal Survey of Youth in 1997 and all subsequent waves or data collection points.

There are other sources of crime statistics as well. For example, crimes committed against businesses can be found in the National Retail Security Survey (USA), which is sponsored by the National Retail Federation (e.g. 2012). This organisation also organises conferences on loss prevention, hence their information is not only useful for criminology research, but informs security practices to reduce shoplifting, employee-related theft and other crimes that affect businesses (see also *Deterrence and prevention*).

Information from hospitals and governmental agencies whose mission includes the health of a population are also invaluable sources for criminological data. Death due to murder or non-negligent manslaughter is one obvious example. For example, the United Nations Office on Drugs and Crime (e.g. 2011) uses both police data and mortality data from governmental agencies responsible for health and medicine to report on homicide rates for almost all member countries (see also *Prevalence, incidence and incident of crime*).

In addition to the sources described above, there are organisations devoted to social science research, including criminology, such as the Inter-University Consortium of Political and Social Research (ICPSR) in the USA, which can be rich sources of criminological and criminal justice information. The ICPSR's goal is to be a repository for data sets which can be used by researchers. It also lists science articles which have been published in these various data sources.

STATISTICS AND CRIMINOLOGICAL THEORY

When used properly, statistics has great potential to test, revise and improve criminological theory. For example, social disorganisation theory is one of the most central theories in criminology (see also *Crime and theory*). It assumes that more cohesive places have less crime and more socially disorganised localities have more crime. This theory lends itself to statistically based testing of hypotheses because researchers are able to examine variations in crimes known to the police and/or arrest data with measures of disorganisation derived from census or population data. Even though the use of census data (such as population density, population mobility or migration, percentage of single-parent households, etc.) is sometimes criticised because it is a 'proxy' for what disorganisation/lack of cohesion is supposed to represent (Tittle 2000), the availability of information at regional and national levels for both dependent and independent variables is almost irresistible to criminologists who favour a quantitative and statistical approach to research.

Almost without exception, every criminological theory and research topic is amenable to statistical examination (and the same can be said of qualitatively derived data). Another example is strain theory. Most criminologists who conduct research on strain theory, for instance, use surveys to measure the difference between respondents' perceptions that their life chances are blocked or constrained in some way (Tittle 2000). DeKeseredy and Rennison (2013) use a critical criminological perspective to statistically examine possible rural–urban differences in violence against women by their male partners, using information from the National Crime Victimization Survey. Conflict theories focus on social class and other features of the social structure of a society to understand crime. Statistical studies using a conflict approach would rely on a Gini coefficient, for example, which would quantify the amount of inequality in the distribution of income and wealth in a society (see also *Poverty and exclusion*).

THE LIMITS OF STATISTICS

Statistics related to crime and the criminal justice system are not perfect, by any means. First, they represent only one of two primary approaches to the study of criminological phenomena. Qualitative approaches which are mostly non-statistical are equally useful for gaining insights and advancing scholarship (see also *Researching crime*). Many criminology scholars point to the equal usefulness of qualitative data, that is, information about various criminological issues that are better answered by information which puts a 'human face' on the research (see also *Prevalence, incidence and incident of crime*).

Second, there is a 'dark side' to most statistical sources. For example, many offences are never reported to law enforcement and the police exercise broad discretionary behaviour in the kinds of crimes on which they focus for enforcement and which enter official records (see also *The criminal justice system*). Self-report studies of substance use and delinquency may fail to survey hard-to-reach young people, such as those who have dropped out of school. Hence, sources for crime statistics are often incomplete. Victimisation surveys must rely on the accuracy of respondent recall.

Third, statistics is not the real centre of the scientific enterprise in criminology. It is valid to criticise criminologists who engage in 'abstracted empiricism', that is, a restriction on what is considered good science to only those research questions where data amenable to statistical procedures is possible, and editorial policies and decision making in criminology journals which are heavily biased in favour of articles which utilise quantitative methodologies, as if their scientific rigour is superior to qualitative investigations. However, as Young (2011: 55) observes: 'but numbers are signs to be interpreted within specific cultural contexts, figures in themselves do not have any magical objectivity'.

Statistics can be abused in other ways as well. Criminological phenomena which are not easily quantifiable are ignored. Criminologists fail to interpret their statistical findings in ways which criticise and revise criminological theory, restricting their considerations to substantive findings which meet an arbitrary criterion of 'significance', such as a .05 probability for a regression coefficient. Resources are wasted on a treadmill of studies which seek incremental increases in the amounts of variance explained, while ignoring more fundamental conceptual issues and underlying assumptions of theory. Hence, a balanced view is to see crime statistics as one way, but not the only way, to conduct scientific research about criminological issues.

IN SUMMARY

Crime statistics require concepts and theories to bring scientific meaning to the numbers, otherwise crime statistics become a form of abstracted empiricism whereby a lot of effort is wasted on numbers which do nothing to advance the science of criminology (Young 2011). In turn, crime statistics help test the validity of criminological theory. Often times, it is the statistical results which compel criminologists to re-think their theories and concepts. The reciprocal relationship of theory and evidence is possible, in part, when properly applied statistics may answer some questions, but raise others.

REFERENCES

Brame, R., Turner, M.G., Paternoster, R. and Bushway, S.D. (2012) 'Cumulative prevalence of arrest from ages 8 to 23 in a national sample' *Pediatrics*, 129(1): 21–7.

Bureau of Labor Statistics (2013) *National Longitudinal Surveys*. Washington, DC: United States Department of Labor. Available at: www.bls.gov/nls/ (accessed 10/04/13).

DeKeseredy, W.S. and Rennison, C.M. (2013) 'Comparing female victims of male perpetrated separation/divorce assault across geographical regions: Results from the national crime victimization survey', *International Journal for Crime and Justice*, 2(1): 65–81.

European Sourcebook of Crime and Criminal Justice Statistics (4th edition) (2010) The Hague, Netherlands: Ministry of Justice, Research and Documentation Centre (WODC). Available at: www.europeansourcebook.org/ (accessed 07/04/13).

Hindelang Criminal Justice Research Center (2011) *Sourcebook of Criminal Justice Statistics*. Albany, NY: University of Albany. Available at: www.albany.edu/sourcebook (accessed 05/03/13).

National Retail Federation (2012) Retail Theft Decreased in 2011, According to Preliminary National Retail Security Survey Findings. Washington, DC: National Retail Federation. Available at: https://nrf.com/media/press-releases/retail-theft-decreased-2011-according-preliminary-national-retail-security (accessed 02/04/13).

Tittle, C.R. (2000) 'Theoretical developments in criminology', in G. LaFree, J.F. Short, R.J. Bursik Sr and R.B. Taylor (eds) *Crime Justice 2000, Vol. 1*. Washington, DC: US Department of Justice, National Institute of Justice, pp. 51–102.

Young, J. (2011) *The Criminological Imagination*. Cambridge: Polity Press.

10 Prevalence, Incidence and Incident of Crime

Definition: *Prevalence refers to the total number of cases or incidents in a population. Incidence may be defined as the number of new cases or incidents in a population during a specified time period. Incident is the single occurrence of a case or event.*

Epidemiology is the study of the distribution of a phenomenon in a population. For example, a medical epidemiologist seeks information about the extent to which an infectious disease, like a variety of influenza, strikes a population, plus where and when a particular strain first appeared and amongst whom it spread.

For herpetologists, epidemiological information about the distribution of snakes and other reptiles informs them about the extent of environmental changes in an area or ecology. Likewise, the criminologist requires information on the epidemiological dimensions of crime in order to test models related to the risk of crime and to consider appropriate crime-reduction strategies (see also *Researching crime*).

PREVALENCE

Prevalence is an epidemiological concept that refers to the total number of cases in a population. For example, in a 2011 report, the United Nations Office on Drugs and Crime (UNODC) estimated the prevalence of homicide for most countries around the world. Since the UNODC is a comprehensive report across many different nation-states with varying forms of governmental institutions, it sought data from either a criminal justice agency, like the British Home Office or the US Federal Bureau of Investigation, or records from a national health agency which would also record death by cause. Country by country, this report, entitled the *Global Study on Homicide*, presents data on the prevalence of homicide by the number of murders known. Homicide prevalence ranges from 0 for the tiny Mediterranean country of Monaco and the southern Pacific Island nation of Palau, to nearly 44,000 for Brazil. Numbers alone, however, are not sufficient. The report also shows homicide prevalence as a rate. For example, Iceland, with only one recorded murder in 2009 (the most recent year information was available for this report), had a rate of 0.3 per 100,000 persons. Not coincidentally, its population is about 320,000 persons. On the other side of the ledger, the prevalence of homicide in Brazil, with a population of nearly 200 million, when expressed as a rate, was 22.7. This rate, even though high, is not the highest. That dubious honour is reserved for the Central American country of Honduras, where the annual prevalence rate of homicide was 82 per 100,000 persons.

Expressing prevalence as a rate is important for an understanding of crime and its causes, especially for studies which examine the extent of crime across different kinds of localities. For example, the number of homicides in the People's Republic of China, the Russian Federation and the USA are about the same (15,000). Because their populations differ in size, Russia's rate is over twice as high – 11.2 per 100,000 persons – when compared to a US rate of 5.0. The US rate is nearly five times higher than China's, which stands at 1.1 per 100,000 persons.

INCIDENCE

Often confused with prevalence, and many times erroneously used to mean the same thing, is the concept of incidence. Incidence refers to the number of new cases in a population during a specified time period. One reason for conceptual confusion is that almost all crimes are discreet occurrences, that is, a single incident does not carry over from one year to the next, in contrast to a serious disease which can continue from one reporting period to the next. Hence, if there are 1,000 homicides in a country of 1 million persons in 2008, and 2,000 homicides in the same country in

2009, the prevalence is 100 and 200 per 100,000 persons, respectively. However, if this was a disease, such as AIDS/HIV, or cancer, the prevalence would be calculated as all persons in a population with that condition, including carry-over from the year before, while the incidence would be the number of new cases within a certain time period, such as on an annual basis.

INCIDENT

Another possible source of confusion is the use of the word incident. An incident is simply a single event. For example, many local newspapers include periodic descriptions of crime incidents which occurred in a neighbourhood (see also *Crime in the media*). In victimisation surveys, such as the US Department of Justice's annual National Crime Victimization Survey (see also *Victims of crime*), information is provided on the number of burglary incidents, and then converted to a prevalence estimate, expressed as the number of incidents per 1,000 persons, based on a complicated formula reflecting how the weighted probability sample of respondents was developed. Other criminologists collect data (usually qualitative) on incidents to tell a 'story' or put a 'human face' on issues related to crime. Hence, research on such vital criminological topics as the impact of methamphetamine addiction or domestic violence utilise an incident as equivalent to a case study for the purposes of describing the context of crime and its cost to victims.

EXAMPLES

All three concepts – prevalence, incidence and incident – are used in criminological research.

Example of prevalence: a large annual study from the University of Michigan, funded by the National Institute on Drug Abuse, involving thousands of school-aged and young adult respondents. The name of the study is 'Monitoring the Future' (MTF). The MTF recently released a report entitled *HIV/AIDS: Risk and Protective Behaviors among American Young Adults, 2004–2011* (Johnston et al. 2012). Chapter 4 is focused on the 'Prevalence/frequency of risk behaviors'. The authors examine three risk behaviours that have already been linked with HIV/AIDS, including needle sharing during injection drug use, men having sex with men, and having sex with multiple partners. To be clear, the researchers used data from both female and male respondents for the first and third risk indicators.

The MTF found that the lifetime prevalence for needle sharing was 0.5% among young adults between the ages of 21 and 30. Second, slightly over 5% of male respondents reported having sexual contact with another male during the previous 12 months. Finally, 24% reported having multiple sexual partners in the previous 12 months.

For all three indicators, a prevalence rate was expressed as a simple percentage of the population, but based on a weighted sample presumed to represent young adults in the USA and delimited by a specified time period. In other sections, Johnston et al. (2012) examined the interrelationship of these risk behaviours and the extent to which the 21–30 age cohort may have changed on each risk indicator, based on two-year moving averages. With a two-year moving average, the researchers are able to examine trends in the three risk behaviours over time, while stabilising variability in the prevalence estimates from one year to the next. Hence, the usefulness of prevalence rates is in assessing both the extent and possible changes in behaviours which are, in turn, known to contribute to a health-related problem (HIV/AIDS), which itself can be expressed in terms of prevalence.

Example of incidence: there is a good example of the application of the concept of incidence to the analysis of crime-reduction strategies in the *Australian and New Zealand Journal of Criminology*. Specifically, Townsley et al. (2000) examine the spatial and temporal patterns of repeat burglary victimisations in Brisbane. They report on the *prevalence* of burglary in both homes and non-residential properties as a percentage of all properties in the study area. Like the Monitoring the Future study, they also report on time-based prevalence as a moving average. To consider crime reduction, they discuss actions which would reduce repeat burglary victimisations at the same address. In a single sentence, Townsley et al. (2000) use all three concepts (prevalence, incidence and incident): 'We showed that by preventing repeat incidents, the overall burglary count could be reduced by at least 25 per cent' (p. 57). Hence, there is a burglary *incident* which may be repeated, a burglary count or prevalence and a burglary incidence (in this case, a 25% decrease). Like the way prevalence and incidence is used in epidemiological studies of disease, burglary during a previous time is carried over as the basis on which an increase or decrease (i.e. *incidence*) is calculated.

Example of incident: DeKeseredy and Schwartz (2009) examined the issue of violence against women in the rural south-eastern (i.e. Appalachian) region in the US state of Ohio. By its very nature, the topic is not well suited to a representative survey administered through a telephone interview, an online survey or a survey sent by mail. The sample was 'purposive', based on recruitment of women as victims through coverage of the research project by a local newspaper, a local television station and local domestic violence service providers. A total of 43 women were interviewed and almost all in a safe place where confidentiality could be maintained and their husbands/boyfriends would never find out that these victims had discussed the abuse perpetrated on them by their partners.

Transcripts from the interviews were used by DeKeseredy and Schwartz (2009) to examine patterns of abuse among rural women, and how their male partners managed to engage in this form of violence with little chance of arrest. As the authors reviewed the interview transcripts, they searched for and subsequently found patterns related to the culture of small rural communities and norms of privacy for family-related issues. They discerned not only a male 'peer support' network which affirmed a culture of male patriarchy, but discovered that abusers often discussed in public places, like a Veterans' Club or the local fast-food franchise restaurant, ways to engage in violence against female partners without getting caught. By doing so, they demonstrated that cohesive, tight-knit localities with high levels of collective efficacy might prevent some kinds of crime, like burglary, but enable other offences, such as intimate partner violence.

CONCLUSION

All three concepts – prevalence, incidence and incident – have their place in criminological research and theory (see also *Researching crime*). Each can contribute to the advancement of knowledge about crime, its causes, its social and cultural contexts, and the development and implementation of policies and practices for its reduction. For example, the DeKeseredy and Schwartz (2009) study shows how specific incidents can challenge the validity of social disorganisation theory. The type of methodology selected by the criminologist is partly determined by the research question and partly by the type of information needed to answer the question. In that sense, prevalence, incidence and incident are three separate but related conceptual tools which can be applied to the criminological enterprise to answer vital research questions.

REFERENCES

DeKeseredy, W.S. and Schwartz, M.D. (2009) *Dangerous Exits: Escaping Abusive Relationships in Rural America*. New Brunswick, NJ: Rutgers University Press.

Johnston, L.D., O'Malley, P.M., Bachman, J.O., Schulenberg, J.E. and Patrick, M.E. (2012) *HIV/AIDS: Risk and Protective Behaviors among American Young Adults, 2004–2011*. Ann Arbor, MI: Institute for Social Research, University of Michigan.

Townsley, M., Homel, R. and Chaseling, J. (2000) 'Repeat burglary victimisation: Spatial and temporal patterns', *Australian and New Zealand Journal of Criminology*, 33(1): 37–63.

United Nations Office on Drugs and Crime (UNODC) (2011) *Global Study on Homicide*. Vienna: UNODC.

11 Risk from Crime

> **Definition**: Risk is the probability of a criminal event occurring which causes harm to a person. The harm can be physical, psychological, economic or social. This definition is sometimes called an actuarial approach because it attempts to account for differences amongst aggregates of the population who vary in their susceptibility to the risk of crime and related harms.

In criminological terms, harm can be broken down into two essential components. The first component is the likelihood that someone will be the victim of a crime. For example, a law enforcement agency can claim that some neighbourhoods have higher rates of break and enter, hence people living there are more likely to be at risk of a burglary victimisation whereby their residence is broken into and their property is stolen and/or damaged. However, the second component of risk must also be considered. This component further specifies risk by the amount of damage or loss that potentially could be incurred by a victim. For example, two residences in the same neighbourhood vary in their risk potential by the value of the property within. Owning and displaying a valuable Picasso on a wall in the main living area of a residence which can be seen through a window by anyone walking or driving by, instead of an inexpensive poster announcing the Picasso exhibition at the local museum, increases the risk of the first component above, not only because the painting makes the property a more attractive target but because of the greater economic value should the real thing be stolen.

Security specialists who focus on risk reduction follow a formula simple in its fundamentals, but often difficult to specify. A risk formula normally involves three factors: (a) *threat* – the potential or likelihood of a criminal event occurring to a person, at a place and during a specific time of the day or season of the year; (b) *vulnerability* – the potential or likelihood of a criminal event occurring successfully, that is, of it not being prevented or deterred; and (c) the *potential cost* of the event should it occur, in terms of property loss/damage and both physical and psychological harm.

RISK AND CRIMINOLOGICAL THEORY

The concept of risk is most closely allied with three criminological theories, namely, crime prevention through environmental design (CPTED), routine activities and situational crime prevention (see also *Crime and theory*).

CPTED is a micro-level theory that focuses on the relationship between physical space and human activities, examining how the specific features of physical space either constrain or enable the commission of crime (Crowe 2000). It starts with the assumption that the physical environment can be modified to produce perceptions and behaviours that reduce crime and, if ignored, increase the risk of crime. CPTED strategies seek to enhance natural surveillance, controlling access to a site and improving people's sense of ownership of an area. For example, a high-risk environment might be a waiting area for a bus or other form of public transport, but the risk can be lessened through a variety of design actions, such as the removal of objects (e.g. a newspaper dispenser or a billboard) that might block natural surveillance, or building a sheltered area with clear plexi-glass so that customers can see who is passing by or who is already there as they walk towards the stop. Security cameras and street lighting are frequently recommended ways that CPTED advocates seek to reduce risk. Risk management/reduction experts (i.e. security specialists) frequently employ CPTED strategies for re-designing public spaces (Schneider 2006) and commercial/retail buildings, and increasingly practitioners seek to build the CPTED philosophy into new residential and commercial developments at the planning stage (Crowe 2000).

Routine activities theory is focused on lifestyles and risk (Felson 2002). Like CPTED, routine activities theory emphasizes the situations in which people place themselves through their everyday activities, and how this is related to their likelihood of victimisation. Although this theory can be very micro in its approach, it also considers macro or structural level factors, such as how social and economic change can influence lifestyles and risk, which in turn are linked to increases or decreases in crime.

Routine activities theory defines risk as a convergence in space and time of potential victims and offenders. Especially for predatory crime, three elements are involved – a suitable target, a motivated offender and a lack of guardianship. Guardianship is defined in a way that is similar to the natural surveillance concept of CPTED, namely in terms of lifestyles/routine activities. Guardians may be either ordinary citizens or security personnel, both public and private, who are willing or paid to intervene (such as by calling law enforcement) if a crime is observed. However, in terms of risk, guardianship is more the idea that motivated offenders are less likely to commit a crime if they believe they will be observed. One risk-related concept shared by both CPTED and routine activities is the 'hotspot'. Hotspots refer to specific localities where unusually high numbers of crimes occur, either in general or of a specific type (Sherman et al. 1989). By identifying hotspots, high-risk areas are designated and appropriate risk-reduction actions can be undertaken.

A third criminological theory which explicitly includes the concept of risk is situational crime prevention (Clarke 2009). Situational crime prevention sees crime as the result of an interaction between the disposition of an offender and the situation. Offenders consciously decide to commit an offence and purposefully look for targets they believe to be vulnerable. Hence, like routine activities theory, it sees risk as a product of rational decision making on the part of offenders who examine the environment and make choices about targets, based on estimates of return and on calculations about the probability of being caught. By analysing specific crimes within particular contexts, forms of risk can be determined, and once determined, resolved or mitigated.

RISK REDUCTION

Although distinctive, all three criminological theories work from the same fundamental definition of risk to develop action agendas that lessen risk. Sometimes called risk reduction, and other times labelled risk management, the idea is to analyse a situation, identify pertinent factors and design appropriate strategies. An example of risk reduction or the action side of this concept is what is typical for the services created for a university community. University campuses entail a great deal of risk, not only because of the physical arrangements of buildings and other structures, but because of the transient nature of students, employees (faculty and staff) and others who access the site, either regularly or less so, as needed. The Catholic University of America in Washington, DC, for example, offers a full menu of risk-reduction services, including 'proactive' community patrol, access control to residence halls, CPTED-based 'surveys' to assess crime risks, emergency telephones strategically placed on the campus grounds, safety and security literature and educational programmes for students and employees, safety escorts in the evenings and in localities where a bus service is not provided, and a shuttle bus service which is operated by campus police. This long list of risk-reduction actions, which can be found on the university's website, is intended as a comprehensive approach to campus safety, with obvious benefits for everyone who studies and works there.

SUBJECTIVE AND OBJECTIVE RISK

All three criminological theories also assume a distinction about the concept of risk by either implicitly or explicitly affirming that risk can be both perceived (i.e. subjective) and real (i.e. objective). In regard to the former, perceptions of a threat or danger can be general (i.e. formless) or very specific. Generally, it is the perception of a specific risk to crime that concerns those involved in risk-reduction strategies because these perceptions are presumed to be directly related to behaviours, from avoidance of an area or of a place at specific times to the kinds of preventive and protective actions which ordinary citizens may adopt (see also *Fear and the fear of crime*).

Also recognised in the distinction between subjective and objective risk is the idea that particular situations can either amplify or attenuate how risk is defined. Amplification includes factors that create greater concern or are more likely to stimulate action to reduce risk. For example, walking in a neighbourhood during daylight hours is generally perceived as less risky than strolling on the same side-walks at night. Frequenting a pub or bar for a drink is perceived as more risky if the customer is alone than with a group of friends (see also *Victims of crime*).

Attenuation of risk refers to factors that reduce the perception, perhaps unrealisti-cally or inaccurately, that there is a danger or threat within a specific situation. An example here is of an area with expensive homes that may be seen as safe from crime. An individual may feel at liberty to walk alone at night without any sense of concern because it is believed that crime does not happen in affluent neighbourhoods.

Perception becomes vitally important in risk-reduction strategies, not only because ordinary citizens take action, such as to avoid a place or an event, due to their concerns about a danger or threat, but symbolically as well. Hence, at many public events with large crowds, a visible police presence provides symbolic assur-ance to citizens, assuaging their fear and encouraging their participation. This can be seen in the various actions in the example from the Catholic University of America in the adoption of emergency telephones and a police shuttle service, on request, where a regular bus service is not provided.

Another consideration in risk reduction is the cost, usually measured in monetary terms but also assessible in terms of social costs, such as constitutional freedoms or restrictions within places believed to be at high risk of a costly incident occurring (such as a terrorist attack). For example, after the events of 9/11 (11 September 2001) in the USA, a considerable number of new security measures were put in place at airports around the world to reduce the risk of future terrorist incidents and to assure the public that air travel was safe. Some of the costs are represented by investments in better detection equipment and a considerable expansion of security personnel at airports around the world, but other costs are now incurred by passengers every time they travel. To reduce risks, arrival at the airport needs to be earlier than before, shoes must be removed and, along with carry-on bags, must be scanned by security personnel. Some people feel uncomfortable with the full body scanners so ubiquitous at airports today, but accept the loss of privacy in the interests of risk reduction and perceptions of safety.

CRITICISMS

Critics have argued that criminology theories which incorporate the concept of risk fail to consider that risk is a socially constructed and contested concept. Hence, some amplifications of risk mask power inequalities, discrimination and the social exclusion of certain groups within a society (Mythen 2013). For example, critics of CPTED argue that it may create a design for safer public places, but does so by framing homeless and other persons as security threats, hence ignoring deeper structural issues about the economic and cultural marginalisation of certain people and how best to help them (see also *Social construction of crime and deviance*; *Fear and the fear of crime*).

REFERENCES

Clarke, R.V. (2009) 'Situational crime prevention: Theoretical background and current practice', in M.D. Krohn, A.J. Lizotte and G. Penly Hall (eds) *Handbook on Crime and Deviance*. New York: Springer, pp. 259–76.

Crowe, T. (2000) *Crime Prevention through Environmental Design*. Stoneham, MA: Butterworth-Heineman.

Felson, M. (2002) *Crime and Everyday Life*, 3rd edn. Thousand Oaks, CA: Pine Forge Press.

Mythen, G. (2013) *The Risk Society: Crime, Security and Justice*. Basingstoke: Palgrave Macmillan.

Schneider, T. (2006) 'Violence and crime prevention through environmental design', in H. Frumkin (ed.) *Safe and Healthy School Environments*. Oxford: Oxford University Press, pp. 250–69.

Sherman, L.W., Gartin, P.R. and Bureger, M.D. (1989) 'Hot spots of predatory crime: Routine activities and the criminology of place', *Criminology*, 27(1): 27–55.

12 Why People Commit Crime

Definition: *Nearly all criminological explanations for why people commit crime can be classified as one of two types: those which seek to explain criminal involvement, and those that attempt to identify places where crime is more likely to occur. (see also* Crime and theory*) Both address the aetiology of crime, that is, factors which explain variations in criminal behaviour. However, it is the former which examines the relationship of individual traits, cultural characteristics and societal-level factors associated with the reasons why some people are at greater risk of committing crime.*

BIOSOCIAL FACTORS

Some criminologists examine the biological characteristics of humans and why they commit crime. These factors are today labelled 'biosocial' because they focus on the possible ways that biology interacts with culture, and various groups and institutions embedded in the social structure of societies, to understand criminal behaviour. Researchers and theorists in this area, whose roots go back to Lombroso and others, are careful about claims of direct links between biological traits and specific expressions of social criminal behaviour, in part because of earlier times in the history of criminology when biological explanations were based on oversimplified and often racist views of people and their criminal tendencies. Nonetheless, serious criminological scholarship to link biological characteristics to why people commit crime is an ongoing scientific endeavour (Walsh and Beaver 2009).

One variant on biosocial explanations are studies which examine the ways in which experiences are differentially internalised, which, in turn, leads to differing behavioural outcomes. For example, emotional stress caused by family conflicts or lack of integration into societal institutions creates a greater likelihood of illicit substance use and envelopment in a criminal subculture (Oetting et al. 1998). Individuals who are biologically predisposed to anger and aggression, or the chemical precursors that enhance these emotional conditions, are more likely to engage in criminal behaviours, especially forms of assault. Aggression is also a socially learned trait, such as through military and police training, which in turn produces chemical reactions in the human body that reinforce the commission of anti-social and even violent behaviours (Walsh and Beaver 2009). Issues of suicide and domestic violence among military personnel returning from combat illustrate these links (see also *Violence/interpersonal violence*).

PSYCHOLOGICAL FACTORS

A second set of explanations is more psychological in focus. One example is the role of self-esteem in criminal behaviour. Low self-esteem is seen as contributing to offending because it is considered to be related to the way an individual is assimilated within key groups in a society, such as school, peer groups and family. Another psychological trait and one that is seriously considered as an explanation for involvement in drug abuse is sensation seeking. Synonymous with social activities that create an 'adrenalin rush', sensation seeking is seen by those who do research in this area to be associated with both the biology of an individual and the way individual propensities interact within a society and culture to create behavioural outcomes that would be defined as criminal (Oetting et al. 1998).

SOCIAL LEARNING

In general, social learning begins with the idea that becoming criminally involved is an outcome derived from the social environments which a society's members experience throughout their life course (Akers and Jennings 2009). Both conforming or law-abiding and criminal behaviours are seen as voluntary in nature, hence derived from what individuals learn (i.e. through socialisation) as members of a society, which, in turn, forms the basis on which they act within the context of particular situations. They learn the values, beliefs and norms of their society through various primary groups, that is, groups in which they engage in face-to-face interaction (Oetting et al. 1998). Further, they are socialised through the media and culture of the society in which they live. These are secondary group relationships. According to social learning theory, the net effect of strongly versus weakly held conventional and unconventional beliefs, values and norms explains the reasons why people commit crime.

Social learning explanations also account for differential reinforcement by considering the influence of perceived and real rewards and punishments associated with actions taken by individuals (Akers and Jennings 2009). There are two types of reinforcement, both of which are linked to the various social groups and cultural milieu in which individuals are situated. Positive reinforcement is the result of consequences directly associated with an action. If shoplifting a chocolate bar at a grocery store is a source of prestige for the pilferer by his peers, this represents a form of positive reinforcement that enables future criminal behaviour. Also, positive reinforcement can lead to conforming behaviour, such as when a teenager resists peer pressure to shoplift and is praised by parents and other authorities for behaving properly. The second type of reinforcement is negative, that is, avoiding something believed or perceived by the individual to be negative. Hence, successfully lying to a teacher to avoid a homework assignment or successfully cheating on an exam can lead to additional behaviours of the same type.

Like reinforcement, the link of punishment to criminal behaviour is considered within various socially and culturally defined situations. A positive punishment is illustrated by someone who is caught shoplifting, incurs a cost associated with this illegal behaviour (e.g. an arrest, a fine, a criminal record, a jail term, the disapproval of parents/authorities) and curtails or reduces the frequency of acting the same way in the future. However, a negative punishment would occur when this same individual attempts to resist pressure from peers to shoplift, which may result in derision and loss of valued friendships, hence shoplifting becomes a means of self-esteem and peer-derived prestige.

Associated with social learning theories is a rich criminological tradition of examining the rationalisations by which individuals justify their behaviours, both conforming and non-conforming. The classic work on rationalisation is Sykes and Matza's (1957) work on 'techniques of neutralization'. Rationalisations are socially learned justifications used by individuals for their behaviours, both conforming and criminal. For example, the shoplifter may decide that stealing is OK because the store is part of a worldwide chain of franchises with multi-billion-dollar annual sales, hence one purloined item will neither be missed nor affect the company's profit margin.

SOCIAL BONDS AND SOCIAL CONTROL

Another set of explanations seeks to explain the reasons why people commit crime, based on their integration or bonding with various groups and institutions within a society. These explanations attempt to explain criminal behaviour by examining the ways in which an individual's integration into primary groups within a society constrains involvement in crime, and how lack of integration enhances criminal behaviour. It is presumed that those with strong bonds to conventional groups in a society will also exhibit conforming, non-criminal behaviour. Their constraint stems from their socialisation into society, hence they are less likely to become criminally involved because they feel less free to engage in anti-social behaviours (Gottfredson 2006). They share moral beliefs with others and worry about how they will be viewed by society at large and by others who they know (see also *Social control, governance and governmentality*).

STRAIN THEORY

Agnew's (2012) general strain theory of criminal behaviour combines aspects of both the social learning and social control models. Overall, strain is seen as a lack of integration into society, which in turn produces motivations to engage in various kinds of criminal behaviour. Strain results from a loss, such as unfavourable treatment or a denial of opportunities to succeed in society. Strain can lead to negative emotional states (anger, frustration), to lessened bonding/integration into the mainstream or conventional groups in a society, and can predispose individuals to learn criminal behaviours through deviant and criminal groups.

Even though loss, treatment and denial are very individualistic in their fundamental formulation, general strain theory views their sources as socially derived. And, to a considerable extent, they are not features of individuals per se, but of aggregates of individuals based on social class and poverty, race, ethnicity, gender and other demographic and social structural features of a society, hence the claim to being a general theory for why people commit crime. These sources of strain may be due to adverse experiences (ranging from child abuse to unemployment), personal problems (running the gamut from an unstable marriage to financial instability), discrimination (such as fewer opportunities to succeed financially, culturally and socially, due to one's ethnicity and social class status) or neighbourhood context (such as living in a high-crime area).

CRITICAL PERSPECTIVES

The final set of criminological perspectives is those whose focus is most keenly on social structural factors. These perspectives range from traditional Marxist explanations of crime as a product of the relations of production (i.e. owners/management vs. workers) to the more recent development of criminological understandings of crime through an array of 'critical' approaches (DeKeseredy and Dragiewicz 2011). At their heart, these explanations consider the differential distribution of power, hence they see crime as rooted in economic, social and political inequalities and social class, racism, hate and other forms of segmented social organisation, reinforced and rationalised by culturally derived relativistic definitions of conforming, deviant and criminal actions, which separate, segregate and otherwise cause governments at all levels and peoples everywhere to differentially and discriminately enforce laws and punish offenders (see also *Social construction of crime and deviance* and *Moral panics*).

From the point of view of various conflict and critical theories, four major arguments are made. The first is that biosocial, individualistic, social learning, social control and general strain explanations are flawed views of criminal involvement when they fail to account for larger, structural features of society which must be considered in order to understand why people commit crime. Second, most other explanations fail to account for the role of government and sources of discriminatory enforcement of laws within a society, which in turn generate much greater involvement in criminal behaviour within certain subsets of a society, especially those who are excluded from mainstream society (see also *Poverty and exclusion*). Third, the emergence of subgroups within complex societies which are considered criminal and dangerous requires a broad perspective that understands how power and politics affect public reaction, the criminalisation of behaviours and the differential enforcement of offences (see also *Social control, governance and governmentality*). Finally, certain kinds of criminal behaviour, such as forms of corporate and environmental crime, require an approach which begins with a structural perspective that can account for the effects of capitalism, inequality and power.

REFERENCES

Agnew, R. (2012) *Foundation for a Unified Criminology: Assumptions about the Nature of Crime, People, Society, and Reality.* New York: New York University Press.

Akers, R.L. and Jennings, W.G. (2009) 'The social learning theory of crime and deviance', in M.D. Krohn, A.J. Lizotte and G. Penly Hall (eds) *Handbook on Crime and Deviance.* New York: Springer, pp. 103–20.

DeKeseredy, W.S. and Dragiewicz, M. (eds) (2011) *Routledge Handbook of Critical Criminology.* London: Routledge.

Gottfredson, M.R. (2006) 'The empirical status of control theory in criminology', in F.T. Cullen, J.P. Wright and K.R. Blevins (eds) *Taking Stock: The Status of Criminological Theory.* New Brunswick, NJ: Transaction Publishers, pp. 77–101.

Oetting, E.R., Deffenbacher, J.L. and Donnermeyer, J.F. (1998) 'Primary socialization theory: The role played by personal traits in the etiology of drug use and deviance II', *Substance Use and Misuse*, 33(6): 1337–66.

Sykes, G. and Matza, D. (1957) 'Techniques of neutralization: A theory of delinquency', *American Sociological Review*, 22(6): 664–70.

Walsh, A. and Beaver, K.M. (2009) 'Biosocial criminology', in M.D. Krohn, A.J. Lizotte and G. Penly Hall (eds) *Handbook on Crime and Deviance.* New York: Springer, pp. 79–101.

Definition: *The fear of crime and its study is a consideration of the ways that people have anxiety or worry about the chances of being exposed to (usually violent) crime – either personally, by close others or 'in society' more generally. Closely related to notions of victimisation, fear of crime is often seen as producing an individual or group response that is disproportionate to the 'real' level of risk, and for some groups (e.g. the elderly) as relatively disabling as one personal response may be to stop going out alone. The fear of crime, however, cannot be understood within a conceptual vacuum and by simply comparing it to levels of crime alone. It is most helpfully understood as sitting within the broader concepts of social fear and risk that help us understand why some crimes are feared more than others and why measuring the incidence of crime is only tangentially related to public perceptions of it.*

THE EMERGENCE OF FEAR OF CRIME AND VICTIMISATION

Interest in the fear of crime as an academic and policy-related issue developed in the 1960s when victim surveys began to reveal for the first time that members of the public felt fearful about crime in various ways and with different levels of intensity (see also *Victims of crime*). It is now a distinct area of criminological study that has produced huge amounts of empirical information globally – most of which suggests that the fear of crime (especially of being the victim of a violent crime) is a worry for a substantial part of most populations. In this sense, the fear of crime is now recognised as a phenomenon that has effects in itself on individuals and populations.

THE EFFECTS OF FEAR AND THE FEAR OF CRIME

Individuals that have been the victims of crime can be particularly fearful of its recurrence, can live in constant fear of this and may no longer move around and act with the kind of freedom to which they were accustomed. Even non-victims can respond to their perception of possible victimhood similarly. Living with relative levels of anxiety or fear that impact on daily life and behaviour, perhaps leading to social isolation and withdrawal, is thus an important aspect of how crime potentially affects society more widely than any crime event itself. It is always important to remember, however, that fear of crime and how people experience and respond to being a victim are neither uniform nor necessarily predictable, but there are some important demographic patterns related to the fear of crime. In general, older populations and women are more fearful of being victims than younger and male populations, in part reflecting perceptions on the parts of those who are fearful that they are generally more vulnerable, regardless of the reality. Younger males who regularly drink and go to pubs and clubs are the most at risk of personal injury and vulnerable to attack yet do not in the main admit to feeling themselves to be at risk, whereas women and the elderly often report high levels of anxiety and fear of personal attack. What these demographic insights therefore reveal is that there is no direct or necessary relation between fear of crime and level of actual risk to particular individuals and groups (see also *Risk from crime*).

MEASURING THE FEAR OF CRIME

One of the problems that research on the fear of crime has to deal with is the methodological difficulty of first defining what kind of an emotional response fear is (does it manifest itself simply through, e.g. worry or anxiety, or does a defiant 'I'm not scared' response by some who then take steps to protect themselves or act as vigilantes also reveal a fearsome response?). It may also be that surveys that ask about crime unintentionally raise levels of fear and/or anxiety by providing a focus on various risks, in addition to the fact that different groups may react variably to similar sets of questions. Each of these issues and more make it difficult to work out how to measure fear of crime in a reliable fashion, and it has been shown that the methodology used to do this is often overly simple, likely to produce some erroneous results and, most importantly, may often exaggerate the level and intensity of fear related to crime (Gray et al. 2008). This is a serious issue for if the level of perceived fear is reported to be higher and more intense than it really is, then policy responses to a specific issue may be either disproportionate or unnecessary (see also *Moral panics*).

In addition to it being important to try to measure the fear of crime as accurately as possible, it is also important to be aware of some of the contextual reasons as to why – in general – the fear of crime/s often exceeds the risks of being a victim of such.

RESPONSES TO FEAR AND THE FEAR OF CRIME

There have been a range of strategies employed to help assuage the fear of crime. These range from community strategies involving putting more police 'on the beat', aimed at increasing the visibility of and interaction with enforcement and 'getting tough on crime', to more empowering approaches whereby communities are enabled in the surveillance of their communities (e.g. Neighbourhood Watch schemes) and their homes (e.g. through anti-theft/prevention strategies), in policing (more volunteer police officers) and through victim support schemes where perpetrators recompense or show remorse to victims and communities. These structural or enabling approaches to the fear of crime are widely seen as preferable to encouraging reactive negative individual responses such as avoidance (e.g. not going out or curbing where individuals choose to go) or personal protection (such as carrying a weapon), as these approaches have, in some studies, through constant reminders of personal restriction/preparation, appeared to encourage a generalised culture of fear and, as a consequence, increase levels of individual fear. A culture of fear can sometimes be connected to real-life events or exaggerated and/or (re)'imagined' fears of particular groups sometimes known as 'folk-devils' or scapegoats (see also *Moral panics*). In such cases, societal and criminal justice responses to fear of crime can include calls for, and sometimes the implementation of, new laws and controls to reduce specific types of criminal activity and subsequent fear. Some fears may resonate very specifically and grow over time and endure and, rather than be the result of a short-term panic or scandal, may be the result, such as in the case of paedophilia (Furedi 2007) or drugs (Coomber 2011), of a moral crusade involving numerous 'moral entrepreneurs' that seek to build a specific (morally based) culture of fear.

Cultures of fear can blossom in very specific contexts or more generally, across society, and arguably it is within this broader sense of fear that fear of crime and fear of particular groups can be better understood.

UNDERSTANDING FEAR OF CRIME WITHIN THE BROADER ANALYTICAL CONCEPT OF FEAR

Although theorising around fear is in its relative infancy, it is now a conceptual area of steady development. Until recently, the concept of fear has often been in the conceptual shadow of risk theorisation (see also *Risk from crime*) and has even been seen as the other side of the same coin. Fear, however, is conceptually different from risk – although clearly they overlap at times – and it provides a separate framework to work within at both the macro and micro levels. Like risk theories, however, contemporary analyses of fear also tend to understand fears within the contemporary cultural space – a context that is 'post-modern', 'late modern' or, at the very least, of 'this time'. 'Culture of fear' theorists thus largely understand current fears – such as fear of terrorism, of GM foods, of spy technology – as products of our (post-)modern times rather than as rooted in the distant past. While this may often be the case, it has been argued that some fears, such as those situated around drugs (Coomber 2011) and, by default, certain other forms of traditional criminality involving the labelling or 'othering' of a population, have a longer history rooted in older, more visceral fearfulness. In this sense, it can be argued that many 'modern' fears in fact take a hybrid form – one that combines traditional or ancient forms of fear with sensibilities related to modern concerns.

Pre-modern fear

The basis of all ancient belief systems was fear. (Douglas 1995: 28)

Using fear to manage and/or control people is as old as society itself but traditional fear is distinct from the more fragmented cultures of fear of late modernity. Pre-modern fears were primarily focused on basic survival and related to things such as famine, flood and the wrath of God. Tom Douglas (1995) has related how it was common in pre-modern societies fearful of (vengeful) acts of God (potentially inclusive of all ills) to ritually transfer blame, sin and thus risk onto scapegoats in an attempt to purify themselves and allay the wrath of their God/s.

Late-modern fear

Without providing a fulsome overview of current positions on late-modern fears, we can summarise them as being products of something new – as distinct from divine intervention or an increased awareness of our vulnerability (through constantly being reminded of it across the various media) in the world and that we are only partially able to manage those vulnerabilities. Whether that be fear of crime/s or fear of climate change or fear of airborne chemicals, we now live with more fear(s) than ever before in the history of human society (Furedi 2007). Fears are also said to be subject to the 'cultural script' – i.e. each of us has learnt about the types of thing that we should be fearful of (such as an intoxicated drug user but not an intoxicated alcohol user) and the script guides us on how we will respond to particular fears – including the fear of crime. Garland (2001) has linked post-modern societies with 'penal populism', where politicians, in dealing with a victim-conscious sensibility or a population deemed to be broadly dissatisfied with the effectiveness of the criminal justice system to control crime, respond by getting tougher on crime. A generalised and fragmented fear (of many things) can then also inflect on more specific fears such as a fear of crime and provide a policy milieu for a more punitive response at the level of society and a fearful 'protective' response at the level of the individual.

CONCLUSION

Fear of crime is thus an important issue for understanding crime in society and the responses to it. Why and how people fear, however, is not straightforward and isn't simply linked to the amount of crime experienced directly or even that being committed in society. Fear of crime is today just one facet of a broader set of fears people live with, fears that are fragmented but that also in many cases (e.g. terrorism, environmental health issues that are all around, technological problems) appear irresolvable to governments and those in authority. This creates for some commentators a more general culture of fear through which people live their lives, and a shift to penal populism and tougher measures on criminals is arguably one response to that broader context of fear that has emerged as a consequence.

REFERENCES

Coomber, R. (2011) 'Social fear, drug related beliefs and drug policy', in G. Hunt, M. Milhet and H. Bergeron (eds) *Drugs and Culture: Knowledge, Consumption and Policy*. Aldershot: Ashgate. pp. 15–31.

Douglas, T. (1995) *Scapegoats: Transferring Blame*. London: Routledge.

Furedi, F. (2007) *Culture of Fear: Risk Taking and the Morality of Low Expectation*. Cambridge: Cassell.

Garland, D. (2001) *The Culture of Control: Crime and Social Order in Contemporary Society*. Oxford: Oxford University Press.

Gray, E., Jackson, J. and Farrall, S. (2008) 'Reassessing the fear of crime', *European Journal of Criminology*, 5(3): 363–80.

Definition: *Poverty is defined in terms of money or income, and refers to the inability of an individual or household to pay for housing, food and other basic necessities. Social exclusion is considered a frequent outcome of poverty. It is a concept which refers to the inability of individuals to access rights and opportunities to participate fully in the economic, social and cultural mainstream of a society. Criminologists have long been interested in poverty, especially in societies based on market economies, because of its correlation with crime. Social exclusion also helps criminologists understand why structural inequalities and discrimination in a society lead to the over-representation of some people in the criminal justice system, both as offenders and as victims.*

POVERTY AND CAPITAL

Poverty is generally defined in terms of a threshold, based on financial or economic capital, such as income and wealth. Income is the amount of money earned or accumulated over a specified period of time, such as a week, a month or a year. Wealth may be defined as a set of assets related to ownership of property, stock in a business, annuities, valuables, etc., which generate income.

Financial or economic capital is an essential indicator of an individual's status in a society, especially in terms of social class location. However, money and wealth alone (or lack thereof) does not completely assure either a high or low social class location within a society. Also important is a person's social capital. Social capital refers to the connections an individual has to others in a society. Often, these links are labelled as bonding capital, which may be defined in brief as the connections and cohesion among members of the same group, and bridging capital, which are links across to other groups, many of which are located at places far from where an individual holder of a bridging link lives and works.

In addition to financial capital and social capital is cultural capital, which includes the level of education of individuals and socially acquired tastes for consumer items which display their social class location in a society, plus their accent, body language and personal appearance. Sometimes, human capital is used to describe the educational level and other skills of an individual, and can be confused with cultural capital. Cultural capital includes a wider array of attributes and is more indicative of a lifestyle which generally identifies an individual's social ranking.

Another consideration in understanding the concept of poverty is the distinction between absolute and relative poverty. Absolute poverty indicates the threshold below which individuals cannot obtain shelter and food for survival. In addition, it is presumed that people in absolute poverty lack not only the financial capital to survive, but also lack the kinds of social and cultural capital necessary to achieve and fully participate in society (Portes 1998).

The difficulty with determining absolute poverty is that standards of living vary so much from one country to another. Instead, social scientists, including criminologists, rely on floating or flexible definitions of poverty. One is relative poverty, which is a threshold determined by the standards of living within a society. Hence, the poverty rate in US society is determined by income thresholds adjusted for the size of a household and the cost of living variations. Most definitions of relative poverty and related thresholds are usually determined by a governmental agency and are used to indicate eligibility for various assistance programmes. In addition, different levels of poverty can be determined based on these metrics, with rates or percentages of the population calculated for each level (see also *Prevalence, incidence and incident of crime*) For example, a certain percentage of the population might be below the general poverty line, but a smaller proportion is below an income level that is 75% or 50% of the poverty line. Hence, poverty becomes relative to a fixed number within a country, which in turn varies from country to country, based on differences in levels of living and economic development.

A second way social scientists examine poverty is by the concentration of income and wealth. Measures of concentration are often expressed in terms of a percentile. As a hypothetical example, in country A, the top 10% of the richest earn or own 60% of all the financial assets. In country B, the top 10% earn or own 25% of everything. Hence, concentration is much higher in country A than in country B. A statistic called the Gini coefficient is often used to measure concentration. The basic formula is quite simple – the Gini coefficient equals A divided by A + B. A is the amount of income and wealth owned by a certain percentage of a population and B is the remaining amount of income and wealth owned by the rest of the population. If the Gini coefficient approaches 0, there is minimal concentration of income and wealth. If the Gini coefficient approaches 1, income and wealth are highly concentrated (see also *Crime statistics*).

The Gini coefficient is a useful way to compare inequality across both space and time, and so too is a rate of poverty. Hence, someone might conduct a study of the rate of crime at the neighbourhood level, using both the poverty rate and the Gini coefficient to test for ways that the economic structure of places is statistically associated with crime.

Criminologists also frequently cite poverty as a correlate or risk for involvement in criminal behaviour (see also *Why people commit crime*). For example, in an attempt to test the relative contribution of poverty, as a measure of 'socioeconomic deprivation', rates of homicide offending (based on arrests) were examined for the black and white populations of US cities of 100,000 or more persons (Ousey 1999). For Ousey (1999), poverty is one of several 'structural' level (i.e. societal level) indicators that are frequently utilised to explain variations in homicide arrests. As a measure of poverty, he used the 'officially defined poverty threshold' (Ousey 1999: 411) for black and white persons. Ousey (1999) also used a measure of income inequality, which was the Gini coefficient for black and white populations in each of the 125 US cities included in his analysis. He discovered that poverty was more important as a structural level factor for predicting homicide arrests for whites than for blacks, suggesting other structural level factors, such as discrimination, may be in operation there.

Many criminological theories consider poverty to be a key predictor of an individual's involvement in crime (see also *Why people commit crime*). Another reason why poverty is a central concept in much of criminology is the ability of researchers to conduct sophisticated statistical operations to test for the relationship of various quantifiable measures of poverty and inequality with equally quantifiable rates of crime (see also *Crime statistics*). Poverty is generally presumed to be positively associated with crime because an area with high poverty lacks the resources necessary to control crime, and criminologists likewise suggest that income inequality in an area reduces the cohesion among people who live there; that is, it assumes their social class differences create a segmented social structure where cohesion is weakened and crime increases (Ousey 1999).

SOCIAL EXCLUSION

However, critics often contend that relying solely on various measures of income, no matter how methodologically sophisticated, are inadequate, especially in societies with heterogeneous populations based on race, ethnicity and other characteristics, such as the UK and the USA. The issue is not economic deprivation per se, but social exclusion. In other words, without connecting the ways that poverty and income inequality are linked to social and cultural capital, and considering the ways that disadvantage is also predicated on non-economic factors, such as discrimination by race, ethnicity, gender, lifestyle and other essential dimensions of social structure, crime cannot be examined in a wider and more critical context. This was the intent of Jock Young's (1999) classic work entitled *The Exclusive Society*, which considered the mechanisms of exclusion, and the intersectionality of factors associated with exclusion, within late-modern societies.

Social exclusion is usually conceptualised in two ways. The first is in terms of lack of economic resources or material deprivation and lack of access to human rights protection and government services and programmes (Jehoel-Gijsbers and Vrooman 2007). This is called structural exclusion and is meant as a way of understanding how the distribution of resources is related to differences by social class, race and ethnicity, and other factors which create structural divisions in complex societies. The second element is the relational dimension (Johoel-Gijsbers and Vrooman 2007), which points to aspects of social and cultural integration into a society. Especially when social exclusion involves not a single individual but a set of people based on similarities in their social class, race/ethnicity and other factors related to social status, it is presumed to be a structural condition of a society.

The concept of social exclusion is meant to capture what happens – the outcomes of poverty and income inequality and other forms of discrimination in a society. Social exclusion does not mean social isolation. Indeed, social exclusion likely creates subcultures, some of which can be deviant by mainstream cultural standards and criminal as defined by the powerful in a society. Hence, alternative forms of social networks representing deviant and even oppositional subcultures develop, partly as a function of exclusion. For example, Shucksmith (2004) describes three kinds of social exclusion – (i) lack of employment which provides integration into a society, (ii) poverty and lack of resources, and (iii) participation in an underclass considered deviant by the mainstream. Shucksmith sums it up by referring to this as 'no work, no money and no morals' (p. 44).

In the *British Journal of Criminology*, an article by McKeever (2007) applies both the concepts of social exclusion and poverty to consider the problem of re-integration of political prisoners in Northern Ireland after their release. His concern is both with the general political environment of Northern Ireland and with the ability of ex-prisoners to participate as citizens in the political process. He recognises that both social exclusion and poverty are 'closely connected to the root of conflict in Northern Ireland' (2007: 434). His use of the concept of social exclusion allows him to analyse the situation from several angles:

> In considering this issue of integration of such political prisoners, standard criminological considerations of how to discourage recidivism through social inclusion have only partial purchase, since, in Northern Ireland, the issue of exclusion elides into the question of political opposition. The very concept of 're-integration' is problematic because it does not address this meeting point of political opposition and social exclusion or recognise that those who faced political, social or economic exclusion prior to their imprisonment were never 'integrated' to begin with; ex-prisoners may have been 'integrated' into their own local social and political cultures, but still not receiving the social, welfare and economic goods nowadays associated with full citizenship. (McKeever 2007: 424)

There is no argument that poverty (and synonymous concepts like income inequality) and social exclusion (and associated concepts like inclusion, citizenship and integration) are theoretical bedfellows in the search by criminologists for the root causes of crime. Yet, even though they consider criminological issues from fundamentally the same causal logic, how they are operationalised and used in research and analysis by criminologists can be very different. Poverty lends itself to quantitative examination, while social exclusion is more conducive to a qualitative and critical analysis of crime and society.

REFERENCES

Jehoel-Gijsbers, G. and Vrooman, C. (2007) *Explaining Social Exclusion: A Theoretical Model Explaining Social Exclusion Tested in the Netherlands*. The Hague: The Netherlands Institute for Social Research.

McKeever, G. (2007) 'Citizenship and social exclusion: The re-integration of political ex-prisoners in Northern Ireland', *British Journal of Criminology*, 47(3): 423–38.

Ousey, G.C. (1999) 'Homicide, structural factors, and the racial invariance assumption', *Criminology*, 37(2): 405–26.

Portes, A. (1998) 'Social capital: Its origins and applications in modern sociology', *Annual Review of Sociology*, 24(1): 1–24.

Shucksmith, M. (2004) 'Young people and social exclusion in rural areas', *Sociologia Ruralis*, 44(1–2): 43–59.

Young, J. (1999) *The Exclusive Society*. London: Macmillan.

14 poverty and exclusion

> **Definition**: 'Victims of crime' is a phrase which can include anyone who is affected directly or indirectly by criminal activity. One branch of criminology focuses exclusively on the victim. It is known as victimology, which is the scientific study of victims which attempts to describe patterns of victimisation, explains social and psychological factors associated with the risk of becoming a crime victim, and examines the underlying political, economic, social and cultural forces which contextualise how society defines who is the victim and who is not.

Up to the 1960s, the scholarly spotlight beamed almost exclusively on understanding offenders (see also *Why people commit crime* and *Crime and theory*). In part, this was due to the influence of readily available data on offences and arrests, such as the Federal Bureau of Investigation's *Uniform Crime Report* in the USA. Civil rights movements on behalf of women and minority groups in many countries of the world brought a sharper focus to the plight of victims. At the same time, there was a growing concern with victims' services and recognition of the simple fact that many crimes are never reported to law enforcement.

DEVELOPMENT OF VICTIMISATION RESEARCH

Even though previous generations of criminologists – including Caesar Lombroso, Edwin Sutherland and Benjamin Mendelsohn – wrote about the victims of crime, it was not until the latter half of the twentieth century that an increasing number of criminologists turned their attention to understanding victimisation, including why some people are more likely to be victimised, the experiences of victims and their post-victimisation actions (including whether or not they notified law enforcement), the perceptions of citizens as important foci in the study of crime, the ways in which both society and the criminal justice system socially construct or define the victim, and appropriate responses to their situation. In regard to the latter, much consideration is given to the notion that some victims are ignored or devalued within a society. In particular, feminist scholars point to the patriarchal forces embedded within the criminal justice systems of many societies around the world, which lead to ignoring and devaluing certain crimes where men are nearly always the perpetrators, such as rape and intimate partner violence (DeKeseredy 2011) (see also *Gender and crime*, and *Social construction of crime and deviance*).

During the 1970s, the US Department of Justice began the National Crime Survey, now known as the National Crime Victimization Study. Following on soon after were victimisation surveys with similar objectives conducted in other countries, such as the British Crime Survey (now called the Crime Survey of England and Wales) which began in 1982. The Scottish Crime and Victimisation Survey (known today as the Scottish Crime and Justice Survey) split off from the British Crime Survey. It has been conducted separately since 1993. A Northern Ireland Crime Survey was also established in 1994. Meanwhile, the European Crime and Safety Survey began in 2005, based in large part on the International Crime Victims Survey, which was started in 1987. Scholars around the world also regularly utilise victimisation surveys for smaller regional and local studies of crime.

VICTIMISATION SURVEYS

Each of these victimisation surveys has common characteristics. They are conducted on an annual, a biannual or some other periodic basis. The surveys generally involve thousands of households and individuals. Weights are assigned to create nationally representative rates of household-level crime, such as burglary, larceny, vandalism and motor vehicle theft. Personal crimes include theft directly from a person (such as pick-pocketing/purse-snatching), plus assault, sexual assault, rape and robbery. Follow-up questions attempt to elicit additional information about the victim's experiences and the circumstances associated with different types of criminal events. The surveys 'bound' their questions, usually to a six-month time period, so that respondents do not mention incidents outside these referenced time periods, which would inflate victimisation rates. One typical way of bounding is accomplished by interviewing the same households and their members (usually only adults) several times over 2–3 time periods, with the first interview setting the bound, followed by a second interview several months later which asks about crime experiences during this time period, followed by additional interviews, each using the previous contact as the time reference, until the household is rotated out of the sample after several years of participation.

There are four important dimensions derived from victimisation studies, beyond alternative crime rate estimates to official police statistics. The first is repeat victimisation. Repeat victimisation, quite simply, is the identification of types of households and persons who are at risk of multiple victimisations. Repeat victimisations may be the same type of crime incident or different types of incidents. However, just as some criminologists identify 'hot spots' as localities where multiple crimes occur, so too some households and persons are highly vulnerable to multiple crime experiences.

Second, victimisation data, along with official crime data, help identify populations who are vulnerable to crime. Potentially correlated with crime experiences from victimisation surveys are sex, race/ethnicity, income, age of household head, size and type of household (i.e. married couple, single person, family with children, etc.) and other demographic and social characteristics. This kind of information, when tracked over time, shows how the status of people within a society varies in their vulnerability to crime.

Third, information about reactions to crime and how people perceive the safety of their neighbourhoods and the effectiveness of law enforcement and the criminal justice system is a core element of most victimisation surveys. In particular, it is possible to compare victims and non-victims on their views about crime and a variety of crime types to adjust these comparisons by the demographic character-istics of survey participants (see also *Fear and the fear of crime*).

Finally, research on understanding the dynamics of victim precipitation is greatly aided by victimisation surveys. Victim precipitation, that is, the ways victims may contribute to or provoke their own victimisation can be erroneously seen as a form of 'blaming the victim'. It is not! Victim precipitation refers to factors ranging from someone who engaged in a loud argument at a pub and subsequently was the victim of an assault, to a woman who is the victim of violence from her male part-ner but is reluctant to leave, to a home burglary where the doors had been left unlocked when the occupants were out shopping or for some other reason were not at home.

VICTIMISATION THEORY AND RESEARCH

Victim precipitation is one factor that is now included in criminological theories which focus on factors related to the victim and the target (Wilcox 2010), such as routine activities theory (see also *Crime and theory*). At the macro level, routine activities theory attempts to explain how long-term changes influence crime rates. For example, the entry of women into the labour force of the US economy in the 1950s and 1960s greatly changed daily lifestyle patterns, decreasing guardianship and increasing the number of attractive targets (see also *Risk from crime*). On the micro level, routine activities theory considers how context contributes to crime through an incredible variety of factors. Hence, researchers might examine how guns escalate arguments and fights into homicides or how height and weight differences between two individuals influence who is the aggressor and who is the victim (Felson 2002).

The theory of lifestyle and victimisation pays special attention to the connection between becoming an offender and becoming a victim of crime. One way to exam-ine this link is to understand the ways that criminal lifestyles contribute to victimisation (Berg et al. 2012), such as violent crime offenders who are also the victims of violent crime, and how becoming a victim may precipitate becoming an offender (Felson 2002) (see also *Risk from crime*).

Factors identified in situational crime prevention (Clarke 2009) and CPTED (Crowe 2000) also identify place-based factors which facilitate or constrain crime victimisation. Part of this tradition of research and theorising involves the ways both offenders and victims see places, especially public spaces, as points of vulner-ability or areas of safety and security. Situational crime prevention also accounts for such factors as criminogenic products (e.g. handguns as a tool of the offender, and credit cards as attractive targets), poor management (e.g. leaving a laptop on the back seat of an unlocked car) and design flaws in buildings and public places (e.g. blind areas, poor lighting) (Clarke 2009).

Also extending a focus on the victims of crime are more specialised themes related to difficult-to-research topics based solely on official police data or the victimisation survey, relying instead on qualitative data, such as key informant interviews. Two examples are research on child abuse (Children's Bureau 2012) and studies of vio-lence against women (DeKeseredy 2011). Their focus is the victim, and their care for accuracy and reliability of data is the same as those who use victimisation surveys to study the victims of crime, but their research goal is more concerned with incidence (i.e. new cases) or collecting incidents (i.e. cases) than prevalence (all cases) (see also *Prevalence, incidence and incident of crime*). In the USA, the 'Fourth National Incidence Study of Child Abuse and Neglect' was based on cases known to child protective services and of children who came to the attention of childcare professionals but for whom no additional action was taken (Children's Bureau 2012). Much of the research on violence against women, such as DeKeseredy's (2011) work, utilises both the National Crime Victimization Survey and various qualitative interviews based on a purposive sampling strategy (usually soliciting confidential interviews with abused women through a local newspaper ad or through flyers left at shelters) to add depth to the survey data and explore particular themes. One such theme is the extent to which males who abuse their partners receive support and even advice from other males in their family and their community for their violent behaviours, which is a localised expression of hegemonic or powerful forms of patriarchy, and contradicts the assumptions of criminologists who assume that collective efficacy only reduces crime (see also *Crime and theory*).

Finally, media depictions of crime shape public perceptions of victims, victim blame and the deservingness or social value (or lack thereof) placed on victims, as well as on offenders. In turn, media and socially derived biases about victims can be seen as influencing the behaviour of courts, the police and other parts of the criminal justice system. These depictions include not only the news, but the ways both police/detective series and so-called reality programming shape societal reactions to crime (Greer 2012) (see also *Crime and the media*).

CONCLUSION

Altogether, the criminological focus on the victims of crime has built up a rich base of knowledge about: who is the victim; the relationship between victimisation and offending; perceptions of crime and criminal justice agencies; ways that victims and their lifestyles influence when, where and to whom a crime occurs; and how factors associated with inequality and bias contextualise the framing of a victim within societies around the world. Most criminological theories related to the victims of crime start with the idea that there will be a certain proportion of people in any society who will commit a crime. By suspending (ceterus paribus) variables contributing to the risk of becoming criminally involved, they are able to examine the other side of the crime question, namely the victims of crime, hence providing a fuller picture of the causes of crime and related solutions.

REFERENCES

Berg, M.T., Stewart, E.A., Schreck, C.J. and Simons, R.L. (2012) 'The victim–offender overlap in context: Examining the role of neighborhood street culture', *Criminology*, 50(2): 359–89.

Children's Bureau (2012) *Child Mistreatment 2011*. Washington, DC: US Department of Health and Human Services, Administration for Children and Families.

Clarke, R.V. (2009) 'Situational crime prevention: Theoretical background and current practice', in M.D. Krohn, A.J. Lizotte and G. Penly Hall (eds) *Handbook on Crime and Deviance*. New York: Springer, pp. 259–76.

Crowe, T. (2000) *Crime Prevention through Environmental Design*. Stoneham, MA: Butterworth-Heinemann.

DeKeseredy, W.S. (2011) *Violence against Women: Myths, Facts, Controversies*. Toronto: University of Toronto Press.

Felson, M. (2002) *Crime and Everyday Life*, 3rd edn. Thousand Oaks, CA: Pine Forge Press.

Greer, C. (2012) *Sex Crime and the Media: Sex Offending and the Press in a Divided Society*. London: Routledge.

Wilcox, P. (2010) 'Victimization, theories of', in B.S. Fisher and S.P. Lab (eds) *Encyclopedia of Victimology and Crime Prevention*. Thousand Oaks, CA: Sage, pp. 978–84.

16 Normalisation

Definition: *There are two general conceptualisations of the term normalisation. For many criminologists, normalisation refers to the way in which crime has become an everyday part of life. For example, Durkheim (1965) argued that deviance was not an inherently pathological condition of the lawbreaker, but a normal feature of society, and that a crime-free society would be impossible to achieve. Similarly, David Garland (1996) and Jock Young (1999) both draw on the phenomenon of escalating crime rates in western societies to argue that crime has now become a normal social fact. Thus, Young (1999) argues that this **normalisation** of crime suggests criminals should now be conceptualised as 'rational offenders', whose characters and behaviours have become blurred with that of the 'normal' citizen.*

*The second general conceptualisation of normalisation oscillates around notions of normal or good citizenship. Howard Becker (1963) proposed that individuals not conforming to social expectations of normal or good citizenship are thrust into a category of deviance by the judgements of others in society. This deviant category marks out these individuals as 'outsiders'. Thus, **normalisation** refers to the normative standards of a society used to measure good or desirable citizenship. Post-structuralists explore this conceptualisation of normalisation in considering societies' responses to crime, especially practices of social control during modernity.*

NORMALISATION OF CRIME AND CRIMINALS

Behaviours regarded as deviant, regardless of whether they are legally sanctioned or not (see also *Crime (definition of)* and *Deviance (definition of)*), can become so frequent that they develop into accepted practices of a society (Rock 1973). According to Young (1999), drug use is a prime example in the normalisation of behaviours that were previously considered deviant. Researchers at the University of Manchester developed the normalisation thesis, asserting that the use of illicit drugs such as marijuana has become part of youth culture and thus a normalised behaviour (Parker et al. 1998). The normalisation thesis draws on empirical evidence, indicating that most young people use illicit drugs at some stage in their lives. This widespread drug use undermines the notion that it is a subcultural practice. Rejecting notions of pathology and social dysfunction as primary factors in the cause of illicit drug use, the normalisation thesis proposes that recreational, illicit drug use is part of a broader search for pleasure, excitement and enjoyment in young people's consumption-oriented leisure lifestyles. Moreover, it suggests that non-drug-using youth could eventually become a minority, and thus the 'deviant' group (Parker et al. 1998) (see also *Crime (definition of) and Deviance (definition of)*).

Critics of the normalisation thesis argue that the thesis exaggerates and misrepresents the extent and normative contexts of young people's drug use (Shiner and Newburn 1999: 142). Research by Simmonds and Coomber (2009) found that a more complex form of normalisation existed within cultures of injecting drug users. Normative judgements of 'clean'/'dirty' and 'responsible'/'irresponsible' drug use stigmatised injecting drug users via a subcultural hierarchy. Injecting drug users who perceived themselves as 'normal' frequently stigmatised other injecting drug users who did not conform to their perspectives of a 'good drug user', such as those who were homeless.

NORMALISATION AND RISK

According to Lea (2002), the blurring of the identity of criminals in contemporary society is a consequence of social groups increasingly encountering one another as risky. This results in confusion between actual criminality and the need to safeguard against the risk of crime and protect oneself against 'risky' people. Those deemed risky and 'dangerous' frequently tend to encompass ethnic groups, those from poorer classes and those who are most visible, such as young people and homeless individuals. In particular, groups that are unknown to the wider community, and do not engage in broad social interactions, may be regarded with suspicion and fear. Thus, Garland (1996) argues that crime is no longer an unexpected or unusual event, but is instead a normal feature of everyday life and a routine part of modern consciousness. It is now an everyday risk to be assessed and managed as another 'normal' danger (see also *Risk from crime*).

The anticipation and fear of crime is heightened by criminal subcultures losing their distinctiveness and resuming features of normality. The normalisation of crime lends support for tighter crime-prevention measures and more punitive responses to crime (Lea 2002). There has subsequently been a growth in strategies to manage the risk of crime and an expansion in the security market in anticipation of incidents of criminality.

DISCIPLINARY POWER

Normalisation as a practice was examined in the work of the French philosopher Michel Foucault (1926–84). In *Discipline and Punish: The Birth of the Prison*

(1977), Foucault introduces the idea of disciplinary power. He argues that 'sovereign power', typically encountered in pre-modern societies as punitive and excessive physical punishment, does not typify the types of power encountered within contemporary societies. Instead, his notion of 'disciplinary power' dominates modern societies (see also *Crime in pre-industrial, pre-modern and post-modern societies*).

Disciplinary power reverses the relations of traditional forms of power. Instead of power being forced down from above through oppressive rule, power is interspersed through the social. Further, with discipline there is an inversion of visibility onto the subjects of power who are presented as 'objects' for the examining gaze. Thus, disciplinary power is productive in that its principle is to 'invest' in things, with 'things' primarily meaning people. It may also be described as a form of power that operates on the basis of minimum expenditure for maximum return.

Discipline operates a microphysics of power penetrating the most 'intimate' spheres of life. It is a power which has as its object and target the human body, seeking to shape and train, in order that it might be made obedient, skilful, responsive and productive. Disciplinary power was first practised in military barracks, hospitals, asylums, schools, factories, offices, and so on, and hence became a crucial aspect of social control in modern societies.

POWER AND THE BODY

Discipline is not the first form of power to have had the body as its object and target. What distinguishes it from preceding forms of power is its capacity to simultaneously objectify and subject the body, which it achieves through the use of technologies that individualise and accumulate, that normalise the body. In order to train and correct, discipline does not only penalise but introduces a double system of gratification-punishment. This mechanism allows for behaviour to be distributed between positive and negative poles. Thus, behaviour is not just demarcated in a binary opposition of permitted and forbidden, but is differentiated according to a normalising scale.

Discipline is not simply practised on populations but is also actively produced by populations as a strategic method of self-constitution. People are not 'conditioned' by repressive methods alone, but are normalised according to a system of censure and praise. The social sciences and its technicians, such as health professionals and psychologists, have been important in extending normalisation as a form of social control with its focus both on abnormal and everyday activities.

The shift to disciplinary power is often captured in the movement in punishment from torture and dungeons to the use of prisons. Prisons attempt to normalise ('rehabilitate') inmates so that they can become 'productive' members of society. Prisons operate a positive form of power with one of the aims being to re-integrate offenders into society, as opposed to acting as a mechanism solely for social exclusion (see also *Punishment* and *Rehabilitation*).

NORMALISATION AND SOCIAL CONTROL

Foucault's ideas have been advanced by criminologists examining contemporary shifts in social control. Increases in official crime rates have occurred despite substantial increases in living standards and considerable expenditure on criminal justice systems (Young 1999: 122). Garland (1996) argues that modern governments and other agencies have responded to the seemingly entrenched nature of high crime rates through the 'new criminologies of everyday life'. Underpinning these new criminologies is the assumption that crime is a normal, routine, commonplace aspect of modern society, and hence a continuous risk to be predicted, calculated and managed through normalisation strategies (see also *Crime in pre-industrial, pre-modern and post-modern societies*).

MODERN CRIME CONTROL

Since the 1970s, dangerousness has been increasingly over-determined and analogised with crime, to the point that an assumption of dangerousness underpins every aspect of dealing with deviance (Lianos 2010) (see also *Crime (definition of)* and *Deviance (definition of)*). Jock Young (1999) argues that in contemporary western societies crime has become a normalised part of everyday life with everyone now perceived as a suspect, with justice subordinated to harm minimisation. Young (1999) explains this as an actuarial stance, which is probabilistic and calculative of risk and manages these risks through surveillance and security techniques. Surveillance includes practices and techniques to collect data about individuals and entities with or without their consent.

Under these new technologies, citizens are expected to take responsibility for preventing and controlling crime by changing their practices to reduce opportunities for crime to occur (see also *Social control, governance, and governmentality*). At the same time, a growth in punitive policies since the 1970s has contradicted the push for individual responsibility and prevention strategies. According to Lea (2002: 159), the normalisation of crime and criminality co-exists with the construction of moral panics and public worry about crime, even when the crime rate is declining.

As part of these new technologies, situational crime-prevention measures aim to reduce opportunities through a range of innovative new security and crime-prevention techniques, which reorient the responsibility for crime control from governments to private agencies and individuals (Garland 1996: 451). Crime control devices are embedded in normal everyday social interactions and enacted through various informal controls. These include public awareness campaigns and citizen groups, and surveillance techniques such as private security agencies and CCTV cameras (Garland 1996: 451–2). These strategies represent a replacement of control mechanisms of repression with practices of normalisation.

REFERENCES

Becker, H.S. (1963) *Outsiders: Studies in the Sociology of Deviance*. New York: Macmillan.
Durkheim, E. (1965) *The Rules of the Sociological Method*. New York: Free Press.

Foucault, M. (1977) *Discipline and Punish: The Birth of the Prison*. London: Allen Lane.

Garland, D. (1996) 'The limits of the sovereign state: Strategies of crime control in contemporary society', *British Journal of Criminology*, 36(4): 445–71.

Lea, J. (2002) *Crime and Modernity: Continuities in Left Realist Criminology*. London: Sage.

Lianos, M. (2010) 'Periopticon: Control beyond freedom and coercion – and two possible advancements in the social sciences', in K. Haggerty and M. Samatas (eds) *Surveillance and Democracy*. Abingdon: Routledge, pp. 52–69.

Parker, H., Aldridge, J. and Measham, F. (1998) *Illegal Leisure: The Normalization of Adolescent, Recreational Drug Use*. London: Routledge.

Rock, P. (1973) *Deviant Behaviour*. London: Hutchinson.

Shiner, M. and Newburn, T. (1999) 'Taking tea with Noel: The place and meaning of drug use in everyday life', in N. South (ed.) *Drugs: Cultures, Controls and Everyday Life*. London: Sage, pp. 140–59.

Simmonds, L. and Coomber, R. (2009) 'Injecting drug users: A stigmatised and stigmatising population', *International Journal of Drug Policy*, 20: 121–30.

Young, J. (1999) *The Exclusive Society: Social Exclusion, Crime and Difference in Late Modernity*. London: Sage.

17 Gender and Crime

> **Definition**: *Gender is socially constructed and refers to the ways in which societies define femininity and masculinity, and how social interaction and social institutions work to reinforce conceptions of femininity and masculinity.*

Early perspectives of gender and crime were influenced greatly by biological determinism. For example, Cesare Lombroso (2006) believed that criminals were born and could be differentiated from non-criminals through physical characteristics. He focused on prisoners largely from one ethnic background, and he neglected the role of poverty and its influence on nutrition and health overall. In a subsequent publication, entitled *The Female Offender* (1920), Lombroso argued that women were morally deficient because they were 'less evolved' than men. The perceived inferiority of women was highlighted in work by Thomas (1923) who viewed poor women in particular as sexually manipulative in the course of criminality. Pollack (1950) argued that women's biology made them more deceitful than men, and suggested that women's position in domestic spheres made it easier for women to conceal their crimes.

The emphasis on biological sex differences in explaining crime ignored power hierarchies pertaining to gender, race/ethnicity and social class. Whereas 'sex' is traditionally viewed as the biological differences that distinguish males and females, such as differences that relate to hormones, genitalia and chromosomes, gender is socially constructed. In other words, societal definitions of masculine and feminine can change over time and vary across cultures; behaviours that are perceived as feminine in one culture can be perceived as masculine in another. Notions of femininity and masculinity are created by and perpetuated during social interaction. Moreover, social institutions (e.g. family, religion, school) reinforce the construction of gender by socialising us to behave in ways that are consistent with our biological sex. Although the distinction between biological sex and gender has been debated, several feminist scholars have been critical of mainstream criminologists' preoccupation with biological sex rather than gender.

In western cultures, most crime is committed by men, and crimes committed by women tend to be less serious than those committed by men. These differences, as well as women's position in social and political hierarchies, served to justify the exclusion of women offenders from mainstream criminological scholarship. Female criminologists in particular began to publicly challenge these views, beginning in the 1970s. Led by female scholars in the UK and the USA, they argued that women's criminality had been neglected and misinterpreted by mainstream criminologists. Carol Smart (1976) noted that studies of criminality had been conducted primarily by men, and were based largely on samples of males. Women's criminality was perceived as unimportant if not irrelevant among mainstream criminologists. During the same decade, Dorie Klein (1973) argued that the limited research into women and crime was guided by sexist and racist attitudes, and that feminist approaches were needed to challenge these perceptions. Other scholars began to examine women's criminality from the perspective of increased employment opportunities that resulted from women's emancipation (Adler 1975; Simon 1975). Adler (1975) proposed that women were adopting the traditional masculine traits of competitiveness and aggression, as they moved out of domestic spheres into male-dominated workplaces. Simon (1975) agreed that increasing opportunities in the workplace paralleled opportunities for involvement in crime, but proposed that changing employment conditions for women would lead to increases in employment-related property crimes, such as fraud and embezzlement. Other writers were critical of these claims and neither argument generated much empirical support. Still, Adler and Simon pushed the boundaries of criminology by focusing on an important topic that had been previously neglected by the discipline.

Scholarly interest in gender and crime has flourished since the 1970s, a change that Heidensohn (2012: 128) referred to as a 'fundamental cultural shift' in criminology. Research publications on gender and crime have appeared in mainstream academic journals, as well as in other journals that have been developed to focus specifically on issues relating to women and crime. A number of authors have published textbooks and edited collections on women and crime, and prominent sections have been developed as part of leading professional associations. Moreover, hundreds of undergraduate and graduate courses on gender and crime have been incorporated into university curricula, or have been embedded into core curricula, developments that reinforce the importance of the topic to emerging scholars. The increased scholarly focus on women and crime has been influenced greatly by feminist scholars, some of whom have challenged the feasibility and appropriateness of gender-neutral theories and the methods used to examine theoretical links between gender and crime.

GENDER AND OFFENDING

Studies of crime conducted in western nations have found that most offenders are male. Although this pattern has been demonstrated regardless of the data utilised (i.e. official crime statistics, victimisation surveys or self-report surveys), the extent of the disparity varies by data source and across cultures. The discrepancy in male and female offending has been referred to as the 'gender gap', and scholars have attempted to explain this gap through assorted theoretical perspectives.

Despite its strong roots in sociology, the field of criminology has been shaped by various disciplinary approaches. Biological theorists view the gender gap as a result of hormonal, genetic or neurological differences between males and females, although contemporary biological perspectives often acknowledge the role of sociological or psychological processes that interact with biological factors to influence behaviour. Psychological perspectives have focused on factors such as personality and emotional attributes (e.g. aggressive tendencies in some males), and differences in cognitive thinking between males and females.

Several sociological explanations for the gender gap have been proposed. These theories have focused on theoretical concepts such as power control, peer and family relations, social learning and strain. Several researchers who examine crime, however, make reference to 'gender' but define it in terms of biological sex, thus they fail to consider how gendered power relations affect criminality or the response to it. Some feminist scholars have viewed this omission as a major criticism of mainstream criminology.

Other theoretical approaches have focused (largely) on male criminality from the perspective of masculinities (Connell and Messerschmidt 2005). These authors view masculinity in different forms, whereby hegemonic masculinity is exalted, valued and culturally constructed. 'Tough guys' and some athletes are contemporary examples of hegemonic masculinity in some western cultures, whereas 'nerds' represent a form of marginalised masculinity which holds less power than hegemonic masculinity. Criminal behaviour, in the form of aggression, dominance and danger, is one way to produce and maintain hegemonic masculinity, thus the ideal form of masculinity can contribute to male criminality. Miller (2002) described how masculine identities emerged among some female gang members in a process she called 'gender crossing'. Masculine traits were associated with greater respect, thus gender crossing was rewarding for female members.

Debates have surfaced regarding the narrowing of the gender gap as it pertains to crime. Increases in arrest rates among females in comparison to rates among males have been viewed as an indication that the gender gap is reducing, that is, the extent of female criminality is becoming more like male criminality. Other studies have demonstrated the importance of using multiple data sources to explore changes in the gender gap. For example, Steffensmeier et al. (2005) used victimisation, self-report and arrest data to examine the gender gap over time. Their study focused specifically on youth and violent offences. The authors found that arrest data showed a narrowing of the gender gap in relation to violent offences (i.e. larger proportions of females had been arrested for violent crimes in comparison to previous years). However, data from sources other than the criminal justice system – that is, self-report surveys and other surveys whereby the victim identifies the age and sex of the offender – showed relatively no change in the gender gap over time. These findings are important because they suggest that the gender gap has remained relatively constant, but that police practices towards girls have altered to include a greater likelihood of arrest of girls whose acts they perceive to be violent.

GENDER AND VICTIMISATION

Daly and Maher (1998) and other scholars refer to the 'blurred boundaries' of victimisation and subsequent criminality among women. In other words, a large proportion of women who offend have previously been subjected to child sexual abuse or neglect, domestic violence, rape or other kinds of serious assault. Moreover, women's victimisation tends to occur in the private sphere of the family or intimate relationships.

Although *liberal feminists* have tended to concentrate on gender and criminality, *radical feminists* have focused on the extent and nature of crime and other structural victimisation of women in the context of patriarchy. A limitation of the patriarchal perspective is that it neglects the role of *agency* with regards to victimisation and the construction of victim identities. Understanding gender as 'situated action' (Miller 2002) incorporates the possibility that women are not necessarily passive victims of crime; rather, they might resist, intervene, report, seek revenge or push for justice.

Gender differences have also been noted in studies that investigate the fear of crime (see also *Fear and the fear of crime*). Although males are more likely than females to be victims of crime, females are more likely than males to fear crime, particularly crimes that involve physical assault. These fears are not necessarily irrational but are shaped by women's perceptions of vulnerability.

GENDER AND OTHER INEQUALITIES

Power hierarchies permeate society, thus crime and victimisation are influenced by the interactions between gender, class, age, ethnicity and race. In several cultures, for example, higher proportions of women from ethnic minorities are likely to be victimised and/or arrested for criminal acts, compared with white women. The complexity of disentangling these effects is a challenge for criminologists. Similarly, people who identify as lesbian, gay, bisexual or transgender have experienced high rates of assault victimisation, relative to their 'mainstream gender' peers. These acts of intolerance also reflect power hierarchies that are explicitly tied to gender and gender identity.

REFERENCES

Adler, F. (1975) *Sisters in Crime: The Rise of the New Female Criminal*. New York: McGraw-Hill.

Connell, R.W. and Messerschmidt, J.W. (2005) 'Hegemonic masculinity: Rethinking the concept', *Gender and Society*, 19: 829–59.

Daly, K. and Maher, L. (eds) (1998) *Criminology at the Crossroads: Feminist Readings in Crime and Justice*. New York: Oxford University Press.

Heidensohn, F. (2012) 'The future of feminist criminology', *Crime Media Culture*, 8: 123–34.

Klein, D. (1973) 'The etiology of female crime: A review of the literature', *Issues in Criminology*, 8: 3–30.

Lombroso, C. (1920) *The Female Offender*. London: Unwin. (First published 1885.)

Lombroso, C. (2006) *Criminal Man*. Durham, NC: Duke University Press. (First published 1876.)

Miller, J. (2002) 'The strengths and limits of "doing gender" for understanding street crime', *Theoretical Criminology*, 6: 433–60.

Pollak, O. (1950) *The Criminality of Women*. New York: A.S. Barnes.

Simon, R.J. (1975) *Women and Crime*. Washington, DC: US Government Printing Office.

Smart, C. (1976) *Women, Crime and Criminology: A Feminist Critique*. London: Routledge & Kegan Paul.

Steffensmeier, D., Schwartz, J. and Zhong, H. (2005) 'An assessment of recent trends in girls' violence using diverse longitudinal sources: Is the gender gap closing?', *Criminology*, 43: 355–405.

Thomas, W. I. (1923) *The Unadjusted Girl*. Boston: Little Brown.

18 Youth and Crime

> **Definition**: *Simply put, there is a link between age and crime over the life span. Street crime occurs largely during late adolescence and young adulthood, and offenders tend to desist from crime as they age.*

The relationship between age and crime is well established; criminality generally begins in adolescence, peaks in late adolescence or young adulthood, and declines as people grow older. This pattern has been referred to as the *age–crime curve*, and has been documented using different kinds of data (e.g. self-report surveys, official reports) and in a number of western cultures. Figure 18.1 illustrates the age–crime curve with hypothetical data.

The age–crime curve reflects the relationship between age and *street crime*. Crimes that result in considerable profit and that are associated with occupations (e.g. bribery, fraud, embezzlement) often commence in adulthood because of age-related opportunities associated with the workplace (see also *White-collar/ middle-class and corporate crime*). The age–crime curve has been observed among both males and females, although criminality tends to decline earlier for females compared with males.

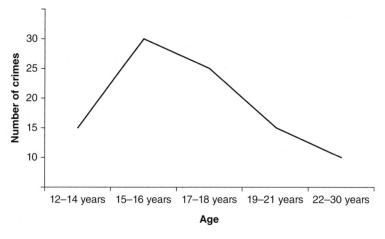

Figure 18.1 Age–crime curve

Youth crime has received considerable research attention since the early 20th century and the work of sociologists who were affiliated with the Chicago School. The topic remains an important line of inquiry among contemporary criminologists, many of whom have tried to explain the onset or continuation of youth offending. Biological explanations have focused on genotypes, and hormonal and neurological changes that occur during adolescence. Psychological explanations have focused on issues such as personality development and impulsivity in teens. Numerous sociological explanations have been proposed to account for the onset of crime among youth. These have focused on issues such as social bonds, informal social control (e.g. variations in parental supervision) and deviant peers. Structural disadvantages (e.g. restricted opportunities for employment among youth, factors associated with schools and neighbourhoods) have also been proposed as explanations for youth crime (see also *Crime and theory*). Additionally, youth may lack the skills to conceal criminality and police may be more likely to suspect them. Despite major interest in trying to explain youth crime, single theoretical frameworks are rarely able to explain a large proportion of it. Integrated theoretical frameworks often explain more variation in youth crime but, still, a relatively large proportion of youth crime remains unexplained.

The social backgrounds of young offenders processed by the legal system are similar across a number of industrialised nations. They tend to be male, unemployed and from ethnic minority backgrounds (White and Cunneen 2006). Muncie (2005) noted the shift in policy that once focused on the welfare of the individual. Contemporary policies reflect a justice model that attempts to prevent, manage and reduce risk believed to be associated with youth crime. Particular types of youth are believed to be 'at risk' for crime and a host of other social problems. 'Risk factors' (e.g. low IQ, single/lone parenthood households, poverty) are said to be associated with certain groups of youth who engage in crime. Moreover, risk is often constructed by researchers, who view risk quite differently than the youth who are alleged to experience it. A 'fixation' on risk among youth ignores societal forces, such as major social inequalities, that can contribute to crime among youth. Programmes that are designed to prevent youth crime are often developed according to experts' views of risk.

Although most crime is committed by youth, Moffitt (1993) observed that some adolescents quickly abandon criminal behaviour soon after their initial engagement with it. Moreover, most youth do not commit crime. Still, we engage in the social construction of youth crime by believing that it is more extensive than it actually is, by assuming that youth are deviant because of their age, by avoiding contact with them or by moving them out of public space.

DESISTANCE

A relatively small number of offenders are believed to commit a disproportionate amount of street crime. Persistent offending can impact on the quality of life of both offenders and victims, as well as of other individuals, and considerable resources are allocated to policing, prosecuting and punishing offenders. Thus, it is important to encourage desistance from crime. Criminologists generally refer to desistance as the cessation or decline of criminality that follows the onset of offending, that is, the downward slope in Figure 18.1. However, scholars have critiqued definitions of desistance. For example, is desistance restricted to crime or does it also include other kinds of deviance in which individuals might engage? If an active offender commits violent crimes for several years, and then commits only minor thefts, has the person desisted? If an individual commits only one criminal act and then abstains from crime, does that behaviour constitute desistance? Or should desistance only apply to active offenders or individuals engaged in serious crime for several years? For what period of time should desistance be measured? Some criminologists have examined desistance over a set number of years, whereas others have argued that desistance is best measured over the life span. Most contemporary desistance scholars suggest that it is a process that can involve frequent engagement with crime that is intertwined with periods of desistance, or a progression that reflects a gradual decline in offending over time.

Several factors have been found to contribute to desistance. The life-course perspective focuses on 'social journeys' that are connected to age-related expectations over a lifetime. These journeys are examined in the context of social structure and historical events that shape individual lives. For example, certain milestones or key life events (e.g. a good marriage or partnership, parenthood, meaningful and stable employment) can strengthen social bonds and attachment to mainstream normative behaviour in everyday life. In turn, these milestones are believed to encourage desistance from crime. Desistance can also be affected by improved family relationships, suitable accommodation and positive peer influence. However, it is difficult to ascertain whether these milestones directly relate to desistance. In other words, another common set of variables might contribute to both desistance and other life changes. Additionally, people desist at different ages so that factors that influence desistance during one life stage (e.g. late adolescence) may differ from factors that affect desistance in another (e.g. adulthood). Structural factors can also affect desistance. For example, a longitudinal study of youth in Edinburgh found that neighbourhood factors (e.g. rates of unemployment and police-recorded crime in the area) had more impact on desistance than did individuals' social class backgrounds (Smith 2006).

Studies based on interviews with former prisoners have contributed to our understanding of the desistance process among 'officially designated' offenders. In one study, former prisoners who had desisted from crime had cultivated 'pro-social' identities that involved a transformation of self. They had developed a sense of purpose in their lives and believed that they had some control over their futures (Maruna 2001). Community and institutionalised stigma can impact negatively on individuals' self-identities and, in turn, reduce the likelihood of desistance: 'Not only must a person accept conventional society in order to go straight, but conventional society must accept that this person has changed as well' (Maruna and LeBel 2010: 76).

REFERENCES

Maruna, S. (2001) *Making Good: How Ex-Convicts Reform and Rebuild their Lives*. Washington, DC: American Psychological Association.

Maruna, S. and LeBel, T.P. (2010) 'The desistance paradigm in correctional practice: From programmes to lives', in F. McNeill, P. Raynor and C. Trotter (eds) *Offender Supervision: New Directions in Theory, Research and Practice*. Cullompton: Willan, pp. 65–89.

Moffitt, T.E. (1993) 'Adolescence-limited and life-course persistent antisocial behavior: A developmental taxonomy', *Psychological Review*, 100: 674–701.

Muncie, J. (2005) 'The globalization of crime control – the case of youth and juvenile justice: Neoliberalism, policy convergence and international conventions', *Theoretical Criminology*, 9: 35–64.

Smith, D.J. (2006) Social Inclusion and Early Desistance from Crime. Report No. 12, Edinburgh Study of Youth Transitions and Crime. Edinburgh: University of Edinburgh, Centre for Law and Society.

White, R. and Cunneen, C. (2006) 'Social class, youth crime and justice', in B. Goldson and J. Muncie (eds) *Youth Crime and Justice*. London: Sage, pp. 17–29.

19 Race/Ethnicity and Crime

Definition: **Ethnicity** is often used to refer to people who loosely share particular characteristics including geographical and ancestral origins, cultural traditions and languages. As these characteristics are not fixed, homogeneous or easily measured, ethnicity is a fluid concept. It is the modern term used to categorise and differentiate between groups, replacing the positivist notion of race. As a biological category,

(Continued)

(Continued)

which emerged during the eighteenth century, **race** has traditionally referred to the division of human populations into sub-species based on visible physical characteristics such as skin colour (Bhopal 2004: 442). The belief was that there was a biological difference between groups of people, often on the grounds of evolution. Ethnicity and race are crucial elements for criminological studies, as it is often those in society perceived as 'different' that are criminalised. Hence, groups whose apparent origins or ethnicities diverge from those of majorities are perceived as 'different', with many of their behaviours viewed with suspicion.

In every nation, some racial and ethnic groups are disproportionately likely to be arrested, convicted and imprisoned for violent, property and drug crimes (Tonry 1994) (see also *Punishment*). Such groups may form a minority population and/or experience social, political and economic disadvantage. However, new immigrant populations initially tend to have low rates of criminal offending, which gradually increase with the length of stay in their new countries (Tonry 1994). Nevertheless, there is little evidence that immigration is linked to higher crime rates and it has been argued that such a link is based on myth (Zatz and Smith 2012).

Perceptions of disproportionate crime involvement by ethnic groups, tend to foster negative stereotypes, discrimination and xenophobia. This in turn can imply a causal link between ethnicity and crime, and undermine feelings of community safety and social cohesion in neighbourhoods with high ethnic populations (Lozusic 2002). Although some racial and ethnic groups may be social and economically disadvantaged in comparison with majority populations, their different experiences with criminal justice systems are more complex than simply differences in wealth, social status and political power (Tonry 1994: 1–2). Socio-economic and demographic characteristics such as poorer neighbourhoods with high migrant populations are likely to impact adversely on crime rates. This can result in an overly simplistic focus on race or ethnicity as the sole cause of crime and, in turn, has wider implications for the ways in which ethnic minority groups are perceived, represented and policed (Mukherjee 1999) (see also *The criminal justice system* and *Social construction of crime and deviance*).

Studies indicate that in predominantly Anglo cultures offenders from racial or ethnic minority groups may receive differential treatment by the criminal justice system (Steffensmeier and Demuth 2001). Steffensmeier and Demuth (2001) argue that ethnicity and employment tend to be linked to judges' perceptions of offenders' dangerousness and potential for reform. In Australia, the Indigenous population is over-represented at every stage of the criminal justice system, including arrest, court appearance and incarceration.

PERCEPTIONS OF ETHNIC POPULATIONS AS THE CAUSE OF CRIME

It is difficult to assess the proportion of crime committed by ethnic groups, first because it is difficult to have standardised definitions of ethnicity, and second because there is no way of knowing the country of birth of everyone who commits a crime (Mukherjee 1999: 49). Additionally, as Tonry (1994) points out, international crime comparisons are difficult to make as most western nations do not retain consistent crime data based on racial or ethnic identification. Canada, Australia and New Zealand are exceptional insofar as they record Indigenous and non-Indigenous identification.

During times of rapid social, economic and political change, people feel threatened and insecure, and minority groups may be perceived as the root cause of the problem (Tonry 1994: 2). According to empirical evidence, there is a link between immigration and reduced crime rates, yet persistent fears of dangerous racialised others have contributed to substantial increases in restrictive immigration policies. In the USA, this has taken the form of a range of immigration-tightening measures, including heightened border enforcement, increased scope for immigrants to be detained or deported for a variety of crimes, and reduced eligibility for welfare benefits for immigrants (Zatz and Smith 2012). The need for such measures is reinforced by negative media reports, and tends to result in differential policing of ethnic communities. These measures may be accompanied by a political discourse of blame towards minority groups, an increase in hate crimes against ethnic groups and alienation of these groups from majority populations (Tonry 1994).

Poynting (2006) argues that political discourses can deliver 'permission to hate' by promoting racial discrimination and failing to act against it. It has been argued that the 9/11 terrorist attacks on New York and the launching of the global 'War on Terror' encouraged a climate of global fear and suspicion about Middle Eastern terrorism and 'invasion'. At the same time, in many jurisdictions, the power assigned to police to arrest and detain terror suspects under anti-terrorism legislation was enhanced (McCulloch 2007). Anti-terrorism measures are evident in a more visible police presence, heightened surveillance and greater police powers to stop and search, monitor, investigate, question, arrest and detain (McCulloch 2007) (see also *Terrorism*).

Cultural stereotyping of ethnic groups has occurred in Australia, the UK and the USA. Poynting (2006) argues that in Australia perceptions of Middle Eastern people as perpetrators of terror and violence have become synonymous with crime gangs. This blurring of the boundaries between terrorism and crime has resulted in greater visibility and intensive focus by police on ethnic groups of Middle Eastern appearance (Lee 2007; Poynting 2006). Smith (1995) argues that there is a strong link in the British popular imagination between Afro-Caribbean populations and street crime such as mugging. This is related to public conceptions of Afro-Caribbean groups as lacking in culture and hence being 'unBritish' (Smith 1995). Afro-Caribbean communities tend to be characterised by low socio-economic status and are more likely than Anglo-background British populations to be arrested and charged with offences that result in incarceration. According to Zatz and Smith (2012), Latino immigrants in the USA are typically portrayed as dangerous with a high propensity for crime, and as 'sneaking' into the country and 'stealing' jobs.

ETHNIC GROUPS AND THE CRIMINAL JUSTICE SYSTEM

The over-representation of ethnic groups by criminal justice systems is, in part, due to their visibility, which tends to attract an intensive focus by police. For example, Australian research has shown that Indigenous people are more likely than non-Indigenous people to be arrested, not so much because of overt discrimination but because of their high levels of unemployment, their high levels of visibility in the public sphere and entrenched practices of over-policing (Hogg and Carrington 2006). Indigenous people are vastly over-represented at all stages of the criminal justice system, including suspicion, arrest, prosecution, conviction and punishment (see also *The criminal justice system*). The Indigenous imprisonment rate (2,303 per 100,000) is over 14 times higher than the non-Indigenous rate (129 per 100,000), with Indigenous people comprising 26% of the total prisoner population (Australian Bureau of Statistics 2010). Comparison studies from the USA have found racial disparities in sentencing practices between white, black and Hispanic offenders (Steffensmeier and Demuth 2001). These inconsistencies are not simply the effect of racial or ethnic discrimination per se, but rather they tend to be shaped by perceptions of an offender's dangerousness, based on their ethnic background and social and economic circumstances.

ETHNIC MINORITY GROUPS AS VICTIMS

While some ethnic minority groups are over-represented within criminal justice systems as offenders, many also tend to have higher rates of victimisation. Additionally, they are often more reluctant to report incidents of crime to police and are often dissatisfied with responses if they do (Makkai and Taylor 2009). Zatz and Smith (2012: 1.13–1.14) argue that anti-immigrant sentiment and harsh new laws, which conflate immigration and crime, make immigrant communities less safe. Hence, law is implicated in the racialisation, economic marginalisation and demonisation of immigrants in the USA and Australia, leaving them vulnerable to violence and exploitation.

Most incidents of violent victimisation toward those of ethnic background involve members of the same ethnic group (Ministry of Justice 2011). However, crimes against ethnic groups also involve hate crimes and racial harassment, the majority of which are perpetrated by people known by, but not closely connected with, the victims (Mason 2005: 855). A study by Mason (2005: 856) found that victims in Britain who report racial harassment are typically of Afro-Caribbean, Indian/Pakistani or dark European ethnic appearance. In Australia, a recent spate of racial attacks on Indian students culminated in the fatal stabbing of a 21-year-old Indian student in Melbourne. With no apparent motive for the murder, commentators concluded that the attack was racially motivated (Mason 2005).

REFERENCES

Australian Bureau of Statistics (2010) Prisoners in Australia 2010. Cat. No. 4517.0. Canberra: Australian Bureau of Statistics. Available at: www.ausstats.abs.gov.au/ausstats/subscriber.nsf/0/F3916FB1F45FAF12CA2577F3000F11F0/$File/45170_2010.pdf (date accessed 09/10/12).

key concepts in
crime and society

Bhopal, R. (2004) 'Glossary of terms relating to ethnicity and race: For reflection and debate', *Journal of Epidemiology and Community Health*, 58: 441–5.

Hogg, R. and Carrington, K. (2006) *Policing the Rural Crisis*. Sydney: Federation Press.

Lee, M. (2007) *Inventing Fear of Crime: Criminology and the Politics of Anxiety*. Cullompton: Willan.

Lozusic, R. (2002) Gangs in NSW. Briefing Paper No. 16/02. Sydney: NSW Parliament.

McCulloch, J. (2007) 'Key issues in a critical approach to policing', in T. Anthony and C. Cunneen (eds) *The Critical Criminology Companion*. Sydney: Hawkins Press, pp. 206–17.

Makkai, T. and Taylor, N. (2009) 'Immigrants and victims of crime: The Australian experience', *Sociology of Crime, Law and Deviance*, 13: 95–105.

Mason, G. (2005) 'Hate crime and the image of the stranger', *British Journal of Criminology*, 45: 837–59.

Ministry of Justice (2011) 'Statistics on Race and the Criminal Justice System 2010'. Available at: www.justice.gov.uk/publications/statistics-and-data/criminal-justice/race.htm (accessed 22/07/14).

Mukherjee, S. (1999) 'Ethnicity and crime', *Trends and Issues in Crime and Criminal Justice*. May, No. 117. Canberra: Australian Institute of Criminology.

Poynting, S. (2006) 'What caused the Cronulla riot'? *Race and Class*, 48(1): 85–92.

Smith, D. (1995) *Criminology for Social Work*. Basingstoke: Palgrave Macmillan.

Steffensmeier, D. and Demuth, S. (2001) 'Ethnicity and judges' sentencing decisions: Hispanic-black-white comparisons', *Criminology*, 39(1): 145–78.

Tonry, M. (1994) 'Racial disproportions in US prisons', *British Journal of Criminology*, 34: 97–115.

Zatz, M. and Smith, H. (2012) 'Immigration, crime and victimization: Rhetoric and reality', *Annual Review of Law and Social Science*, 8: 1.1–1.19.

20 White-collar/Middle-class and Corporate-class Crime

Definition: *White-collar and corporate offences are crimes that occur in the context of business, the professions or corporate affairs. They often involve individuals who hold organisational power, and generally involve a violation of trust with the intent of producing individual or corporate gain.*

Edwin Sutherland (1949) introduced the concept of white-collar crime in his presidential address to the American Sociological Association in 1939. The address was important in that Sutherland described previous notions of crime as misconceived because they ignored the crimes of individuals in the course of business and professions. It followed that theories of crime were flawed because research samples comprised largely individuals from working-class backgrounds. To Sutherland, white-collar crimes in the course of business included behaviours such as falsified financial records, bribery, embezzlement and tax fraud. He also suggested that some physicians engage in white-collar crime by engaging in false reporting and performing or recommending unnecessary medical procedures. In general, Sutherland proposed that white-collar crimes are committed by people with power (which allows them immunity) and involve a breach of trust. Although Sutherland held an influential position in sociology (i.e. president of the American Sociological Association) and had this work published in a leading sociology journal, his work did not lead to immediate research interest in white-collar crime. Instead, scholarly and governmental interest in white-collar crime emerged some 30 years later in the USA, coinciding with major social and political changes in that country (Simpson and Weisburd 2009).

Although definitions of white-collar crime have been debated, the crime occurs in the context of occupations and professions, and is intended to benefit the individual who commits the crime. White-collar crime might also benefit the business or profession with which offenders are affiliated; however, the motivation for individual gain is often the defining factor. Corporate crime is similar in that it involves crime in the context of professions, businesses or industry. However, corporate crime is generally defined as crime that is committed by corporate representatives or executives, in order to benefit the corporation. Examples of corporate crime include the marketing of unsafe products or medicines, intentional violations of safety in the workplace, and bribes and other deceit by corporations. Albanese (2005: 108) noted that 'the laws governing these offenses are designed to ensure fairness and safety in the conduct of business so that the desire for profits does not lead to dangerous or unjust actions'.

The terms white-collar and corporate crime are sometimes used interchangeably even among criminologists. Additionally, an act (e.g. selling faulty car products) can be linked to individual advantage, corporate gain or both. This issue contributes to a conceptual confusion between the two crimes. Importantly, white-collar and corporate crime are inherently linked through the concept of power, in that several but not all offenders hold positions of occupational power. Some scholars prefer to describe these acts collectively as 'elite deviance' (which extends to violations of regulations that are not illegal) or simply as 'crimes of the powerful' (which is broad, and can include crimes that occur outside corporate or professional settings).

PUBLIC PERCEPTIONS

Survey results from a representative sample of US residents demonstrated the perceived seriousness of white-collar and corporate crime among the public (Piquero et al. 2008). Survey respondents were provided with descriptions of a number of hypothetical acts that involved corporate/white-collar crime and street crime. They were then asked to compare the seriousness of the acts. In most instances, respondents viewed corporate and white-collar crimes to be equal to or more serious than street crime. The perceived seriousness of white-collar and corporate crime varies across individual characteristics (e.g. gender and age), and western and non-western cultures; such perception of seriousness also depends on the types of offences or harms that are highlighted.

RESPONSE BY THE LEGAL SYSTEM

White-collar and corporate crimes often go unnoticed because they occur in private settings which are hidden from the public gaze. Complaints by witnesses or victims are rare compared with street crime, because people are not often aware that they have been victimised, or they lack the power to voice complaints. White-collar and corporate crime can be difficult to detect because of the intricacies of the offences which can sometimes be concealed through legitimate business operations. Additionally, law enforcement may lack the resources to investigate these offences.

Some governments have introduced measures that attempt to prevent or detect white-collar and corporate crime. Piquero et al. (2008) noted initiatives by the US government in its efforts to protect investors from corporate fraud through the Sarbanes-Oxley Act of 2002. In the UK, the Corporate Manslaughter and Corporate Homicide Act was passed in 2007 and relates to deaths that result from a serious 'breach of duty' by corporations. Sentencing options include fines, compensation and 'publicity orders'; however, imprisonment is not an option under the Act, which contrasts sharply with sentencing options available for deaths that are linked to street crime. In 2013, the UK government initiated a public consultation on sentencing options for organisations and individuals that have been convicted of environmental crimes. The outcome of the consultation is likely to have some influence on sentencing ranges for white-collar and corporate offenders who engage in environmental offences.

Guidelines in the USA specify the range of sentences for selected corporate and white-collar crimes. For offences relating to finance, sentencing guidelines are based in part on the monetary loss to victims. Several years ago, criminologists described patterns of lenient sentences for white-collar and corporate offenders. More recent evidence from the USA suggests that the pattern may have changed, with increasing numbers of offenders being sentenced to lengthy terms of imprisonment (Buell 2014). Still, extensive media reporting has highlighted other perhaps outlying lenient sentences for white-collar and corporate offenders. For example, Richard Adelson was convicted of large-scale fraud and faced a sentence of life imprisonment under US guidelines. However, the judge sentenced him to 3½ years, arguing that he considered a life term to be 'barbaric' for the offender. In another recent US court case, Michael Peppel was sentenced to a heavy fine, seven days' imprisonment and three years' supervisory release for issuing fraudulent accounts over a two-year period. Peppel's crimes depleted thousands of dollars from employees' pension and savings accounts, and shareholders lost an estimated $18 million after the fraud was exposed to the public. Under sentencing guidelines, Peppel should have received a prison sentence of 8–10 years, however the US District judge awarded leniency with a prison sentence of seven days. After a relatively rare instance of government appeal of a sentence for a white-collar offender, the appellate court found that the District judge had erred, and ordered her to impose a new prison sentence. Although these two cases are at odds with Buell's (2014) conclusions, they hint at the empathy imposed on individuals whose social status and privileged positions are similar to those of the judges who sentence them. Similar connections have been described by C. Wright Mills in his treatise on the 'power elite' (Mills 1956). Additionally, a sole focus on sentencing decisions ignores the advantages that several white-collar and corporate offenders accumulate at various stages of the criminal justice process. For example, these offenders are likely to be able to afford bail and their courtroom demeanour can invoke sympathy from jurors (Buell 2014). In contrast, individuals who cannot afford bail remain in custody which can negatively impact on their cases.

SOCIAL HARMS

Some corporate acts are legal despite causing serious social harm to others. Friedrichs (2010) and other scholars have questioned whether definitions of white-collar and corporate crime should include social harms that do not violate the criminal law. Braithwaite's (1984) international study highlighted the negligence (e.g. manufacture of unsafe medicine) of the pharmaceutical industry. More recent reports on the practices of 'Big Pharma' have drawn attention to the testing process for new drugs. For example, Shah (2006) noted that although pharmaceutical medicines are used disproportionately by patients in western cultures, an estimated 30–50% of new drugs are tested on people residing outside the USA and Europe.

Prior to the regulatory approval of a new drug, pharmaceutical companies are required to conduct dozens of clinical trials in which the drug is tested on human volunteers. Shah (2006) described how multinational pharmaceutical companies rely on Contract Research Organisations ('body pullers') to recruit and retain volunteers from developing nations. She described cases in which study volunteers – including children – have died from the effects of a drug. Several others have experienced serious health effects as a result of their participation in clinical trials.

Other writers have focused on the environmental harms that have resulted from corporate pollution, death and injury associated with intentional violations of health and safety in the workplace, and the exploitation of workers in developing nations who produce goods designed largely for western nations. These social harms are linked via the corporate pursuit for profit.

REFERENCES

Albanese, J. (2005) *Criminal Justice*, 3rd edn. Boston: Allyn & Bacon.

Braithwaite, J. (1984) *Corporate Crime in the Pharmaceutical Industry*. London: Routledge & Kegan Paul.

Buell, S.W. (2014) 'Is the white collar offender privileged?', *Duke Law Journal*, 63(4): 823–89.

Friedrichs, D.O. (2010) *Trusted Criminals: White Collar Crime in Contemporary Society*, 4th edn. Belmont, CA: Wadsworth.

Mills, C. W. (1956) *The Power Elite*. Oxford: Oxford University Press.

Piquero, N.L., Carmichael, S. and Piquero, A.R. (2008) 'Research note: Assessing the perceived seriousness of white-collar and street crimes', *Crime and Delinquency*, 54: 291–312.

Shah, S. (2006) *The Body Hunters: Testing New Drugs on the World's Poorest Patients*. New York: New Press.

Simpson, S.S. and Weisburd, D. (eds) (2009) *The Criminology of White-Collar Crime*. New York: Springer.

Sutherland, Edwin H. (1949) *White Collar Crime*. New York: Holt, Rinehart & Winston.

Section Two

Types of Crime and Criminality

> **Definition**: **Trafficking** is a somewhat elusive term that is used to encompass human trafficking and recruitment of people into sex work and other exploitative labour. It is a term used to define activity that is the modern equivalent of **slavery**. The notion of human trafficking is sometimes confused with **people smuggling**, which loosely refers to the procurement of the illegal entry of another person for profit, but does not involve sex trafficking or other labour exploitation (Larsen and Renshaw 2012). The difference between trafficking and smuggling is the procurement of individuals for exploitative labour by others.

Statistics on human trafficking activities tend to be absent or unreliable, due first to high levels of under-reporting, and second because of politicisation of the trafficking problem which misrepresents trafficking as simply an issue of exploitative sex work (Feingold 2005). Although human trafficking into non-sex sectors accounts for the majority of trafficking activity, Chuang (2010) argues that international anti-trafficking laws and policies have tended to focus on sex trafficking and prostitution (see also *Sex work*). An American coalition of 'neo-abolitionists' comprising conservatives, feminists and evangelical Christians have pursued the anti-trafficking debate to promote global abolition of prostitution (Chuang 2010: 1658).

It has been argued that the focus on prostitution tends to cloud the debate and subsequently impede broader efforts by anti-trafficking advocates to prioritise protection of the human rights of trafficked persons and prevent atrocities resulting from human trafficking (Chuang 2010; Feingold 2005). A study by the International Labour Organization (ILO) (2004) found that of the estimated 9.5 million victims of forced labour in Asia, less than 10% were trafficked for sexual exploitation. Worldwide, sex trafficking victims comprise less than half of all trafficking victims (Feingold 2005).

LEGAL PROTECTIONS

New legal definitions of trafficking codified in United States law in 2000, and simultaneously a new international law on trafficking from the UN (the United Nations Protocol to Prevent, Suppress and Punish Trafficking in Persons, Especially Women and Children), signalled attempts to define trafficking more broadly to encompass gender and non-sex sectors (Chuang 2010). Article 3 of the UN Protocol comprises three components: recruitment, transportation, transfer, harbouring or receipt of persons; the use of improper means, such as force, abduction, fraud or deception; and the objective of exploitation, such as sexual exploitation, forced labour, servitude or slavery. The Protocol requires signatories to take steps to protect and support victims of trafficking with entitlements to confidentiality and protection against offenders. This includes protection generally as well as specific witness protection if the person is providing evidence to police or courts. There are also optional requirements that victims receive social benefits such as housing, medical care and legal or other counselling support (United Nations 2000).

QUANTIFYING TRAFFICKING

Assessing the quantity of human traffic globally is complex. There are a range of definitions based chiefly on labour, migration and criminal justice, all of which conceptualise trafficking within their own domain. Different countries also use different definitions regarding the scope and meaning of trafficking, the activities involved, the purpose, and the consent of victims, all of which confound quantification of this activity. In Thailand, for example, men are excluded from trafficking statistics because its national laws do not recognise men as trafficking victims (Feingold 2005). Nevertheless, there is global consensus that human trafficking involves coercion, deception or force to exploit people. It enslaves victims through labour exploitation, sexual exploitation, or both, hence it is considered a modern form of slavery.

GLOBAL FIGURES

The number of trafficked persons globally has been estimated broadly at between 500,000 and four million (US GAO 2006). It is estimated that 56% of all persons in forced labour are women and girls, with most from low socioeconomic backgrounds. It is thought that victims are trafficked from 127 different countries and experience exploitation in 135 countries around the world (UNODC 2006). In 2009, the ILO found that the annual profits from human trafficking were at least US$32 billion (ILO 2009). The trafficking of a child can earn a trafficker up to $US30,000. In recent years, there has been a growth in child trafficking for the purposes of labour exploitation, adoption, drug smuggling, sex and organ theft (McCabe 2008: 89–90).

Generally, the purposes of trafficking include sexual exploitation, organ theft, forced recruitment into armed militia, begging and labour exploitation. The industries predominantly using trafficked persons are hospitality, construction, forestry, mining and agriculture (Larsen and Renshaw 2012). It has been suggested that there are more slaves today than were ever taken from Africa (Bales 1999).

SEX TRAFFICKING

Trafficking can be difficult to identify and define. Carrington and Hearn (2003: 6) argue that the boundaries between smuggling, trafficking and exploitation can be blurred as many women who believe they are migrating to another country to work legally or illegally in the sex industry can find themselves victims of other forms of exploitation such as debt bondage.

Recent debate has centred on whether prostitution is always coercive and therefore a form of trafficking, or whether the definition of trafficking should be applied only to forced prostitution (Chuang 2010: 1657–8). Women's experiences in sex work are diverse and complex (see *Sex work*). This was evident in a case study of Vietnamese women in a Cambodian brothel which found that women who were originally coerced into selling sex later decided independently to continue doing so (Buszar 2004: 232). The study found that many of the women chose to work as prostitutes and did not fit the UN Protocol's definition of being trafficked into sex work; however, they were frequently referred to as trafficked workers to protect Cambodia's international reputation (Buszar 2004).

Buszar (2004) cautions against addressing the problem of human trafficking through approaches that equate all sex-work migration with trafficking and exploitation; such an approach only complicates efforts to meet the immediate needs of sex workers. For example, as Cambodia is a signatory to the UN Protocol against Trafficking in Persons, Buszar claims that Cambodian police and NGOs regularly raid Cambodian brothels under the guise of 'rescuing' 'trafficked' Vietnamese women. These raids result in violence, with the women forced to pay bribes to get out of prison, further depriving them of work and wages.

PEOPLE TRAFFICKERS

Those involved in people trafficking range from highly organised criminal groups to loosely connected networks, individuals, and family and friends of victims (Larsen and Renshaw 2012). According to Feingold (2005), human trafficking in Southeast Asia mostly involves 'disorganised crime' and traffickers can range from truck drivers to village 'aunties', to labour brokers and police officers. Feingold (2005) cites studies of Burmese domestic workers in Thailand, and African workers trafficked to the Middle East, which found that workers were subjected to beatings, sexual assault, forced labour without pay, sleep deprivation and rape. Boys from Cambodia and Burma are also frequently trafficked onto commercial fishing boats, and, according to research, 10% never return; boys who become ill are often thrown overboard (Feingold 2005).

State agents may be paid substantial amounts to help someone immigrate illegally and find employment, and Asian women may be particularly at risk of various forms of abuse. According to an ILO report (2004: 54), domestic workers in Kuwait have been subjected to a variety of forms of abuse, particularly instances of intimidation and violence, withholding of wages, restrictions on their freedom of movement, inadequate living conditions, sexual abuse, trafficking and forced labour. There have also been reports of domestic workers having their organs removed. Following an incident of a dead Sri Lankan domestic worker being returned home from Kuwait with no kidneys, the ILO (2004) reported that it appears workers' organs are being removed for profit.

COMBATING TRAFFICKING

Global efforts to address human trafficking have focused primarily on criminalisation, along with measures to protect and assist victims. However, there is little evidence that prosecutions have had any significant impact on levels of trafficking (Feingold 2005). The problem of human trafficking is complex and criminal justice paradigms alone cannot provide solutions. Anti-trafficking policy has focused on prevention, protection and prosecution, which are limited to short-term interventions rather than longer-term solutions.

Trafficking victims working illegally in foreign countries are often detained and deported, an action which simply places them back in the same conditions that initially endangered them, particularly in situations of armed conflict or political unrest (Feingold 2005). Further, some victims may have no home to which they can return and no way to prove their nationality and hence no legal status. A lack of proof of citizenship in itself makes people highly vulnerable to trafficking, and renders women particularly at risk of trafficking for exploitative sex work or abusive forms of labour (Feingold 2005). Feingold (2005) argues that simply promoting birth registration in developing countries is an effective means of combating human trafficking.

A MODERN CRUSADE

Chuang (2010) argues that 'slavery' has become conflated with prostitution in conservative debates about the problem of human trafficking. This has resulted in a transformation of the anti-trafficking movement into a modern worldwide moral crusade against prostitution. Chuang explains that this approach is problematic because ideology has come to substitute evidence and formed a basis for neo-abolitionist policy. As Busza points out, the reasons why women engage in sex work are complicated (see *Sex work*) and are not necessarily captured in international definitions of trafficking, definitions which do not indicate how best to meet the needs of victims' communities (2004: 232). Rather, there is a need to address trafficking as a problem rooted in broader structural issues, such as poor migration management, ineffective labour protection for poor and unskilled workers, and endemic gender, race and class discrimination that facilitates a demand for exploited labour (Chuang 2010: 1721, 1725).

According to Anderson and O'Connell Davidson (2004: 7–8), the demand for trafficked persons' labour and services is almost absent in sectors where workers are strongly unionised and labour standards, such as workplace health and safety, working hours and work contracts, are monitored and enforced. Sex work and domestic work in private residences are frequently perceived as sub-categories of work, and workers may not be seen as real workers and hence as holders of rights. Unless there is international consensus on how states should respond to sex and private domestic workers, it is difficult to make policy recommendations on trafficking. There is a need for coordinated dialogue and thinking by national and international policy makers, ministries of labour, foreign affairs, justice departments, employment and welfare services. There also needs to be consultation with trade unions, sex workers' rights activists and NGOs, in order to protect vulnerable workers and exploited persons.

REFERENCES

Anderson, B. and O'Connell Davidson, J. (2004) *Trafficking: A Demand Led Problem? Part 1 Review of Evidence and Debates*. Stockholm: Save the Children. Available at: http://resourcecentre. savethechildren.se/content/library/documents/trafficking-demand-led-problem-part-1-review-evidence-and-debates (date accessed 13/05/13).

Bales, K. (1999) *Disposable People*. Oakland, CA: University of California Press.

Buszar, J. (2004) 'Sex work and migration: The dangers of oversimplification – A case study of Vietnamese women in Cambodia', *Health and Human Rights*, 7(2): 231–49.

Carrington, K. and Hearn, J. (2003) 'Trafficking and the sex industry: From impunity to protection'. Current Issues Brief, No. 28, 2002–03. Canberra: Department of the Parliamentary Library. Available at: www.aph.gov.au/binaries/library/pubs/cib/2002-03/03cib28.pdf (date accessed 13/05/13).

Chuang, J. (2010) 'Rescuing trafficking from ideological capture: Prostitution reform and anti-trafficking law and policy', *University of Pennsylvania Law Review*, 158: 1655–83.

Feingold, D. (2005) 'Human trafficking', *Foreign Policy*, Sept./Oct.: 26–32.

International Labour Office (ILO) (2004) Gender and Migration in Arab States: The Case of Domestic Workers (S Esim and M Smith, eds). Geneva: ILO. Available at: www.ilo.org/public/english/region/arpro/beirut/downloads/publ/publ_26_eng.pdf (date accessed 13/05/13).

International Labour Office (ILO) (2009) The Cost of Coercion: On Fundamental Principles and Rights at Work. International Labour Conference, 98th Session, Report I (B). Geneva: ILO. Available at: www.ilo.org/wcmsp5/groups/public/---ed_norm/---declaration/documents/publi cation/wcms_106268.pdf (date accessed 13/05/13).

Larsen, J. and Renshaw, J. (2012) 'People trafficking in Australia', *Trends and Issues in Crime and Criminal Justice*, June, No. 441. Canberra: Australian Institute of Criminology.

McCabe, K. (2008) *The Trafficking of Persons: National and International Responses*. New York: Peter Lang.

United Nations (2000) Protocol to Prevent, Suppress and Punish Trafficking in Persons, Especially Women and Children, Supplementing the United Nations Convention against Transnational Organized Crime. New York: United Nations. Available at: www.uncjin.org/Documents/Conventions/dcatoc/final_documents_2/convention_%20traff_eng.pdf (date accessed 13/05/13).

United Nations Office on Drugs and Crime (UNODC) (2006) Trafficking in Persons: Global Patterns. Available at: www.unodc.org/pdf/traffickinginpersons_report_2006-04.pdf (date accessed 13/05/13).

United States Government Accountability Office (US GAO) (2006) *Human Trafficking: Better Data, Strategy and Reporting Needed to Enhance US Antitrafficking Efforts Abroad*. Washington, DC: US GAO.

22 Sex Work

Definition: *The business of selling 'sex' or sex-related activities in exchange for money or services is known as **sex work**. The term sex work was originally coined by Carol Leigh (aka Scarlet Harlot), a prostitutes' rights advocate, at a conference in San Francisco in 1978. Her motivation was to create a discourse which would be inclusive of women working in sex trades. The term gained wider currency during the 1980s. One of the first texts to use and popularise the term was* Sex Work: Writings by Women in the Sex Industry *(Delacoste and Alexander 1987). The term sex work has been widely adopted in the sex industry and among some academics and other professionals. However, the more pejorative term remains 'prostitution', which is still used in broader society and by mass media.*

PROSTITUTION

The organisation of sexual labour is highly variable, both historically and cross-culturally, as are the meanings given to it and formal and informal reactions towards it. Historically, the sale of sex has typically been referred to as 'prostitution'. Gagnon and Simon offer a useful definition of the term as 'the granting of sexual access on a relatively indiscriminate basis for payment, either in money or barter ... with the payment acknowledged to be for sexual performance' (1974: 213). However, prostitution is a term that is morally loaded, conjuring up images of crime and sexual degradation and exploitation.

Prostitution is strongly associated with the idea that commercial sex runs against notions of romantic love and intimacy, sex being a caring and private activity. Furthermore, the term prostitution, as with other terms such as 'whore', emphasise an identity – typically, a social and psychological characteristic of women. As such, the social construction of 'prostitute' denies agency and fails to acknowledge the variability of experience (Kempadoo and Doezema 1998).

SEX WORK

Advocates prefer the term 'sex work' as it is more neutral than prostitute, placing greater emphasis on the work, as opposed to the sex. Sex work indicates a social position – an income-generating form of labour for men and women. The focus is on recognition of work, basic human rights and working conditions. The term also emphasises the variability of sexual labour, with sex work being one of a range of income-earning activities women and men might engage in throughout their lifetime. Sex workers can include strippers, lap dancers and phone-sex operators. Sex work may range from 'straightforward' penetrative sex to more specialised and, sometimes, less tactile types of services involving the fulfilment of fantasies or fetishes. The sex industry involves a host of players, including clientele, owners, managers and staff of commercial establishments, and regulatory agents such as police.

Worldwide, although male and transgendered people work in the sex industry, the vast majority of sex workers, often estimated at 90%, is female and the vast majority of clients male. As such, gender has been a key issue in attempts to understand sex work in terms of supply and demand. The difference between male and female sex work is that male sex work is typically carried out on a same-sex basis. The demand for sex work has frequently been justified and legitimised with reference to the innate and irrepressible sexual needs of clients. Little is known about the population size and geographic distribution of sex workers, although numbers of persons working in sex industries are influenced by economic conditions and legislation (tax, public health and criminal) and its enforcement.

The structure and organisation of sex work varies historically and cross-culturally. Street workers are found in most regions. Frequency of street work is tied to economic conditions, with greater numbers of street workers seen as an indication of economic breakdown or difficulty. Brothel work is more likely to be found where sex work is tolerated or decriminalised, while escort work is typically linked with developed countries. Some very distinct forms of sex work have been identified regionally or nationally, such as the geisha in Japanese cities, 'beer girls' (young girls hired by companies to promote products in bars and clubs, who sell sex on the side) in Cambodia and Uganda, 'femme libre' (single or divorced women who exchange sex for gifts) in central America and 'beach boys' (young men from developing countries who offer services to women in resort settings) (Harcourt and Donovan 2005).

The motivations of both sex workers and clients vary significantly. Most women participate in sex work for economic reasons, simply to increase their income, to support a family or because they are unemployed. Research has suggested a strong association between sex work and a lack of marketable skills, suggesting the choice to enter into sex work may result from limited options. However, not all sex workers come from socio-economically deprived backgrounds and many are well educated. For some women and men, sex work may bring increased autonomy. Interestingly, studies indicate that up to a third of women have engaged in sex work as a result of personal curiosity. Despite popular understandings, relatively few women engage in sex work to support a drug habit. Most engage in sex work as a casual activity, providing an irregular form of income. As such, few would view sex work as an occupation.

REGULATION

Historically and cross-culturally, most societies view engaging in sexual activities for financial reward as problematic. Sex work has been considered as the archetypal form of female deviance, with relatively strict forms of social control for women engaging in such activities. (see also *Crime (definition of)* and *Deviance (definition of)*). As such, almost every jurisdiction in the world has developed a legal strategy to govern this behaviour and its associated activities. Abolition seeks to disallow this activity in any form. Criminalisation seeks to restrict the activities of people buying or selling sex. Decriminalisation removes such activities from criminal codes, but typically employs other laws and regulations to regulate the activity. Decriminalisation implies neither approval nor disapproval of sex work, holding, rather, that private sexual conduct carried out by consenting adults should not be the concern of the law (Abel et al. 2010).

Selling sex has been considered problematic in relation to morality, public order and/or amenity, and public health. During the nineteenth century, prostitution became a metaphor for urban disintegration and disorganisation. By the middle decades of the twentieth century, it was commonly claimed that the majority of sex workers were coerced, forced or ensnared into a trade, which could only be entered into for financial reasons, rather than chosen voluntarily or for mental or physical satisfaction. Sex work was seen as diametrically opposed to 'loving' relationships, which were regarded as providing the basis of a healthy and well-functioning society. Sex conducted for profit could not involve pleasure, and was therefore personally unsatisfactory. Sex workers, because they supposedly engaged in sexual contact that lacked intimacy and was unfulfilling, became associated with a promiscuous, predatory or kinky type of sexuality. With the appearance of HIV/AIDS during the late twentieth century, sex workers were viewed as reservoirs of disease, despite a lack of evidence showing that sex workers are more responsible for the transmission of disease than other groups.

The policing of male and female sex work has been found to be discriminatory, involving corruption and the abuse of discretionary powers (see also *The criminal justice system*). Where sex work has been criminalised, it has typically been the most visible aspects of the trade that have borne the brunt of law enforcement. The vast majority of arrests (85–90%) has involved street workers, who represent a more socio-economically disadvantaged group within the sex industry. Despite this over-representation in terms of arrests, street work typically accounts for about 10% of the overall sex industry (Dennis 2008). Although street workers form the largest group involved in sex work, clients have tended to remain invisible in public discourses surrounding prostitution and, unlike sex workers, are rarely subject to social control.

Sex workers suffer high levels of violent victimisation, particularly with regard to rape, abuse and physical injury. This activity stems from wider misogynistic and homophobic attitudes held in the community, and relates to the legal and social status of sex workers. Crimes against sex workers are frequently under-reported and under-policed, and often sex workers are blamed for acts of violence perpetrated against them. Sex workers who suffer violence are reluctant to report it to police or other authorities for fear of prosecution and stigmatisation (Quadara 2008). Recently, internet escorts, who now constitute a considerable proportion of the sex industry, have utilised discussion boards and 'black' lists to vet clients. Clients, who can be at risk of robbery, assault and blackmail, have also used websites to screen sex workers and report incidents of abuse and violence (Cunningham and Kendall 2011).

ACTIVISM

There is a long tradition of political activism centring on sex work, which dates from the mid-nineteenth century. The organisation of sex workers since the 1970s into political lobby groups has been aimed at promoting the human rights of sex industry workers and occupational health and safety issues through legislative reform. By the mid-1970s, sex-worker rights groups had emerged such as Call Off Your Old Tired Ethics (COYOTE) in the USA, ACTION in Britain and the Australian Prostitutes Collective (CAP) in Australia. In 1996, Australia became the first country to unionise sex-workers. Reformers emphasise that the criminalisation of sex work entrenches the stigmatisation and social exclusion of sex workers, further impeding their access to community networks and social resources.

FEMINISTS AND SEX WORKERS

Feminists have viewed sex work as a gendered institution, which variously exploits, oppresses or discriminates against women. Feminists seem to agree that there is something 'wrong' with sex work; however, there is marked disagreement concerning what exactly is wrong with sex work, why it is wrong and what solutions should be adopted to address the wrongs. There are two camps to this debate:

those who emphasise the free will of women (agency) and those who emphasise more deterministic constraints (structure).

The shift to 'industrial' or 'occupational' perspectives allows closer ties to be forged between feminists and sex workers. Those emphasising agency have adopted a pragmatic approach to sex work, still critical of sex work as an institution but sensitive to the plight of sex workers. Overall (1992) argues that the coercion of women by men is a typical aspect of patriarchal or capitalist societies. However, while some sex workers may lack choice, others have clear social alternatives presented to them, deliberately choosing to engage in sex work. Thus, sex workers are constituted as not *necessarily* disempowered and may even be exercising significant control over their lives.

Sex work, it is pointed out, may be problematic, but so are most forms of work in patriarchal and capitalist societies. Since sex work is no different from other forms of paid labour, the right of sex workers to work should be defended. With respect to this, decriminalisation has been adopted as an appropriate strategy to address problematic features of the current organisation of sex workers. For example, it is argued that if sex work were to be decriminalised, sex workers would be able to form collectives and gain access to rights and entitlements equivalent to those enjoyed by other members of the workforce. A self-regulating sex industry is viewed as a desirable political outcome, especially in terms of the health of sex workers, and inefficient and corrupt policing practices.

Strategies have been adopted to undermine ideological representations of sex workers which have characterised the prostitute as 'other'. Sex work has been redefined as a sale of 'skill' rather than 'body'. Sex work is presented as a 'work choice', the argument being that to deny a woman her right to work under conditions of her choosing is a violation of her civil rights (Jenness 1990: 405, 416). Sociologists have recently presented sex work as a form of labour, which includes activities and jobs for which care and feeling are required, commodified and commercialised. Social relations involving sexual labour need not necessarily be gendered, despite the fact that women historically have been sellers of this product and men its buyers (Kempadoo and Doezema 1998).

CRITICISMS

Not all scholars favour use of the term 'sex work'. For example, Marxists have generally studied sex work in terms of systems of production and related forms of labour. They have seldom viewed sex work as valid work, instead associating it with alienation, an effect of moral decay or cultural collapse under particular social conditions. Marxists argue that prostitution would cease to exist in a world free of economic, gender and sexual exploitation, and as such the problem of sex work would be solved with the resolution of more pressing political problems. Opposition towards sex work is adopted as part of a more general opposition towards capitalism and the familial and property relations that it creates (Shrage 1996: 41–3) (see also *Crime and theory*).

For feminist Catherine MacKinnon (1987), women cannot exercise agency and control in commercial sexual encounters. She argues that prostitution is not simply a male-dominated practice, but a patriarchal institution, upholding and perpetuating imbalances in sexual power. Women's freedom or liberation cannot be achieved while women are objectified in male-dominated sexual practices and relations. Prostitution is viewed as an exemplary form of male oppression, the site from which all other forms of male domination emerge. The existence of prostitution legitimises the exploitation of women in other spheres of society such as the family, educational institutions and the workplace (Shrage 1989).

Activists working in this tradition have tended to view prostitutes as victims of patriarchy, as sexual slaves, as victims of pimps, drug addiction and organised crime. It is with this in mind that strategies directed at the abolition of all activities involving prostitution have been presented as viable with regards to the long-term political reform of prostitution. Accordingly, feminists working in this tradition have adopted policies seeking to 'protect' prostitutes from exploitation and oppression. This might involve the establishment of social services providing 'outreach' facilities for prostitute women or legislative reform. However, in contrast to liberal feminists, cultural feminists have rejected decriminalisation strategies to demand increased penalisation of clients, pimps, brothel-keepers and other persons deemed to benefit in one way or another from the sexual exploitation of prostitutes.

Because of the impacts of technological innovation through the internet, much existing research on male sex work is dated, especially with regard to demographic characteristics of sex workers and motivational reasons for entry into this profession. Computer-mediated communications may increase sex-work rates by allowing information and awareness of services to reach a wider socio-demographic audience (Cunningham and Kendall 2011). Early research has attracted significant criticism because of its sampling bias (largely delinquent populations) and its *a priori* assumptions. To use the example of male sex work, research has shifted from a rather simplistic account of heterosexual sex workers servicing homosexual clients to a more sophisticated account of the male sex industry, in which both sex workers and clients are acknowledged as having complex and variable sexual histories.

REFERENCES

Abel, G., Fitzgerald, L., Healey, C. and Taylor, A. (eds) (2010) *Taking the Crime out of Sex Work: New Zealand Sex Workers' Fight for Decriminalisation*. Bristol: Policy Press.

Cunningham, S. and Kendall, T.D. (2011) 'Prostitution 2.0: The changing face of sex work', *Journal of Urban Economics*, 69: 273–87.

Delacoste F. and Alexander, P. (eds) (1987) *Sex Work*. San Francisco, CA: Cleis Press.

Dennis, J. (2008) 'Women are victims, men make choices: The invisibility of men and boys in the global sex trade', *Gender Issues*, 25(11): 11–25.

Gagnon, J.H. and Simon, W. (1974) *Sexual Conduct: The Social Sources of Human Sexuality*. London: Hutchinson.

Harcourt, C. and Donovan, B. (2005) 'The many faces of sex work', *Sexually Transmitted Infections*, 81: 201–6.

Jenness, V. (1990) 'From sex as sin to sex as work: COYOTE and the reorganisation of prostitution as a social problem', *Social Problems*, 37(3): 403–20.

Kempadoo, K. and Doezema, J. (1998) 'Introduction', in K. Kempadoo and J. Doezema (eds) *Global Sex Workers: Rights, Resistance, and Redefinition*. New York and London: Routledge.

MacKinnon, C., (1987) *Feminism Unmodified: Discourses on Life and Law*. Cambridge, MA: Harvard University Press.

Overall, C. (1992) '"What's Wrong with Prostitution?" Saluating Sex Work'. *Signs Journal of Women in Culture and Society* 17(4): 705–24.

Quadara, A. (2008) *Sex Workers and Sexual Assault in Australia: Prevalence, Risk and Safety*. Melbourne: Australian Institute of Family Studies.

Shrage, L. (1989) 'Should feminists oppose prostitution?', *Ethics*, Jan.: 347–61.

Shrage, L. (1996) 'Prostitution and the case for decriminalization'. *Dissent*, 43: 41–5.

23 Victimless Crime

> **Definition**: Victimless crimes are behaviours that violate the criminal law but inflict no harm on the consenting parties. The concept has been debated, with some commentators arguing that behaviours are not considered criminal unless they result in victimisation.

Sociologist Edwin Schur has been credited with introducing the concept of victimless crime. Schur (1965) argued that some illegal acts are best described as 'crimes without victims', in that they involve the willing exchange of services or commodities producing little or no harm to participants. At the time of his publication, he argued that crimes such as drug use, abortion and homosexuality involve voluntary participants rather than crime victims or complainants. Schur emphasised that the criminalisation of these behaviours has implications for civil liberties, stretches the boundary of criminal law into the private lives of adults, and, in turn, can harm individuals by labelling them as deviant (see also *Deviance (definition of)*).

Schur and Bedau (1974) debated the issue of victimless crimes in their subsequent work. Schur acknowledged the deviant nature of some victimless crimes but noted the difficulty in enforcing laws that proscribe them. He argued that decriminalisation of these crimes would lead to fewer resources being expended on law enforcement. Bedau agreed that behaviours should not be subjected to criminal penalties when the acts involve willing exchanges between adults. However, Bedau observed the complexities with conceptualising victimless crime. He argued that the concept lacked clarity and noted the difficulties in determining acts that are truly victimless. Bedau also noted that defining 'victimisation' is critical for understanding the concept of victimless (see also *Victims of crime*). Quinney (1972) argued that acts cannot be considered to be criminal unless they produce victims. Thus, both crime and victimhood are socially constructed, leading Quinney (1972: 315) to prefer the phrase 'officially designated' victims.

DEBATES OVER THE MEANING OF VICTIMLESS

The notion of victimless rests on two principles: consent and an absence of harm. Various acts that are proscribed by criminal law involve participants who willingly engage in the behaviour or exchange. For example, individuals who knowingly buy stolen goods or imitation designer clothes generally consent to the transactions. Similarly, willing buyers and sellers are required for illicit drug markets to flourish. Some acts, however, may involve subtle or overt coercion rather than full consent. For example, sex work is illegal in some countries but, regardless of legal status, sex work has been depicted as a 'hierarchy' of physical and economic coercion (see also *Sex work*). Moreover, drug dependence and addiction can impede the ability to consent in drug market transactions. Assisted suicide is proscribed in several countries yet many individuals do not believe that the act should be criminalised. Still, the consent to die among individuals who seek assisted suicide may be affected by the severe pain or medication associated with debilitating illness. Discussions on victimless crime generally focus on consenting adults. In several countries, youth are not viewed as being capable of providing consent, which has led to legal and social debates around the behaviour of 'sexting' among young people.

The idea of crimes without victims implies that little or no harm results to the parties involved in the transaction. Assessments of harm, however, can depend on context, place, cultural expectations and characteristics of the assessors (e.g. religiosity). To view sex work as a victimless crime means that we ignore the underlying exploitation and violence that characterise sex-for-money exchanges. Sex work is often accompanied by violence from customers, business owners who provide settings for sex work to take place and other individuals who control earnings from sex work.

The principle of 'little or no harm' is generally restricted to the actors involved in the behaviour. Some perspectives suggest that this restriction is too limiting, and that crimes are not victimless when individuals are harmed who are situated outside the immediate context of the behaviour or exchange of goods or services. For example, drug use can impact negatively on families, children, co-workers and members of other social networks to which the user is attached. This extended notion of harm led Meier and Geis (1997) to suggest that it might be more accurate to refer to 'victims without crimes' rather than 'crimes without victims'. Acts that are perceived as victimless can also contribute to additional crime (e.g. human or drug trafficking, organised crime, extortion) because goods or services which are proscribed by law tend to increase the price of these commodities. However, this argument is limited in that legal behaviours can also contribute to crime by others – for example, the quest to own materialistic or expensive commodities can provide the impetus for theft and burglary.

Some crimes are perceived as victimless because of the invisibility of the victim. For example, knowingly buying stolen goods or imitation clothing is justified on the basis that no person was harmed in the transaction. Illegal downloading of music and videotaping films in cinemas are also affiliated with invisible victims. The lack of face-to-face confrontation between offender and victim makes it easier to neutralise the criminal act. Moreover, theft of proceeds from wealthy designers may be justified as victimless because of the economic status of the victim ('designers have enough money'). Similar reasoning has been used to justify shoplifting from large chain stores, a behaviour that has the potential to result in higher prices of goods, which has implications for other consumers.

CONSENSUS AND CRIME SERIOUSNESS

Victimless crimes are generally considered to be examples of *mala prohibita* in that the majority of people view these acts as being less serious or inflicting less harm than property/acquisitive and violent crimes (*mala in se*). A large body of research has investigated the perceived seriousness of crime among members of the public. Braithwaite (1989) argued that there is general public consensus in most countries about the seriousness of behaviours that should be considered as crimes, and about the seriousness attached to particular criminal acts. The seriousness of murder, for example, tends to generate high consensus among members of the public. However, victimless crimes are characterised by 'doubtful consensus' (Braithwaite, 1989: 4), whereby members of the public are more likely to disagree on the level of seriousness of these acts, in comparison to other crime categories. Stylianou (2010) outlined four kinds of public opposition to victimless crime. *Libertarian* views focus only on the harm associated with the behaviours. *Paternalistic* opposition prioritises self-protection over individual liberties. *Moralistic* perspectives emphasise the importance of protection to self and society, and the need for consistency with other societal morals. Finally, public opposition can reflect all three perspectives (the *community welfare perspective*).

IMPLICATIONS FOR ENFORCEMENT

It is difficult to enforce criminal laws that pertain to illegal acts that involve consenting adults and result in no harm. Illegality encourages parties to engage in the acts in private settings that are away from the gaze of the public and agents of formal social control (e.g. police). Complaints from victims or witnesses are often lacking. Law-enforcement agencies have invested considerable resources in their attempts to prevent and control some acts that are perceived to be immoral and offensive. For example, huge policing expenditures have been allocated for sting operations and other initiatives that are designed to reduce sex work. In several liberal democracies, arrest, prosecution and prison expenditures are spent on individuals charged with possession of marijuana or cannabis. The allocation of these resources is inconsistent with public consensus regarding the seriousness of these offences. The criminal justice focus on these incidents has increased net widening, and has the potential to stigmatise the actors involved. Moreover, criminal records can serve to bar people from employment, which can have long-term consequences for young people in particular.

REFERENCES

Braithwaite, J. (1989) *Crime, Shame and Reintegration*. Cambridge: Cambridge University Press.
Meier, R.F. and Geis, G. (1997) *Victimless Crime? Prostitution, Drugs, Homosexuality, Abortion*. Los Angeles, CA: Roxbury Publishing Co.

Quinney, R. (1972) 'Who is the victim?', *Criminology*, 10: 314–23.

Schur, E.M. (1965) *Crimes Without Victims: Deviant Behavior and Public Policy.* Englewood Cliffs, NJ: Prentice-Hall.

Schur, E.M. and Bedau, H.A. (1974) *Victimless Crimes: Two Sides of a Controversy.* Englewood Cliffs, NJ: Prentice-Hall.

Stylianou, S. (2010) 'Victimless deviance: Toward a classification of opposition justifications', *Western Criminology Review*, 11: 43–56.

24 Drug-related Crime and Violence

> **Definition**: *Crime is strongly correlated with certain types of drug use. It is overly simple, however, to suggest this fact reveals that drug use alone causes a crime relationship. Looked at closely, the evidence suggests that the relationship is in reality far more complex, with a range of research confirming small levels of criminality for most drug users and the existence of pre-drug use criminality for those most involved, while certain structural conditions can combine to increase or decrease drug-related criminal activity, including that of drug-related violence. Given this, some researchers have argued that there is no necessary or direct causal link between drug use and crime but a complex web of interconnections.*

INTRODUCTION

The issue of drug-related crime is an important one. The idea that drug use causes crime underpins approaches to much policing and sentencing policy in many societies around the world and normally results in a particularly punitive, and arguably disproportionate, approach towards those arrested and prosecuted for drug-related offences. The broader context for this situation (see also *Moral panics*) is the long-standing historical portrayal of 'drugs' as being overly homogenised (grouped as essentially similar) in terms of the broad risks they present to individuals and society and also as containing inherent powers to transform individuals (to make them aggressive or violent, to rob them of morals, to make them less caring, to make them stronger, to easily make them addicts, to make them kill, etc.) and wreck families and communities. Other long-standing misconceptions/myths about drugs such as heroin and the drug market (e.g. that street drugs are 'cut' with poisons and other dangerous substances; that heroin/crack is instantly addictive; that dealers commonly seek out young non-drug users to hook on addictive drugs) have led to exaggerated fears (see also *Fear and the fear of crime*) of drug users and those who inhabit the drug market (Coomber 2011). Together, this has contributed to the general sense that drugs cause crime because drugs are often (over)attributed with 'powers' to make people do things and because crime and criminality do often show strong statistical correlations. Statistical correlation, however, is not necessarily an indication of causation. Just because two things often occur together does not mean one is caused by the other. What we need to do now is consider more specifically how the relationship between drugs and crime might be understood more usefully and from a policy perspective more fruitfully.

DRUGS AND VIOLENT CRIME

One of the strongest beliefs around drug use and crime relates to the idea that drugs (and alcohol) make people violent. Media portrayals of violent acts committed by people thought to be 'high' (intoxicated) on drugs are common and have been for many years. Early portrayals, however, were often confused: cannabis, for example, was portrayed in 1930s America as turning people into frenzied killers after a single use (a now wholly discredited notion); cocaine (again, in early twentieth-century America) as turning black men into rapists and killers (showing how drug use has often been uninformed and tainted with racist undertones); and addiction as robbing people of the sensibilities that stop normal people from hurting others. Contemporary portrayals continue to rely on these long-standing assumptions about how drugs transform people and to misunderstand the nature of drug-related violence. Typically, the cause is assumed before the evidence is known, as in the following event and subsequent headline:

> Miami man shot dead eating a man's face may have been on LSD-like drug: Witness describes incident as 'really, really horrific' as police and doctors suggest attacker was on drug called bath salts. (*Guardian* 2012)

Policy-wise (built on fear and hysteria), there were immediate calls to ban the substance. This abated somewhat, however, a short time later when, apart from some traces of cannabis, the assailant had tested negative for the presence of any other illegal (or legal) drugs.

Cross-cultural and other evidence shows that even alcohol – the substance most associated with aggression and violence – does not produce such outcomes at all in certain cultures and circumstances, and in other societies does so to a lesser extent than found in many North American and north European countries, despite comparable or higher consumption levels. Research, in fact, strongly suggests that violence following drinking is often related to beliefs around alcohol, situational factors (e.g. confrontational events) and a drinker's pre-existing disposition towards aggression and violence. Other cross-cultural research has found that street drugs often associated with violence – such as 'Angel Dust' (PCP/ Phencyclidine) – when taken by groups with a less violent pre-disposition, do not produce violent outcomes. As with alcohol, when pre-existing disposition to aggression and violence is taken into consideration, illegal drugs do not appear to increase these characteristics either uniformly or consistently or to a degree to which they are explanatory. Although heroin – along with numerous other recreational drugs – has at times been strongly associated with violence, at other times it has been found that there is less violence in the heroin community than even in the non-drug-using population. Probably the greatest factor connecting illicit substances to violence relates to what Goldstein et al. (1985) called the 'systemic violence' of the drug trade. Essentially, the nature of some parts of the illicit drug trade, where violence can be elevated by a context of mistrust, competition and cultures of violence, means that much drug-related violence comes from the trading of drugs in a black-market context, not from their use.

NON-VIOLENT DRUG-RELATED CRIME

The type of crime most commonly associated with drug use is acquisitive crime. Acquisitive crime is where property or money is acquired illegally. For the most part, this relates to acts like shoplifting, burglary, robbery and (e.g. stolen credit card) fraud. Estimates of the impact of drug-related crime vary widely but drug-related crime is commonly seen as the single most important contributor to crime figures overall with up to 70% of crimes committed seen as drug related. One UK politician felt confident in asserting: 'the greatest cause of crime, as all law-abiding people know, is drugs' (Hawkins 2004). These estimates, however, are problematic for a number of important reasons. Given that most (especially recreational) drug use does not show a meaningful correlation to criminal activity, the crime figures tend to relate to assumptions around so-called problem or addicted drug use. In particular, they tend to relate to heroin, crack-cocaine and (powder) cocaine use.

Most formal estimates rely on arrestee data and the fact that numerous studies show a high proportion of arrestees are problem or dependent drug users. Extrapolation of the arrestee data provides estimates of how much crime has been committed and, in turn, the proportion of all crime that has been committed by those using drugs dependently or problematically. It is from such data that the proportion (e.g. figures of 70% of all crime) of drug-related crime is largely derived. Unfortunately, the data tends to be problematic in a range of important ways. To begin with, a range of research suggests that drug users are over-represented (as a consequence of, for example, targeted policing tactics and their visibility as 'at risk' populations) by as much as a factor of two and, as such, estimates on this basis alone would have to be revised dramatically downwards. It is also the case that many formal extrapolations/estimates assume that a crime committed by, for example, a heroin user would not have been committed if they were not using heroin. This is based on the economic-compulsive model which assumes that heroin users (or crack-cocaine users, etc.) are forced into criminality because their compulsion to feed their addiction makes them commit crime to obtain money to buy drugs. Unfortunately, this model is unable to sufficiently account for those (the majority) who had a pre-existing criminal career and would have committed a proportion of the crimes anyway; or for those who do not undertake crimes such as shoplifting but instead find other ways to fund their purchases (this may be through so-called 'victimless' crimes such as sex work or 'user dealing', where users sell to other addicted users and do not become involved in acquisitive crime; for others, the level of consumption is kept within affordable means; while still others may have some form of paid work or act as 'runners' for established dealers). Again, factoring in the choices that some dependent drug users have (it is nonsense to assume drug-dependent users are *compelled* to commit crimes such as shoplifting or burglary) will affect how much crime is extrapolated from being a drug user in a meaningful way. It is also the case that formal estimates – for the sake of producing a model of extrapolation – assume a certain general level of consumption, a level that is often higher than the average level of consumption revealed by research. If the general attributed level of consumption is over-estimated, then the extrapolated figures will then also be an over-estimate. There are a number of other confounding factors that can further impact on these extrapolations but those listed here are the most damning. If dependent/problem drug-using arrestees are over-represented as a proportion of those criminally active; if levels of consumption are over-estimated; if levels of general (acquisitive) criminality (because of alternative choices available) are over-estimated; and if we factor in the amount of crime that already active criminals who become dependent/problem drug users would have committed anyway, then the proportion of drug-related crime attributed directly to drug use would have to fall significantly. A fall of the kind likely (perhaps to around 10–20% instead of around 60–70%) would potentially impact meaningfully on the public psyche and on political decision making and policing at both local and national levels. There would arguably, and as a consequence, be a shift away from seeing dependent and problem drug use as a predominantly criminal justice issue to one that was a public health and medical issue.

UNDERSTANDING THE DRUGS–CRIME CONNECTION(S)

Clearly, there is a relationship between drug use and crime. The relationship, however, is not the simple causal one that is often assumed, nor is the amount of drug-related crime likely to be of the level reported by many formal estimates. Most users of illicit drugs have no or little more of a relationship to criminality (other than for possession or supply of drugs) than do non-drug-using members of the population – including most users of powder cocaine. Those that do – for example, heroin or crack cocaine users – tend to be dependent or otherwise problem drug users. However, many of these individuals were criminally active *prior* to being drug users and while periods of frequent/dependent use tend to *increase* the amount of crime these individuals commit, such use does not cause it to start. Similarly, and for the same reasons, research also tends to show that for these individuals engagement with treatment such as methadone maintenance where a user is provided with substitute drugs to replace their street drugs (taking away the need to steal to get their drugs), criminality tends to be *reduced* not stopped. It is reduced only because pre-existing (pre-drug use) levels of criminality are resumed. By removing the simple, one-way, 'drugs cause crime' idea, we are forced to move away from a pharmacologically orientated model (drugs cause crime) and acknowledge that the links or connections are more complex and have their roots in wider social conditions. Some researchers have chosen to argue that rather than suggesting drugs cause crime, it is in fact preferable to see it the other way round – that criminally active individuals are more likely to become drug users.

One consequence of this exaggerated drug-centric understanding of crime is that general discourses around drugs and drug users have become increasingly criminalised and less medicalised. A focus on punishing drug use rather than helping drug users is justified (Stevens 2007).

REFERENCES

Coomber, R. (2011) 'Social fear, drug related beliefs and drug policy', in G. Hunt, M. Milhet and H. Bergeron (eds) *Drugs and Culture: Knowledge, Consumption and Policy*. Aldershot: Ashgate. pp. 15–21.

Goldstein, P. (1985). 'The drugs/violence nexus: A tripartite conceptual framework', *Journal of Drug Issues*, 21 (2): 345–67.

Guardian (2012) 'Miami man shot dead eating a man's face may have been on LSD-like drug', 29 May. Available at: www.guardian.co.uk/world/2012/may/29/miami-man-eating-face-lsd (accessed 31 December 2012).

Hawkins, N. (2004) *Commons Hansard: 18th October 2004, Column 690*. London: The Stationery Office.

Stevens, A. (2007) 'When two dark figures collide: Evidence and discourse on drug-related crime', *Critical Social Policy*, 27(1): 77–99.

25 Gangs

> **Definition**: *While many people might initially or even intuitively feel they know what a gang and a gang member is, the reality is that these definitions are highly contested. Gang structures, behaviours, motivations and membership forms can differ widely, along with meaningful differences in the level of intensity for each aspect. The stereotype New York or Los Angeles gang doesn't transpose easily onto the streets of London, Paris or Sydney, while some other 'gangs' may be better defined as organised crime groups and others more reasonably as 'connected' youth.*

CONTEXTUALISING GANGS

Children have gangs. These gang forms often have some basic structural characteristics that we would recognise as meaningful. Membership of the gang is perhaps the defining feature. You are either 'in' a gang or not. Being in it means inclusion and a sense of identity and having privileged access to some of the benefits that begets almost any gang member, such as loyalty and support from other gang members and an expectation that you and the gang will 'do things' together. Such gangs often have a leader or leaders of sorts. It is 'their' gang. In this way, formations of early childhood identity, such as being part of a similarly minded group, having peers to 'hang out' with, look up to and take a lead from (or do the leading for) can be highly meaningful. Childhood gangs can be innocent, loose membership opportunities to play and have adventures, as depicted in the middle-class characters in Enid Blyton's *Famous Five* novels or the mischievous William Brown and his gang, the 'Outlaws', in Richmal Crompton's *Just William* series. They can also, depending on the context, provide early life protective belonging for vulnerable 'street' children growing up in areas of poverty. In such contexts, 'adventure' or just everyday activity may mean early engagement with gang-related crime. In childhood gangs, the level of hierarchy, rules of inclusion and control will vary enormously, as will the levels of naughtiness or even criminality. Transpose the gang and gang membership into adolescence and young adulthood and some of the same attributes clearly apply but the structures and activities, as we shall see, can become more serious to both gang members and to wider society.

OVER-HOMOGENISATION

It is important, however, not to overstate the prevalence and supposed essence of gangs, just as it is for other 'subcultures'. Subcultural theory emerged in early criminology from the study of youth gang behaviour and it is from here that the first clearly defined characteristics of (usually deviant) gangs are derived. Subcultures have traditionally been understood as youth groups that adopt alternative styles (fashions, apparel), values and behaviours to the dominant culture of 'normalcy'. Sometimes they do this because they are already in many respects 'excluded' from many of the life chances available to others (the 'poor' excluded) or because they feel suffocated by normalcy (e.g. middle-class subcultures), or both. A subculture is thus, in part, seen as a form of resistance to the dominant culture and a way of challenging its dominance through membership and adherence to an alternative identity and lifestyle. Subcultures, because of how they confront normalcy, often offend or challenge the dominant culture and can be seen as 'other' and a threat to society and its normative values. The fear that this creates for many often leads to a scapegoating and stereotyping of the groups involved and to an exaggeration of the real threat involved (see also *Moral panics* and *Fear and the fear of crime*). Subcultural theory, however, along with lay attribution, suffers from assuming that punks, bikers, goths, etc. have greater levels of membership and commitment to the group or gang than is often the case, and therefore imagine a subculture when something much looser in fact exists. By artificially grouping what are often loosely connected individuals with a commitment to *some* aspects of the collection or subculture in question, an impression is created of something more coherent and definable. Even where the opposite appears true, for example when a young man is stabbed and killed by a group of young men on the streets of London, loose gang affiliation may be present, but the roots of the violence may be more explicable through reference to how these young people resolve conflict generally – through violent means – rather than seeing it as a direct expression of gang membership or gang-directed behaviour. A contrast could be made with a gang-ordered killing or a gang-related territorial battle. Seeing all violence and crime that loosely (or even strongly) connected gang members commit as the result of being in a gang is to misunderstand the broader living context of those members. Non-gang members commit crimes of violence and loosely associated youths sometimes/often group together, for example on housing estates and in schools, but would not consider themselves as part of a definable gang.

Early writing on gangs depicted 'unsupervised youth developing organization through conflict with other groups and authorities ... [and excluded] criminaliza-tion as a necessary characteristic' (Hagedorn 2005: 155), while later definitions, particularly official and criminal justice definitions, have often considered crimi-nality to be one of the defining criteria. We can see this in the USA where the following definition of 'gang' adopted by the California state legislature has been adopted (albeit often modified slightly) in a number of different states throughout the country:

> 'criminal street gang' means any ongoing organization, association or group of three or more persons, whether formal or informal, having as one of its primary activities the commission of one or more of the criminal acts [...], having a common name or common identifying sign or symbol, and whose members individually or collectively engage in or have engaged in a pattern of criminal gang activity. (Kinnear 2009: 201)

Academia (sociologists and criminologists in particular) produces more contested definitions and many of these definitions are in flux as the world and societies within it change. Broadly however, we might say that the research literature accepts the following as a minimalist definition:

- A gang has to comprise of three or four members, typically for 'youth gangs', between the ages of 12 and 24, but many gangs have much older members and may typically not be 'youth gangs' at all (e.g. Hell's Angels).
- Gang members share an identity. This will usually be linked to a specific gang name. Insignia associated directly with the gang is also common and loyalty to, affiliation with and membership of the gang can be demonstrated by adorning (wearing clothes, colours, bearing tattoos, etc.) associated insignia on their person.
- Gang members self-identify as members of a specific gang and are identified as such by others.
- For a gang to be a recognised entity, it has to have some longevity/stability over time and be organised at least to some degree rather than simply being a loose affiliation of people.
- Most gangs are associated with an elevated level of criminal activity (but this is not a necessary component, just a common one).

GANGS DIFFER

In the USA, where most of the research literature has been focused until recently, gangs that broadly correspond to the definitions given above are prevalent and more of them fit the 'drive-by-shooting, drug supply involved, violent essence' of the gang stereotype than in some other countries. Nonetheless, huge differences exist between gangs, even in the USA. In 1996, it was estimated that across the country, more than 31,000 gangs were in existence with around 846,000 gang members. With an average age of 17–18 years overall, in those cities with long-standing and established gangs the average age rises and having gang members in their 30s is not uncommon. Gang sizes also differ significantly. Some of the most well-established, city-wide, gangs can number up to tens of thousands, while a territorially based gang from a defined city area is more likely to number around the 200 mark. 'Speciality' gangs specialising in, for example, drug-related crime are more likely to number up to 25. Some gangs are all male, some are all female and many have proportions of female membership with varying levels of female roles within those memberships – from highly unequal and traditionally gendered to more equal and less traditionally gendered roles.

In other countries such as the UK, as has already been suggested, the issue is more contested amongst criminologists and sociologists. Many UK academics have traditionally preferred not to see or to label loose affiliations of youth as gangs. In part, this is because they do not always see them helpfully defined as gangs, but also because of an awareness that public policy responses to 'gangs' can produce overly punitive criminal justice responses. 'Gang' academics can thus sometimes talk past each other in terms of definition and engage in unhelpful posturing. Following Densley (2013), then, it might be best to acknowledge that few gangs are the same – especially internationally – but to also recognise that for alliances of young people that self-define as being in a gang; have some degree of gang-focused organisation; where their operations are at least semi-clandestine or criminal in nature; and where they use internal 'policing' to resolve conflict within the group and with other 'gangs', then a gang label is not unhelpful.

GANGS – A GROWING WORLDWIDE PHENOMENON

According to Hagedorn (2005), gangs are now a globalised phenomenon, with gang members likely numbering in the tens of millions, tied to unprecedented worldwide urbanisation and the problems that that can bring. Industrialisation and urbanisation bring a variety of problems but in the less-developed, and developing, world nearly as many people now live in urban slums than those who don't, and in some parts of Africa nearly three-quarters of the population are living in slum conditions. This means that, from the street children and drug gangs of the favelas of Brazil and the 'child soldiers' in the Democratic Republic of Congo to the excluded of India, conditions are rife for people – especially the disconnected and relatively unprotected young – to engage in a connective practice that provides camaraderie, support, identity, status and belonging where otherwise there might be none, or too little. In the USA too, gangs are prevalent and thrive in the poorest, most excluded neighbourhoods (see also *Poverty and exclusion*).

GANGS AND CRIME AND VIOLENCE

Although there is a strong correlation between gangs, gang membership and crime and violence, just as with the link between drugs and crime and violence, this relationship is not a necessary one. It is not causal in the literal sense (see also *Drug-related crime and violence*) as many gang members would be criminally active prior to gang membership but gangs/gang membership can increase levels of criminality and involvement in violent events. Gangs normatively have strong traditional, masculine hierarchies and structures and conflict is often resolved through recourse to violence. The often 'hypermasculine' cultural norms and culture of violence present in many gangs, however, is not simply produced by the gang but is mostly reflective of the existing cultural context from which the gangs emerge. Gang involvement and the structures they adopt nonetheless no doubt help to reproduce such values and reinforce them in younger members, including 'traditional' values on how women should be treated (Miller and Brunson 2000). Involvement in crime and violence is meaningfully elevated in spaces where people are politically marginalised and have poor life chances. When gangs become either nominally or very organised, both crime and violence rise. While there are many gangs as described above that comfortably conform to this image, there are nonetheless more moderate manifestations in many developed countries such as the UK, Australia and elsewhere.

GENDER

In terms of gender, research has consistently found that gangs are largely male-dominated in their structure, prevalent status hierarchies and general activities. Because of this, research has also tended to focus almost entirely on male involvement, to the detriment of an understanding of female roles and interaction within gangs. Women do, however, belong to gangs and also sometimes form gangs. Gang membership, as for males, tends to increase involvement in delinquency but for women this tends to be in lesser forms of criminality, and Miller and Brunson (2000) have suggested that women sometimes use gendered roles and expectations to allow them to avoid becoming embroiled in serious crime and to control what they wish to become involved in. In many studies, it is also the case that women enter gang life earlier than males and exit it earlier too. Actual gang membership in 'mixed gender' gangs is sometimes unclear, with women sometimes taking marginal positions, not just in criminality but also in terms of full membership. Women's roles and status in gangs can also vary depending on gender saturation and the cultural/patriarchal bent of the gang itself, but, in general, gendered inequality within gangs in one study did mean that women were less likely to become victims of violent crime than the young men.

CONCLUSION

Gangs are complex phenomena that have been the subject of a great deal of academic debate. Simple definitions are quickly undermined by the great variety of forms and structures found and some agreement now exists that too rigid a focus on stereotyped images is unhelpful and that self-definition, along with some other broad criteria, have a credible role to play in identifying where gangs exist and who belongs to them. Although gangs have long existed, they continue to proliferate and develop globally, with ongoing urbanisation and industrialisation continuing to produce relatively disenfranchised populations with few life chances and opportunities. As a consequence, large numbers of excluded people are forced to live together in challenging circumstances worldwide. Gangs, it is recognised, provide their members with structure, support and identity, and many young adults, who might otherwise feel even more dislocated, find a 'home' in gang life that resonates with their own circumstances. Gang life, however, often also increases involvement in criminality, as well as the chance of being a victim of violent crime – particularly for young males.

REFERENCES

Densley, J. (2013) *How Gangs Work: An Ethnography of Youth Violence*. Basingstoke: Palgrave Macmillan.

Hagedorn, J.M. (2005) 'The global impact of gangs', *Journal of Contemporary Criminal Justice*, 21(2): 153–69.

Kinnear, K. L. (2009) *Gangs: A Reference Handbook* (2nd edition). Santa Barbara: ABC-CLIO.

Miller, J. and Brunson, R.K. (2000) 'Gender dynamics in youth gangs: A comparison of males' and females' accounts', *Justice Quarterly*, 17(3): 419–48.

26 Environmental Crime and Green Criminology

> **Definition**: The examination of crimes against the environment and violations of environmental regulations is a rapidly growing subfield within criminology. The study of environmental crime is often referred to today as 'green criminology'.

There are two areas in criminology which use the word 'environmental', so it can be confusing. Environmental criminology is generally considered to be concerned with examining crime and its relationship to places, especially small places (see also *Crime and theory*). Hence, it is focused on the ecology of crime events, 'hot spots' and the use of GIS technology to understand time and place variations, at the micro level, in which crime occurs, and how to prevent crime through physical security and other preventative measures (Wortley and Mazerolle 2008).

Studies of environmental crime share with environmental criminology the fundamental notions that crime occurs at specific locations and can be highly situational in nature, but, otherwise, they are very different approaches to defining crime and justice issues. Environmental crime studies can range from understanding the motivations of poachers to environmental harms perpetrated by corporations who exploit land and natural resources for profits (Potter 2010; White 2009). Many criminologists who are interested in environmental crime today identify with the phrase 'green criminology'. Although it is difficult to pinpoint when the green criminology movement began, it is a term many criminologists began to use during the 1990s, and it continues to grow as a specialisation within criminology today.

However, not all criminologists interested in environmental crimes are 'green' criminologists. The main reason for this is the way that green criminology has expanded the domain of criminology. To quote Potter (2010: 11):

> Only a minority of instances of environmental harm are accounted for by criminal activities – the vast majority of fishing, deforestation, pollution and so on are actually legal, and often seen as important economic activity. More tradition-minded criminologists do not see this sort of activity as the business of criminology at all.

Hence, everything depends on the definition (see also *Crime (definition of)*). On the one hand, the criminological study of environmental crime can be defined more narrowly and traditionally as 'an act in violation of an environmental protection statute that applies to the areas in which the act occurred and that has clearly identified sanctions for purposes of police enforcement' (Clifford and Edwards 1998: 25). The criminal can be an individual or a corporation, but the action must somehow violate a law (White 2009).

On the other hand, criminologists who identify with green criminology declare that environmental harm is in itself a crime (White 2011: 4). This view, as Potter (2010) noted, takes a more critical perspective that considers how social structure, political power, the profit motive, an increasingly globalised economy and other society-wide factors contextual crime in ways that a more legalistic definition of environmental crime cannot. White (2009) points out that a definition of harm derives directly from the concepts associated with 'eco-justice', which are extensions of fundamental human rights and of concepts related to the sustainability of physical and human systems which include considerations of animal rights and species survival (see also *Social construction of crime and deviance*). Briefly, eco-justice (and synonymous terms, such as environmental justice and ecological justice) stresses the relationship of humans to the natural environment and the rights of all species 'to a life free from torture, abuse and destruction of habitat' (Heckenberg 2009: 11).

Between these dramatically different conceptualisations of environmental crime is a vast array of issues on which criminologists can focus. In fact, both advocates for a more legalistic approach and proponents of the 'harm to the environment' approach would likely agree as much as disagree on what constitutes environmental crime. Further, some issues which are now subsumed under the rubrics of both the legalistic and harm approaches to environmental crime were the subject of empirical analysis long before green criminology came along, such as poaching/violations of wildlife and hunting regulations, animal abuse and illegal dumping (see also *Rural crime*).

Although the reasons for the coalescing of criminology's focus on environmental crime today is complex, events and trends over the past few decades from around the world have certainly contributed, including: the growth of environmental laws and environmental advocacy groups in many countries; issues of climate change, illegal logging, the depletion of rainforests, species extinction from over-development and other human influences; health problems and other deleterious consequences from the accidental or purposive release of oil, chemicals and radioactive materials into the biosphere; site location of hazardous waste facilities and their impacts on the surrounding population who are often poor and lack political power; and the threat of land acquisition (whether legal or illegal – known as land theft) for natural resources development and exploitation in areas where many traditional and indigenous groups are located.

EXAMPLES OF GREEN CRIMINOLOGY

Here are three examples of the ways in which the criminological study of environmental crime has changed, especially under the influence of green criminology.

Traditionally, studies of poaching/violations of wildlife and hunting regulations have focused on either the motivations of those who violate wildlife laws or the policing styles of game wardens, wildlife conservation officers, park rangers/constables and rural law-enforcement officers. Today, informed by a green criminology approach, poaching studies have expanded the scope of their subject matter and their theoretical view of poaching as an environmental crime. Poaching can be seen as the beginning of a 'commodity chain', that is a national and transnational set of activities which extends from the source of production to its subsequent sale and consumption. In this regard, it is a form of economic exploitation in which animals are killed or captured, mostly in rural localities, as raw products and shipped to urban centres as value-added products (see also *Rural crime*), representing a form of profit-driven exploitation. In many countries, such as Uganda, poaching for food is also a survival response of local people who were displaced both geographically and/or economically by the establishment of a park. For example, Lemieux (2011) describes elephant poaching as a partial response to the forcible relocation of people in Africa from their traditional lands for the establishment of tourism and economic development, set up either during colonial times or by post-colonial governments. Finally, the illegal harvesting of animals can be viewed as a form of oppositional behaviour displayed by poachers who are from poor and working-class rural backgrounds. Excluded from mainstream opportunities for success, they learn to poach for both profit and the self-efficacy derived from the activity, especially if they are not caught (see also *Poverty and exclusion*).

From a traditional criminological standpoint, animal abuse is seen as a type of precursor behaviour among children for more serious interpersonal violence later in their lives. Animal abuse from a green criminology perspective expands the debate to consider features of feminist theory, insofar as it promotes a view of human–animal interaction in terms of rights (both human and animal rights) and the general concept of harm. For example, Bierne (2009) describes four primary perspectives, including: (1) an examination of animal abuse as an action that violates the law; (2) a view that the pain and suffering of animals inflicted by humans is not practical in most cases, which by implication means there will be exceptions, i.e. occasions when it is acceptable; (3) the perspective that animals have rights, especially higher-order mammals, and therefore deserve protection; and (4) a feminist view that animal abuse is similar in kind to the coercive behaviour seen in male violence against women, especially domestic violence. Bierne (2009: 193) concludes: 'a criminology that ignores animal abuse will be a speciesist discourse utterly irrelevant to the understanding of much harm and suffering inflicted by humans on nonhuman, but nevertheless valuable, forms of life'.

A third area where the discourse on environmental crime has expanded due to green criminology's influence is the issue of illegal dumping. A more legalistic approach would examine the illegal disposal (also known as 'fly-tipping' and 'fly dumping') of rubbish and hazardous waste as a form of victimisation. In particular, environmental studies of dumping are very much like environmental criminology in focus because locations where illegal disposal is frequent are considered 'hot spots'. There are also costs to the victims, most of whom are the landowners, in terms of clean-up and damage to property. Additional costs are incurred to the surrounding community through greater risks associated with water quality and human health.

A green criminology approach would consider the same factors as related to both victims and offenders, plus expand the context by considering two concepts that also inform the dialogue (see also *Crime (definition of)*). The first is the concept of environmental inequality. This concept parallels other measures of inequality and concentration, such as income. In this case, environmental inequality refers to variations by place in the quality of the physical environment, hence in the way that the environment affects the health of humans as well as non-human populations.

The second concept is that of environmental justice, which is concerned with issues of environmental inequality based on social exclusion and discrimination related to race/ethnicity, among other factors. Now dumping can be seen as a convergence of factors associated with the economic and political conditions and associated powerlessness of a place and the characteristics of people who live there, of local offenders and their links to wider networks of environmental offenders (including organised crime), and of issues related to zoning regulations and political considerations which push disposal sites to places near where poor and disenfranchised people live, and create negligence in the enforcement of regulations, and even bribery.

For example, Pellow (2009) describes the case of the dumping of highway construction waste in black and Latino neighbourhoods of Chicago by a company which never bothered to obtain proper permits and was bribing the local alderman to the sum of US$5,000 each month. The owner of the business attempted to bribe the local residents by providing monies for various beautification projects, such as free flower and vegetable seeds. However, complaints about the health effects of the crushed construction material continued. Eventually, through persistent activism, the local neighbourhood won its battle, new and more strict regulations were developed and enforced, and the illegal sites were cleaned up. Pellow (2009) makes a bigger point, in addition to his description of a success story in the fight for environmental justice, which is that this situation would never have occurred in the predominantly white, upper-income neighbourhoods of Chicago.

THE BOTTOM LINE

Arguably, there is no issue which has risen to the top of the criminological agenda faster than that of environmental crime. Most green criminology scholarship takes a more macro and critical approach to environmental crime, incorporating concepts related to harm, environmental inequality and environmental justice.

REFERENCES

Bierne, P. (2009) 'For a nonspeciesist criminology: Animal abuse as an object of study', in R. White (ed.) *Environmental Crime: A Reader*. Cullompton: Willan, pp. 175–99.

Clifford, M. and Edwards, T.D. (1998) 'Defining "environmental crime"', in M. Clifford (ed.) *Environmental Crime: Enforcement, Policy, and Social Responsibility*. Gaithersburg, MD: Aspen Publishers, pp. 5–27.

Heckenberg, D. (2009) 'Studying environmental crime: Key words, acronyms and sources of information', in R. White (ed.) *Environmental Crime: A Reader*. Cullompton: Willan, pp. 9–24.

Lemieux, A.M. (2011) 'Policing poaching and protecting pachyderms: Lessons learned from Africa's elephants', in R.I. Mawby and R. Yarwood (eds) *Rural Policing and Policing the Rural: A Constable Countryside?* Farnham: Ashgate, pp. 183–92.

Pellow, D.N. (2009) 'The politics of illegal dumping: An environmental justice framework', in R. White (ed.) *Environmental Crime: A Reader*. Cullompton: Willan, pp. 360–73.

Potter, G. (2010) 'What is green criminology?,' *Sociology Review*, 20(1): 8–12.

White, R. (2009) 'Introduction: Environmental crime and eco-global criminology', in R. White (ed.) *Environmental Crime: A Reader*. Cullompton: Willan, pp. 1–8.

White, R. (2011) *Transnational Environmental Crime: Toward an Eco-Global Criminology*. London: Routledge.

Wortley, R. and Mazerolle, L. (eds) (2008) *Environmental Criminology and Crime Analysis*. Cullompton: Willan.

27 Rural Crime

> **Definition**: *Rural refers to those places with a lower population size and population density than urban localities. Social scientists, including criminologists, presume that the number and density of people living in an area influence crime rates and the kinds of crimes mostly likely to occur there. Hence, understanding similarities and differences in expressions of crime in rural and urban places is important.*

In historical terms, the urbanisation of the world is nothing short of breathtaking. As recently as 1800, only 3% of all people lived in places other than farms and small rural villages (Population Reference Bureau 2013). Sometime during 2008, for the first time in human history, a majority of the world's population was estimated to be living in urban centres (United Nations Population Division 2009).

Defining what is rural and what is urban is not easy. Each country has its own way of classifying a population. In England and Wales, any town, village or hamlet with less than 10,000 persons is considered to be rural; in the USA, rural is defined as all places containing less than 2,500 persons that are not contiguous to a larger place. The US Census Bureau also classifies every county or county equivalent (of which there are more than 3,200) into two basic categories: metropolitan or urban and non-metropolitan or rural. Regardless of definitional differences, these countries were among the first to transform into majority urban societies, with England and Wales reaching the urban–rural tipping point by 1850 (Law 1967), and the USA achieving the same status sometime during the decade of 1910–1919 (Donnermeyer and DeKeseredy 2014).

AN URBAN-CENTRIC CRIMINOLOGY AND THE RISE OF RURAL CRIMINOLOGY

It should not be surprising that criminology is mostly urban-centric in its focus, given that so much of its early development was in the countries of Europe and North America where the industrial revolution began and urbanisation took root early on (Donnermeyer and DeKeseredy 2014). Criminology presumed that areas with smaller and less dense populations had less crime, and that their crime problems were less serious.

It is still common for criminologists to refer to the sociological theorist Ferdinand Tönnies, and his well-known distinction of *gemeinschaft–gesselschaft*, as catch-all descriptors for rural and urban, respectively. For Tönnies, *gemeinschaft–gesselschaft* refers to types of societies based on two kinds of human will, known as *kürville* or essential will, which expresses a person's character, and *wesenville* or arbitrary will, which represents the purposive selection of actions based on efficient approaches to achieve a goal on the part of an actor (Donnermeyer and DeKeseredy 2014). Today, *gemeinschaft* is erroneously considered synonymous with small town and rural living, primary group relationships, cohesive communities and less crime; with *gesellschaft* over-generalised to the urban as designating secondary group relationships and less cohesion (i.e. greater disorganisation).

Assumptions about urbanism and urban life form the intellectual pillars of social disorganisation theory and many other mainstream theories about crime and society (Sampson 2012). Urbanism starts with the notion that densely populated places manifest more heterogeneous populations, and with this diversity comes a greater chance for the development of criminal subcultures and individualistic forms of deviance. It was the 'transformation' of societies from rural to urban (and by implication *gemeinschaft* to *gesellschaft*) that had great sociological significance for the Chicago School of Sociology, from Park to Sutherland to Wirth, and its echoes can still be heard in the work of latter-day criminologists with Chicago roots (Sampson 2012).

Also contributing to the urban-centric focus of criminology is the persistent gap in the *prevalence* of official crime (i.e. crimes known to the police) between the rural and urban sectors of countries like the USA and the UK (see also *Victims of crime* and *Crime statistics*). Studies of crime and delinquency, gangs, policing styles and most other criminological issues are also mostly urban in their orientation.

However, like other rural-related areas of criminology (see also *Environmental crime and green criminology*), rural criminology scholarship has increased greatly over the past few decades (Donnermeyer and DeKeseredy 2014). Criminologists who focus on rural and urban crime continue to acknowledge key differences in the social and cultural context of place by size and/or population density, even though gross generalisations based on well-worn dichotomies derived from Tönnies have been replaced by more cautious differentiations.

One set of rural–urban distinctions important for understanding crime and society is illustrated by Weisheit et al. (2006). For example, when compared with urban localities, rural communities are more likely to have a greater density of acquaintanceship, that is cohesion based on primary group relationships. The same individuals participate in a wide array of activities; hence in a typical rural community people interact with each other in a great variety of roles, rather than in a single role or in a few specialised roles. Rural economies are more likely to depend on agriculture, fishing, logging, mining and other forms of natural resource extraction, or on a single employer, making them more vulnerable to economic dislocations. Finally, a globalised economy and electronic forms of communication make the social and cultural boundaries of all places highly permeable and susceptible to outside influences.

Donnermeyer and DeKeseredy (2014) point out that even softly stated rural–urban distinctions can lead criminological thought and empirical work astray for two important reasons. First, rural places are very diverse – simply put – and there are so many more villages, hamlets and small towns than large cities. For argument's sake, it could be claimed that on a general scale, which considers the sheer number of locations in societies around the world by population size and density, there are more rural places, hence as much, if not more, diversity exists between them than between cities. Second, to assume that rurality translates into less crime, while urbanity automatically implies more crime, is completely false. The real diversity in expressions of crime in any society is at the local level, of which its size or density is only one dimension. Hence, rates of crime for some offences may be higher in specific rural places when compared with the same crime in cities and suburbs.

SIGNIFICANT AREAS OF RURAL CRIMINOLOGY

There are several significant areas where criminological research which considers both the rural and urban context, or focuses mostly on the rural, has advanced the general field of criminology. This is in addition to criminological work on environmental crime and green criminology, much of which is located in rural places and affects rural peoples and communities.

First, criminologists who want to understand crime and society have asked questions about variations in crime rates with size of place and urbanism.

Urbanism refers to factors such as tolerance for differences, anomie, weak social bonds and lessened social control. Rotolo and Tittle (2006) concluded that 'It may be inaccurate to claim that city size is monotonically related to crime rates or to assume that increases or decreases in population may portend corresponding increases or decreases in crime rates' (p. 359). Their parting statement is even more interesting: 'Current urban theory does not even fully anticipate or explain our findings, much less anticipating and explaining more complicated possibilities' (2006: 360).

Second, studies of violence often focus on the rural context. For example, in the USA, criminologists have examined the 'subculture of violence' hypothesis, attempting to link strong cultural traits associated with the history and rural heritage of a region to contemporary expressions of interpersonal violence. Other criminologists have examined the extent to which some forms of crime diffuse from urban centres to rural places, hence expressions of rural crime and its prevalence frequently and persistently lag behind urban crime, yet grow with time. Homicide studies find that murder can be higher in localities with persistent poverty, high levels of gun ownership (in the USA) and acquaintanceship of the victim and offender – characteristics which define many rural places (Donnermeyer and DeKeseredy 2014). Similarly, there is a rich body of research on the relationship of violence to social change due to the initiation of mining and other natural resource-extraction activities in rural places (Carrington et al. 2013).

Third, there is a large volume of rural studies which has attempted to use social disorganisation theory and noted that it does not work as well. Donnermeyer and DeKeseredy (2014) challenge the generalisability of social disorganisation theory to rural communities, based on their review of over two dozen rural-located statistical studies, and other rural research. They contend that Sampson (2012) and associates have it wrong when they use collective efficacy to talk only about the ways the collective characteristics of places, rural and urban, reduce crime.

Substance use and drug production is a fourth area where crime in the rural context has been frequently researched (Weisheit et al. 2006). National-level data sets, such as the Monitoring the Future study of adolescent substance use in the USA, show little difference in rates of substance use between rural and urban youth. There are now numerous studies of drug production/trafficking in rural communities, especially methamphetamines, and of needle-sharing and drug-using networks among rural people, which challenge mainstream criminological notions of disorganisation by noting the ways forms of cohesion and collective efficacy facilitate criminal behaviours.

The work of criminologists on violence against rural women in societies around the world, especially involving current/former male partners, reveals forms of tight-knit social networks among male abusers in rural communities to engage in abuse of women without public knowledge or detection by officials (Donnermeyer and DeKeseredy 2014). This research shows the extent to which there are multiple forms of collective efficacy which exist side by side in rural (and by extension, urban) localities, hence a form of diversity which cannot be accounted for or measured by census data, or even massive surveys of neighbourhood residents (Sampson 2012). Although crime rates may be lower for 'crimes known to the police', that is crimes that may threaten the public order, there are other crimes like violence against women that represent a more private sphere (the family) and where collective efficacy discourages reports to the police, hence facilitating their occurrence (see also *Crime statistics* and *Social construction of crime*).

Research on agricultural crime shows the same dynamics. For example, Barclay's (2003) research not only found that farmers in New South Wales would steal from each other, using opportunities presented by the large size of agricultural operations and the daily work routines of farmers, but that there were strong community norms against 'dobbing in' or reporting crime. Hence, it was tolerated. All of the criminological work on agricultural crime also demonstrates ways that the industrialisation of agriculture has made agricultural operations more attractive targets (see also *Risk from crime*). Plus, farmers themselves may be offenders through violations of environmental regulations and using the farm operation for various illegal activities, such as drug production (Donnermeyer and DeKeseredy 2014).

Regardless of the lop-sided, urban-biased nature of criminology, both today and in the past, there is a growing recognition of the need to examine criminological phenomena within the context of smaller places in order to understand more fully the nature of crime and society, and to improve the criminological imagination through more comparative rural and urban research.

REFERENCES

Barclay, E. (2003) Crime with Rural Communities: The Dark Side of Gemeinschaft. PhD dissertation. Armidale, NSW: The University of New England.

Carrington, K., McIntosh, A., Hogg, R. and Scott, J. (2013) 'Rural masculinities and the internationalisation of violence in agricultural communities', *International Journal of Rural Criminology*, 2(1): 1–25.

Donnermeyer, J.F. and DeKeseredy, W. (2014) *Rural Criminology*. London: Routledge.

Law, C.M. (1967) 'The growth of urban population in England and Wales, 1801–1911', *Transactions of the Institute of British Geographers*, 41(Dec.): 125–43.

Population Reference Bureau (2013) *Human Population: Urbanization*. Washington, DC: Population Reference Bureau. Available at: www.prb.org/Publications/Lesson-Plans/Human Population/Urbanization.aspx (accessed 21/01/13).

Rotolo, T. and Tittle, C.R. (2006) 'Population size, change, and crime in US cities', *Journal of Quantitative Criminology*, 22(4): 341–67.

Sampson, R.J. (2012) *Great American City: Chicago and the Enduring Neighborhood Effect*. Chicago: University of Chicago Press.

United Nations Population Division (2009) *Urban and Rural Areas 2009*. New York: United Nations, Department of Economic and Social Affairs.

Weisheit, R.A., Falcone, D.N. and Wells, L.E. (2006) *Crime and Policing in Rural and Small-Town America*. Long Grove, IL: Waveland Press.

> **Definition**: *Internet or cyber crimes are criminal offences committed through various electronic forms of communication and economic transactions. Also called computer crime, these crimes involve illegal activities, ranging from identity theft to purchases of illegal or prohibited products, which are committed through online networks.*

There is a phrase – 'New wine in old bottles' – which represents an apt description of internet or cyber crime. The nature of the actual offences which we know as internet crime – fraud, theft and even forms of violent crime – are nothing new. What is new is the context of the crimes provided by the development of electronic means of communication.

None of what we know today as internet crime would have occurred without a long series of technological innovations representing the unerring transformation of societies around the world from rural and agricultural to urban and industrial. These include the telegraph and the telephone in the nineteenth century, the radio in the first decades of the twentieth century, and then television in the 1950s and 1960s. Even though email was developed in the 1970s, it did not begin to revolutionise the workplace and the ways people connect with each other until the 1980s, and today it represents a cluster of electronic forms of communication which have made it possible for everyone in the world to be almost instantaneously connected to everyone else, through various forms of social media, such as Twitter and YouTube.

A World Bank (2012) report estimated that 75% of the world's population has access to mobile phones. Plus, there are millions of Facebook users in countries across the globe (Social Bakers 2012). The phenomenal growth in electronic communication provides many new opportunities and situations for crime, even though the kinds of crime which can be committed through electronic media will be fundamentally the same. Only the context will change.

There are three levels of victims for internet crime. Individuals can become the victims of cyber bullying, identity theft and scams. Corporations are also the victims of theft, and of attempts to gather privileged information or to disrupt their daily operations through sabotage of computer systems. Cyber terrorism is also a concern of government agencies at the local, national and international levels. Perpetrators of internet/cyber crime can also be found at all three levels, namely, individuals, corporations and governments.

VARIETIES OF CYBER THEFT

There are many kinds of internet crime. One of the most frequent is identity theft. Identity theft is the unauthorised use of information about another person's identity, without permission, to commit fraud. Identity thieves may sell a person's identity or use it themselves to apply for a job with false information, obtain pre-scription medications without having to pay for them or file false claims for reimbursement with a medical insurer. Theft of personal information, such as credit history, credit card numbers and bank account numbers, can result in a con-siderable loss of money for victims, even though there are laws in many countries limiting a victim's financial liability from stolen credit and debit cards. It is also costly to repair or clean up personal records which have been improperly used, and there can be considerable psychological stress suffered by victims of identity theft.

A recent variation on identity theft is child identity theft. In this case, the iden-tities of newborns and young children, such as their national identification number, are used by thieves to open false bank and credit card accounts, fraudulently col-lect government benefits, apply for bank loans and forge identity papers for passport and visa applications. Identity information can be stolen in a variety of ways – such as from hospital or school records, applications for sports league par-ticipation and paperwork for separation/divorce of parents.

The variety of email scams is almost endless. Perhaps the most popular form of email scamming is a plea for help. Someone in a country far away from the tar-geted individual has had a tragedy occur. Their parents, who are rich, were killed by their financial advisor who is attempting to steal the family fortune, or the sender of the email is dying of cancer or some other irreversible malady. The sender wants to transfer the family funds to the target for safe keeping, and in return for a substantial fee. Bank account numbers must be exchanged to complete the transaction. Once that happens, the scam is successful and the account number of victims is used to steal funds from their savings. Other common email scams from the recent past include offers for pre-approved home loans and credit cards for a small fee, winning a lottery requiring information about bank account num-bers for the transfer of the false largess, and 'phishing' attempts from seemingly reputable sources (based on the scammer's email address on the message) to obtain password information or account numbers.

PORNOGRAPHY, BULLYING AND STALKING

The internet and computers have also facilitated another type of crime which predates modern times. It is pornography. The ability to access and store porno-graphic materials on the internet is easy and, for some people, addictive. There are over 4 million porn sites on the internet, with as many as 10,000 added every week. The revenue from pornography exceeds all of the largest companies in the world. Since watching pornography is positively associated with males who psychologically and physically abuse women, the easy accessibility of internet-sourced pornography enhances particular forms of violence (DeKeseredy and Olsson 2011).

The internet also augments or facilitates the commission of other offences by providing places for forms of virtual identity among users who engage in hidden and extreme forms of deviance. One example from the USA is the ability of far right-wing hate groups to use the web to recruit and sustain members. Another is the purchase of illegal or prohibited goods, such as through an online black market programme known as 'Silk Road', and internet services like 'Tor' which are designed to keep the identity of participants and purchases hidden.

Two forms of violent crime related to computer technology are cyber bullying and cyber stalking. Bullying is a type of violence because it is a repeated and aggressive form of behaviour (threats, intimidation and assault) by one or more persons against a targeted individual. Targeted individuals may have been singled out due to a characteristic that makes them different, such as their race/ethnicity, a disability or some other physical trait. Cyber bullying is the same thing as bullying in general, except that the aggression or intimidation is through electronic means of communication, hence it mostly does not include direct violence by a perpetrator against a victim. However, incidents of cyber bullying which make the news often describe harassment by teenagers against someone they are aggressively excluding from their group, and the psychological and social costs incurred by the victim, including cases of suicide. Despite media coverage of cyber bullying as an adolescent-based behaviour within the context of a school setting, victims can be any age and there are frequent instances of cyber bullying involving adults, some of which is workplace related (Australian Institute of Criminology 2010) (see also *Violence/interpersonal violence*).

Cyber stalking is similar to cyber bullying in two important ways. First, stalking was around well before the advent of electronic means of communication. In its non-electric form, stalking is whenever a victim is repeatedly contacted by and/or harassed by someone else, and the victim feels threatened and has indicated that the contact is not welcome. Sometimes stalking occurs between two individuals who were previously in a relationship or who dated, and the stalker does not want the relationship to end. Stalking can also be based on the imagination of the stalker who is strongly attracted to the other party based on their perceived physical attractiveness, celebrity status or some other special characteristic. Regardless of the motive, the impact on victims can be substantial – economically, psychologically and sociologically (Morewitz 2003).

Cyber stalking is the electronic equivalent of stalking, with the main difference being that the contact is through electronic means, especially email. YouTube, Facebook and other web-related venues, plus mobile phones, can also be used. Even though cyber stalking is largely electronic in origin, prolonged harassment can be both proximal and electronic. The motivations of stalkers and the effects on victims are much the same, regardless of the medium through which the stalking occurs.

CORPORATE AND GOVERNMENTAL TARGETS OF CYBER CRIME

The targets of internet/cyber crime include not only individuals, but governments and corporations as well. Corporate targets may be for-profit organisations, such as a bank or manufacturing company; and not-for-profit entities, such as a university, political party or social movement group. A special report from the Bureau of Justice Statistics, US Department of Justice (Rantala 2008) indicated that of the 7,818 businesses in the National Computer Security Survey, 67% had detected at least one cyber crime incident, including 58% who experienced a cyber attack, with over 323,000 hours of computer system downtime. A cyber attack is an attempt to access a company's computer and software systems in order to damage or destroy their ability to operate, hence inflicting considerable financial harm on them by disrupting day-to-day business operations. Cyber attacks can be motivated by hackers or individuals who enjoy the challenge of breaking into computer systems for bragging rights with others who enjoy the same kind of thing, or can be an individual working on behalf of a competitor or foreign government to inflict economic damage (Choo 2011).

A syntactic attack refers to the use of viruses (self-replicating programs), worms (which can be used to spy on the computer traffic of a business) and Trojan horses (programs or computer functions which appear legitimate but are also a way for viruses and worms to breach an organisation's computer security system). These same kinds of attacks can be directed at government entities, and can represent a form of terrorism, with the actions based on a political ideology. Governments may also attack each other. One famous international incident describes attempts by the US and Israeli governments to sabotage the nuclear-processing capabilities of Iran (Arthur 2013).

A cyber attack which is semantic refers to the modification and/or falsification of information on the computer system of a corporate entity or government. The ability of a very bright high school or college student to hack into the computer system of an educational institution to change a grade is one example. Falsifying a picture for political purposes and posting it on a website or sending out false information through various networks, like Facebook, is another way. It is sometimes difficult to say when a semantic form of a cyber attack is nothing more than the kind of 'bare knuckles' politicking often associated with the promotion of political and social movement messages, and not illegal even though false, and when such actions are criminal.

Cyber theft against corporate and government entities represents attempts to acquire financial resources, intellectual property, computer software systems and other properties. About 11% of the business who participated in the National Computer Security Survey said that they had been victims of computer theft in the past year, with an estimated monetary loss of nearly $0.5 billion (Rantala 2008).

IN SUMMARY

It is difficult to estimate the future forms and costs of internet/cyber crime. Yet, the 'old wine in new bottles' adage still holds – offences based on computers will be mostly the age-old crimes of theft, fraud, bullying, stalking and terrorism.

REFERENCES

Arthur, C. (2013) 'Symantec discovers 2005 US computer virus attack on Iran nuclear plants', *Guardian*, 26 February. Available at: www.guardian.co.uk/technology/2013/feb/26/symantec-us-computer-virus-iran-nuclear (accessed 04/03/13).

Australian Institute of Criminology (2010) *Covert and Cyber Bullying.* Research in Practice (Tip Sheet No. 09). Canberra: Australian Institute of Technology.

Choo, K.R. (2011) 'Cyber threat landscape faced by financial and insurance industry', *Trends and Issues in Crime and Criminal Justice*, No. 406 (Feb.). Canberra: Australian Institute of Criminology.

DeKeseredy, W.S. and Olsson, P. (2011) 'Adult pornography, male peer support, and violence against women: The contribution of the "dark side" of the internet', in M.V. Martin, M.A. Garcia Ruiz and A. Edwards (eds) *Technology for Facilitating Humanity and Combating Social Deviations: Interdisciplinary Perspectives*. Hershey, PA: Information Science Reference, pp. 34–50.

Morewitz, S. (2003) *Stalking and Violence: New Patterns of Trauma and Obsession*. New York: Kluwer Academic/Plenum.

Rantala, R.R. (2008) *Cybercrime against Businesses, 2005*. Washington, DC: US Department of Justice, Office of Justice Programs. NCJ 221943.

Social Bakers (2012) Facebook Statistics by Country. Available at: www.socialbakers.com/facebook-statistics/ (accessed 09/12/12).

World Bank (2012) *Mobile Phone Access Reaches Three Quarters of Planet's Population*. Washington, DC: The World Bank. Available at: www.worldbank.org/en/news/press-release/2012/07/17/mobile-phone-access-reaches-three-quarters-planets-population (accessed 07/12/12).

29 State Crime

> **Definition**: *Crimes conducted by states are acts of commission or omission that cause serious harm to individuals. State crime is committed by government elites or other representatives of the state while engaged in the business of the state. In general, state crimes violate domestic and/or international law; however, some legal acts by the state can also inflict serious harm. Crimes committed by state officials for personal gain are not considered to be state crime.*

Studies of crime have focused primarily on 'street crime', with considerably less research emphasis on crimes of the powerful, including institutions, organisations and governments. William J. Chambliss is often credited for drawing criminologists' attention to state crime. His presidential address to the American Society of Criminology highlighted the importance of researching 'state-organized crime' (1989: 183–94), i.e. behaviours that violate criminal law and are 'committed by state officials in the pursuit of their jobs as representatives of the state'. Importantly, Chambliss' definition excluded crimes by government elites that are committed for individual advantage.

During the last two decades, the concept of state crime has evolved considerably and scholars have expanded on Chambliss' definition of state crime. For example, Kauzlarich et al. (2003) proposed that state crime involved harmful acts of commission or omission by government, its agencies or its agents, involving a violation of trust that is associated with state responsibilities. They suggested that violations of trust are shaped by cultural expectations of the state, thus some violations of trust may be considered criminal in one state and tolerated in another. Their definition includes harmful acts, as well as acts of omission, i.e. when the state fails to intervene on behalf of its residents. This component is important because of its emphasis on the responsibility of the state to protect people who are seriously harmed. The authors also suggested that states can engage in crime for 'self-interest' or to protect and maintain the interests of the elite.

Other scholarly work has sought to distinguish between state crime and state–corporate crime (see also *White-collar/middle-class and corporate-class crime*). Three decades ago, research into state crime tended to be conducted separately from studies of corporate crime, ignoring the ways in which these phenomena are sometimes linked (Kramer and Michalowski 1990). For example, state crime can be assisted by corporations, and corporate crime can be aided, condoned or ignored by the state. In their subsequent work, these authors defined state–corporate crimes as harmful or dangerous acts committed by the state in conjunction with organisations that are motivated by profit (Michalowski and Kramer 2007).

EXAMPLES OF STATE CRIME

All states engage in crime, regardless of the political system in place. Similar to patterns of street crime, the nature and extent of state crime varies across regions. Many states have instigated, supported, condoned or ignored serious violations of human rights, including genocide, assassinations by police and other death squads, torture and extraordinary rendition (see also *War crime*). States have also contributed to crime committed by other states, e.g. by selling weaponry to governments that are known to engage in systematic violations of human rights. Extrajudicial killings and forced disappearances have been documented in Turkey, Argentina and dozens of other countries. Victims have included political activists and other individuals who are deemed by a state to be a threat to its political or economic objectives.

Other acts of commission include the intentional exploitation of vulnerable populations for the purpose of identifying cures for disease. For example, scholars of research ethics are familiar with the 40-year experiment conducted by the US Public Health Service that involved approximately 400 African American males who were infected with syphilis (i.e. Tuskegee Syphilis Study). Despite the discovery of penicillin in the 1940s, the men were not provided with this treatment, nor were they given details about the true purpose of the research. A second study was conducted in Guatemala by the US Public Health Service in conjunction with Guatemalan officials. The study recruited over 1000 Guatemalan prisoners, sex workers, army personnel and patients in mental health facilities, although informed consent was not provided (Reverby 2011). Researchers intentionally infected the study participants with syphilis or gonorrhoea and are believed to have provided some treatment for approximately half the participants.

More recently, the US government's National Security Agency (NSA) ordered telecommunication companies (e.g. Verizon, AT & T, Sprint) to provide millions of telephone records, including customers' names and other personal identifiers that were linked to telephone calls and text messages from US telephone numbers. The information is stored in various locations and was obtained without warrants. The policy commenced in 2001 with former President George Bush and continued during the Obama Administration. Several commentators have argued that the collection of this information violates the fourth amendment of the US Constitution. However, the US government maintains that the data are considered transactions rather than communications, and hence the activity does not violate the law. The government requests are considered 'classified' information, thus legislators who were aware of the state's activities were prohibited from disclosing the details. Several state legislatures in the USA are attempting to enact laws that will prohibit domestic spying efforts by the federal government. Allegations of domestic mass spying have also surfaced in Europe.

The failure of a state to *intervene* on behalf of residents who are exposed to serious harm is also considered to be state crime. In 2011, the head of state in Ireland issued a state apology to hundreds of individuals who had been sexually and physically abused as children while in the care of religious-order institutions in the country. A second apology was delivered in 2013 for the conditions in Ireland's Magdalene Laundries;[1] however, that apology did not acknowledge the state's role in coercing some women to be sent to the Laundries, or the state's failure to close the Laundries, which remained open until the 1990s. States have a responsibility to provide assistance to citizens during natural disasters, although some states lack the economic means and infrastructure to do so. The *New York Times* has collated information on the US government's response to Hurricane Katrina, including the failure to intervene when evidence indicated that the state of Louisiana was unable to cope with the effects of the hurricane.

In regions affected by widespread political conflict, sexual violence perpetrated by military personnel and other representatives of the state has been described as a 'tool of war' that is intended to punish and ethnically cleanse opponents and promote camaraderie among troops. In some regions, sexual violence by state agencies continues or re-surfaces during periods of conflict transition. For example, Lenning and Brightman (2009) discussed numerous reports of sexual violence perpetrated by members of the 'security' forces in Nigeria. They found that the criminal law was ineffective in addressing these crimes and described the inaction of the Nigerian government as state crime.

State–corporate crimes include the exploitation of and violence directed at local citizens in the pursuit of natural resources, such as oil, gas, metals and precious minerals. Corporations, including multinationals, purchase the rights to extract the resources, and their endeavours are often supported by the state. Local populations can be exploited in the process and they generally derive no economic benefit. The British Petroleum oil spill in the Gulf of Mexico paled in comparison with the disastrous and frequent oil spills in the Niger Delta, yet state intervention in the former was far more effective. State–corporate crime that relates to natural resources has escalated the level of violence in conflict-ridden regions (Patey 2010). For example, 'conflict' or 'blood' diamonds have been used to purchase weaponry that has been used in civil wars and other conflicts.

STATE DENIAL

Although state crime has been described as the most heinous kind of crime, states tend to deny their role in criminality. According to Cohen (2001), states engage in a range of 'techniques of denial'. States might take part in *literal denial*, by refuting that a harmful act occurred or accusing opponents of committing the act. *Interpretive denial* involves acknowledging an act but underestimating the seriousness of it through, for example, manipulating words or jargon, e.g. 'global warming' to 'climate change' (Poole 2007: 45). *Implicatory denial* occurs when a state admits that a harmful act occurred but blames others for it. For example, states might collude with local paramilitaries or mercenaries who engage in extrajudicial violence and blame them if the violence is publically exposed (Jamieson and McEvoy 2005).

RESPONDING TO STATE CRIME

States are reluctant to consider their actions to be criminal, hence few government officials have been prosecuted for their involvement in state criminality. Extensive state-led human rights abuses have occurred for years in some nations and other states are often slow to respond. International responses to state violations of human rights are challenging because of the fundamental principle of state sovereignty. However, states have a duty to intervene if they support international conventions – and most states recognise international law. The reach of the internet and other technology has the potential to put pressure on the international community by highlighting state crimes to a global audience.

Truth and reconciliation commissions and state-led tribunals are two national methods of responding to state crimes. These methods are designed to provide a public inquiry into state-led human rights violations, and to provide a voice for victims, their families and the wider community. Truth and reconciliation commissions have been established by subsequent democratic governments in Guatemala, Argentina and Chile. South Africa's truth and reconciliation commission was launched after popular vote. The Chilean commission focused on over 3,000 incidents of extrajudicial killings, torture and forced disappearances that occurred under the dictatorship of Pinochet.

Some states have established tribunals with goals similar to those of truth and reconciliation commissions. Tribunals in the Republic of Ireland and Northern Ireland have investigated incidents such as extrajudicial killings, institutionalised police corruption and the unlawful financial transactions of politicians. The Saville Inquiry investigated extrajudicial killings by British soldiers in Northern Ireland when 13 unarmed civilians died. Tribunals and truth commissions can last several years and are expensive. For example, the Saville Inquiry took 12 years to complete and cost an estimated £195 million. Although these methods are important, persons accused are often granted immunity from prosecution.

State-led human right abuses can be prosecuted in the International Criminal Court (ICC), implemented in 1998. The ICC considers cases that involve major violations of human rights, e.g. genocide and other crimes against humanity. Although the ICC has the authority to prosecute and punish, it has no arrest powers. Rather, it depends on states to arrest individuals and transport them to the ICC, located in The Hague. Persons sentenced to prison by the ICC serve their sentence in the state of origin. Most states have ratified the Rome Statute, the body of law or treaty that officially founded the ICC. The USA, Israel, China and Russia have not ratified the Rome Statute and hence they do not recognise the jurisdiction of the ICC.

NOTE

1. Magdalene Laundries were religious-order institutions that housed women who were unwed and pregnant, deemed to be 'wayward' or violated minor social norms. Women were forced to work in the institutions and several survivors' reports indicate sexual and other types of abuse during their incarceration. Thousands of women were sent to Ireland's Magdalene Laundries over a period of nearly two centuries. Some women remained in the Laundries for decades. Babies were placed for adoption. See Justice for Magdalenes at: www.magdalenelaundries.com/index.htm

REFERENCES

Chambliss, W.J. (1989) 'State-organized crime: Presidential address to the American Society of Criminology, 1988', *Criminology*, 27: 183–208.

Cohen, S. (2001) *States of Denial: Knowing About Atrocities and Suffering*. Cambridge: Polity Press.

Jamieson, R. and McEvoy, K. (2005) 'State crime by proxy and juridical othering', *British Journal of Criminology*, 45: 504–27.

Kauzlarich, D., Mullins, C.W. and Matthews, R.A. (2003) 'A complicity continuum of state crime', *Contemporary Justice Review*, 6: 241–54.

Kramer, R.C. and Michalowski, R.J. (1990) 'State–Corporate Crime.' Paper presented at the annual meeting of the American Society of Criminology, Baltimore, MD, November.

Lenning, E. and Brightman, S. (2009) 'Oil, rape and state crime in Nigeria', *Critical Criminology*, 17: 35–48.

Michalowski, R.J. and Kramer, R.C. (2007) 'State–corporate crime and criminological inquiry', in H.N. Pontell and G. Geis (eds) *International Handbook of White-Collar and Corporate Crime*. New York: Springer, pp. 200–19.

Patey, L.A. (2010) 'Crude days ahead? Oil and the resource curse in Sudan', *African Affairs*, 109: 617–36.

Poole, S. (2007) *Unspeak: Words are Weapons*. London: Abacus.

Reverby, S.M. (2011) '"Normal exposure" and inoculation syphilis: A PHS "Tuskegee" doctor in Guatemala, 1946–1948', *Journal of Policy History*, 23: 6–28.

30 War Crime

Definition: *War crimes are major violations of international laws directed at citizens or combatants during armed conflict. War crimes can include genocide and other crimes against humanity.*

War crimes are criminal acts that are committed by individuals during armed conflict and are directed at civilians or combatants. These crimes are proscribed in international humanitarian laws or conventions, including the Hague Conventions of 1899 and 1907, the Geneva Conventions of 1929 and 1949, and the Rome Statute of 1998. The Hague Conventions attempted to codify customs of war, including the treatment of prisoners of war and restrictions on weaponry. Designations of war crimes emerged from the International Military Tribunal, established in 1945 to prosecute several Nazi leaders who had led or engaged in mass atrocities in Germany and its occupied territories. The Tribunal was held in Nürnberg, Germany and became known as the Nuremberg Trials. The Tribunal was guided by a Charter which defined the Tribunal's jurisdictional reach and noted the differences between crimes against peace, crimes against humanity and war crimes. War crimes were designated as 'violations of the laws or customs of war', including acts such as murder, ill treatment, slave labour, deportation and malicious destruction of private or public property that could not be justified militarily. The Soviet Union, France, the UK and the USA were signatories to the Charter which in 1950 was adopted as the International Law Commission of the United Nations (also known as the Nuremberg Charter 1950). The Tribunal was the first international court that tried cases involving crimes against humanity by a government against its own citizens and citizens of occupation. War crimes also violate the Geneva Conventions which were designed to protect civilian populations, prisoners of war and medical personnel (e.g. the Red Cross).

The decade of the 1940s reflected a critical time for human rights law. The United Nations was created in 1945, followed three years later by the United Nations Declaration of Human Rights. The Genocide Convention of 1948 acknowledged that genocide was a separate international crime that involved the intent to eliminate particular groups of people based on religious, racial or ethnic identity. As an international crime, genocide can occur in the context of armed conflict or during times of peace. Note that groups that are targeted based on gender, gender identity and social class are not protected under the Genocide Convention of 1948. Under international humanitarian law, such offences would be considered crimes against humanity (described below) rather than genocide.

The International Criminal Court (ICC) was established in 2002 by the Rome Statute of 1998. The ICC is important because it is the first international court that has responsibility for serious criminal acts that violate international humanitarian law. The Rome Statute specified four types of crimes that could be investigated and tried by the ICC: (1) crimes against humanity, (2) genocide, (3) war crimes, and (4) crimes of aggression. *Crimes against humanity* are criminal acts that are 'widespread' or 'systematic'. Widespread can mean that several acts are conducted over lengthy periods of time, or it can refer to one act that involves several victims. It can refer to an act that occurred in various communities or a single act within one detention facility. Crimes against humanity are not random acts of violence; rather, 'systematic' implies that acts are organised as opposed to random. Crimes against humanity can affect civilians, or soldiers who are wounded or captured, but they do not need to be linked to armed conflict. Crimes against humanity can include murder, deportation, slavery, apartheid, sexual violence or torture. Victims of genocide can include civilians or members of the military. *Genocide* is described above and can occur during armed conflict or during peace time. Genocide is one type of crime against humanity. *War crimes* include acts such as intentional killings and serious injuries without military justification, attacks against civilians, torture, major destruction of property without military justification, the use of poisons as weaponry, unlawful deportation, transfer or detention, trials that lack due process, the degrading of people, involving children as participants in armed conflict, and the capture of hostages. Many of these offences are proscribed by the Geneva Conventions. Other offences were added following court decisions that were based on the interpretation of humanitarian law. The Rome Statute also specifies the sentences for persons convicted of these crimes, i.e. imprisonment (including life sentences), asset forfeiture and fines.

The Rome Statute was initially ratified by 60 nations, and by November 2012 a total of 121 countries had ratified the Rome Statute. States that thus far have refused to ratify the Rome Statute include the USA, Israel, China and others. According to the US State Department, the USA supports the ICC when prosecution serves US interests. Although the Rome Statute represents a significant step in prosecuting violations of serious human rights abuses, international law is in its infancy compared with criminal codes at national levels.

THE INTERNATIONAL CRIMINAL COURT AND TRIBUNALS

The International Criminal Court is located in The Hague, in the Netherlands, and is a permanent and independent court that targets individuals rather than states. As described above, the Court has jurisdiction over serious international crimes, i.e. war crimes, genocide, crimes against humanity and crimes of aggression, for which national courts have been unable or unwilling to prosecute. There are temporal as well as geographic restrictions to the jurisdictional reach of the ICC. First, the ICC does not have the authority to investigate crimes that occurred before 1 July 2002, the date that the Court was established. Some states ratified the Rome Statute after 2002. The ICC can only investigate crimes that occurred after the date of ratification in those states. Second, the ICC cannot prosecute individuals who are citizens of states that have not ratified the Rome Statute. Referrals for prosecution come from states that have ratified the Rome Statute, the UN Security Council or the Court itself.

The first criminal conviction was delivered in 2012 – ten years after the Court was established. By March of 2012, indictments had been issued to 28 individuals – all of them from African nations. That trend may change in the future, with Palestine being given state status by the UN General Assembly in 2012 (paving the way for its ratification of the Rome Statute and the subsequent involvement of the ICC). Additionally, a report by the ICC's Office of the Prosecutor (ICC 2011) indicates that preliminary investigations have been conducted in Colombia, the Republic of Korea and elsewhere.

International criminal tribunals are ad hoc in that they were created by the United Nations Security Council to address crimes that occurred in a specific place at a particular time. Their aims are to provide an official record of mass atrocities, highlight victims' perspectives, administer criminal proceedings and promote peace in regions where international security has been threatened. The International Criminal Tribunal for Rwanda (ICTR) was established in 1994 and has primarily focused on genocide that occurred during 1994. Proceedings are held in the United Republic of Tanzania and trial outcomes for all individuals are available in the public domain. The International Criminal Tribunal for the former Yugoslavia (ICTY) was created in 1993 and has investigated war crimes, genocide and crimes against humanity in the Balkans. The ICTY was the first international criminal tribunal since the Nuremberg (1945–6) and Tokyo trials (1946–8). The seat of the ICTY is in The Hague, in the Netherlands. Other tribunals or special courts have been created to address mass atrocities in Cambodia and Sierra Leone.

The ICC and international criminal tribunals have been criticised for the disproportionate focus on individuals who hold mid-rank positions within military groups or political parties. People in senior leadership positions are more likely to have the finances and networks to remain hidden from investigatory gaze. The ICC has also been criticised for its failure to target major social and economic injustices during times of peace. Starr (2007) argues that such injustices include human trafficking, forced prostitution, widespread oppression of women in some countries and the fraudulent theft of national funds by government leaders that contributes to poverty, ill health and early mortality among citizens. She notes that the ICC has the authority to prosecute and seize assets of the perpetrators of these offences, although it has not done so. Critics have also highlighted the inefficiency of international tribunals. Trials have lasted several years, which causes frustration for victims and results in substantial financial costs. Additionally, criminal tribunals can reinforce ethnic divisions when the accused individuals share the same ethnic background. This issue prompted Desmond Tutu to support truth and reconciliation efforts in South Africa rather than an international criminal tribunal (McMorran 2003).

Collectively known as the Arab Spring, widespread public protest for political, social and economic reforms commenced in 2010 in Tunisia, and later spread to Algeria, Egypt, Libya and elsewhere. In Syria, political protest led to extreme interventions by its government. Observers from Human Rights Watch and Amnesty International have documented cases of torture and summary executions of civilians and rebels by government forces. Mass atrocities have also been committed by rebel forces, although Amnesty International argues that considerably more human rights violations have been committed by the government. Although investigative journalist Robert Fisk has noted the difficulty in ascertaining accurate death counts during armed conflict, the UN General Assembly in 2013 estimated that 80,000 people had died in Syria and approximately one million people were recorded as refugees. In the same year, 57 nations requested that the UN Security Council refer the Syrian atrocities to the ICC. At times, the nature of armed conflict makes it difficult to distinguish between crimes by individuals and crimes against humanity.

ELITE NATIONS: RESISTING THE LABEL OF WAR CRIMINAL

Scholars have argued that the US-initiated war in Iraq was unjustified (i.e. Iraq posed no immediate threat) and lacked authorisation from the UN Security Council (Kramer and Michalowski 2005). Bonn (2010) argued that the invasion of Iraq was fuelled by moral panic created by US political elites and media. In the futile attempt to locate weapons of mass destruction (that were never found), Bonn notes that over one million Iraqis and some 4,100 US military personnel were killed. Moreover, Iraq's political, economic and social infrastructure has been devastated. Even if the ICC were interested in investigating war crimes and acts of aggression committed by the USA, it would not be permissible because the USA has not ratified the Rome Statute.

The US and the UK militaries utilised depleted uranium shells during the Iraq conflict of 1991 and the war in 2003. Some reports have linked depleted uranium to birth defects, negative health effects among soldiers and contamination of land and water. In 2012, 138 nations supported the UN in its request for precautionary use of depleted uranium weaponry. Three nations opposed the resolution: France, the USA and the UK.

'Collateral damage' is not legally considered to be a war crime, although it might also be used as a 'flag of convenience' when military personnel err in judgement. Collateral damage refers to fatalities and other significant harm involving civilians who were not the intended target. Collateral damage has occurred from shootings and cluster and other bombs that have destroyed neighbourhoods, mosques and markets during armed conflict. The practice is justified when governments can provide evidence of 'military necessity'. Finally, the US use of extraordinary rendition has been documented by human rights groups as well as by individuals who have been subjected to the practice (Satterthwaite and Fisher 2006). The mechanisms of extraordinary rendition and the resources of elite nations mean that some governments have the capacity to work around international laws while engaging in the forced transfer of individuals without due process.

REFERENCES

Bonn, S.A. (2010) *Mass Deception: Moral Panic and the US War on Iraq*. New Brunswick, NJ: Rutgers University Press.

International Criminal Court (ICC) (2011) *Report on Preliminary Examination Activities*. The Hague: International Criminal Court, Office of the Prosecutor.

Kramer, R.C. and Michalowski, R.J. (2005) 'War, aggression and state crime: A criminological analysis of the invasion and occupation of Iraq', *British Journal of Criminology*, 45: 446–69.

McMorran, C. (2003) 'International war crimes tribunals', in G. Burgess and H. Burgess (eds) *From Beyond Intractability*. Boulder, CO: Conflict Information Consortium, University of Colorado, Boulder. Available at: www.beyondintractability.org/bi-essay/int-war-crime-tribunals (date accessed 27/09/14).

Starr, S. (2007) 'Extraordinary Crimes at Ordinary Times: International Justice Beyond Crisis Situations', *Northwestern Law Review*, 101 (3): 1257–314.

Satterthwaite, M. and Fisher, A. (2006) *Tortured Logic: Renditions to Justice, Extraordinary Rendition, and Human Rights Law*, 6 THE LONG TERM VIEW 52. Available at www.mslaw.edu/MSLMedia/LTV/6.4.pdf (date accessed 27/09/14).

key concepts in crime and society

31 Terrorism

> **Definition**: **Terrorism** is generally defined as the use of violence and intimidation to disrupt or coerce a government and/or identifiable community into a particular course of action. It is often a response to specific grievances among an identifiable subgroup of a larger population, such as an ethnic minority. It is underpinned by political or religious beliefs or ideologies. It used to be argued that for something to qualify as terrorism, violence had to be perpetrated by some organisational entity with some conspiratorial structure and identifiable chain of command beyond an individual acting on their own, however this perspective has now changed (Burgess 2003). A new form of terrorism has emerged, embodied in the practices of extreme Islamic fundamentalist groups such as Al Qaeda and distinct from earlier terrorist organisations such as ETA. Instead of operating locally with united ideological objectives and strict hierarchies, new terrorist groups are defined by their nebulous strategies, their disparate organisation and global activities. For example, at its peak, Al Qaeda was thought to have terrorist cells in over 90 countries, giving it the potential to strike anywhere and at any time (Mythen and Walklate 2006).

Terrorism is difficult to define, having many different styles, actors and targets. The term has been applied to a diverse range of activities, including apartheid, pornography, rape and state-sanctioned acts. Terrorism is distinguished from routine criminal violence to the extent that it is driven by political and/or religious motivation. Such acts are largely directed at civilian targets and populations with the intent to inflict injury and insecurity (Mythen and Walklate 2006). This view of terrorism as political violence relates to its roots as a political term applied to the activities of the tribunals during the French Revolution's 'Reign of Terror' (Burgess 2003).

The definition can apply to numerous groups who are deemed to be terrorists, for example: the Basque separatists in Spain; the Irish Republican Army; the African Nationalist Party; Mau Mau African Nationalist Movement; Liberation Tigers of Tamil Eelam in Sri Lanka; Al Qaeda; and Hamas in Palestine. However, these minority groups argue that they have fought because they have been marginalised in some way by dominant groups, such as by being denied: equal rights in employment; housing; legal, religious or human rights; their own separate state; or citizenship.

There is little doubt that some of the actions of these groups come under the definition of terrorism, but the actions of dominant groups can also be categorised as terrorist actions. While typically the definition of terrorism is restricted to non-state activities, some have argued that this suggests a state-centric reading of terrorism, which is western in outlook and would be questioned by those who regard themselves as politically disenfranchised. Typically, political violence against the state is labelled terrorism, rather than political violence committed by the state. Despite this, some have argued that activities such as the dropping of atomic bombs on Japan by the USA, constitute acts of terrorism.

American professor Noam Chomsky (2002) has publicly argued that the USA is guilty of horrendous terrorist acts. He uses examples of US violence in Nicaragua, the effects of which, according to Chomsky, are much more severe even than the 9/11 tragedies. When the World Court found the USA guilty of 'unlawful use of force' in Nicaragua and ordered it to pay compensation, the USA refused, showing contempt for the order. People in western nations would not call the US government a terrorist organisation; however, in the eyes of many Nicaraguans, it is.

UNDERSTANDING TERRORISM

While terrorism can be considered an act of political violence, not all acts of political violence are terrorist acts. War, for example, is a form of political violence but is distinguished from terrorism as it is regulated by a series of international laws regulating how war activities can be conducted, most notably the Geneva Convention. Supposed 'terrorists' generally ignore these laws, often deliberately targeting civilians (Burgess 2003). Additionally, terrorism differs from general crime in its aims and motivations. General crime is often motivated by concerns for pecuniary gain or in relation to conflicts in interpersonal relationships. Terrorism, on the other hand, is a reaction to a wider social order.

Terrorism is often (but not always) a response to specific grievances among an identifiable subgroup of a larger population, such as an ethnic minority discriminated against by a majority or ruling group. Usually, there is a lack of opportunity for the subgroup to participate politically or bring about its desired end, such as a separate state or the removal of a ruling group. A social movement then develops with terrorist activities often the actions of an extremist faction of this broader social movement. Terrorist organisations with religious motivations can be different to these socio-political movements. Those motivated by religion primarily have their beliefs as the driving force behind their actions, such as ridding the world of non-believers or enforcing a specific religious doctrine on a broad community or communities.

THEORETICAL PERSPECTIVES

Politico-economic theories argue that the material conditions of some societies support the growth of terrorism. According to these theories, political alienation and economic marginalisation of individuals and groups by dominant or ruling groups may cause ostracised groups to adopt alternative, illegitimate strategies to achieve their political goals. Terrorism is then viewed as one of a number of viable strategies to redress the perceived political imbalance. This theory can be used to explain the violence in Northern Ireland and Spain, and the West Bank clashes between Palestine and Israel.

Cultural explanations attribute terrorism to ideological and value clashes between terrorists and their targets. This is often referred to as 'the Clash of

Cultures' thesis. According to this perspective, when there is a clash of values between cultures conflict can arise. This thesis can be used to explain conflicts with Muslim extremist organisations like Al Qaeda. These clashes occur because these extremist organisations view individualised, materialistic, western cultures and traditions as antithetical to their own cultural, religious and family values. Thus, the aim is not to bring about a form of political rule, but a cultural shift underpinned by religious beliefs.

The problem with these two theories and other explanations is that they omit some important features of terrorism. For example, not all terrorism involves a clash of cultures and terrorism is not always carried out by marginalised groups.

UNDERSTANDING TERRORISTS

It is very difficult to specifically define the personality or psychological and social characteristics of a 'terrorist'. What we do know is that terrorists vary considerably in their socio-economic and personal characteristics and circumstances. Terrorist acts have traditionally been primarily carried out by men. For example, the profile of the Middle- Eastern suicide bomber is typically a young man who is unmarried and poor, with strong religious beliefs. However, the terrorists of the 9/11 attacks did not fit these 'typical' features insofar as they were well educated, had good employment histories and came from wealthy middle-class backgrounds. Suicide bombings, however, only make up about 3% of all terrorist incidents worldwide, even though they are responsible for around half the deaths caused by acts of terrorism. Furthermore, most of these acts, prior to 2001, were 'home-grown', i.e. the terrorist and the target were from the same society. For example, pre-2001, most terrorist acts conducted in the USA were by its own citizens for their own political or religious reasons. International terrorism, as we now understand it, is generally a recent phenomenon.

Attachment of the label 'terrorist' is a subjective and relative proposition. Those who commit terrorist acts have variously been described as 'commandos', 'extremists', 'fundamentalists' and 'guerillas' (Burgess 2003). Those who carry out terrorist actions may be viewed by those with the same political perspective as heroes, martyrs, defenders of their nation or freedom fighters. Movement between the poles of terrorist and freedom fighter is likely to shift over time, as has been the case with political shifts in places such as South Africa, Northern Ireland and Kosovo (Mythen and Walklate 2006).

Terrorist groups usually define themselves in terms of race and/or ethnicity. Even though people of the same ethnic or racial group might share the goals of a terrorist organisation, most do not agree that terrorism is the best means by which to achieve the organisation's goals. While observers may be divided as to who is and who is not a terrorist, those labelled 'terrorists' uniformly oppose such labels, instead justifying their actions by claiming such actions were forced on them as actions of last resort. Victims of terrorist acts, however, are more inclined to label their attackers 'terrorists', with all the negative connotations the term implies (Burgess 2003).

THE NEW TERRORISM

Since 9/11 (11 September 2001), terrorism has been reconstructed as a new problem for western nations with a focus on the actions of groups linked to the Middle East, Islamic fundamentalism and the Arab–Israeli conflict. The events of that day prompted a global 'war on terror', which is characterised by increased local policing and surveillance, international military action and the global implementation of tightening national and local security measures. There has also been an increase in public suspicion, casting doubt on ordinary people, with weakened interactional trust making people wary of particular groups, and encouraged racial vilification (see also *Race/ethnicity and crime*). The fear of terrorism is disproportionate to the actual threat and is fuelled by political, public and media discourses of 'terror'. US research indicates that the public has transferred its fear of crime onto terrorism. Lee (2007) argues that terrorism and security are highly politicised phenomena constituting moral panics which generate and elevate societal fear.

POLICING TERRORISM

Counter-terrorism policing has been characterised by the merging of law enforcement with paramilitary policing. Counter-terrorism laws have shifted the policing focus from the individual law-breaker and monitoring crime to investigating the activities of particular communities who are targeted as potential suspects. The expansion of police powers in many western countries since 9/11 allows the police more opportunities for overt and covert surveillance, monitoring and searching (Pickering et al. 2008). This type of policing is selective in its criminalisation of particular groups who fit popular notions of who and what constitutes a risk (see also *Race/ethnicity and crime* and *Social construction of crime and deviance*).

This blurring is evident in anti-terrorist legislation that gives police and security forces the power to detain individuals suspected of being terrorists, who are thought to have links to terrorist organisations or are alleged to have information about terrorist activities. The problem with this legislation is that it broadens definitions of terrorism and pre-empts what people might do – one does not need to have committed a crime; there merely needs to be a suspicion that one might do so. By defining terrorism as an act to further a political, religious or ideological cause, the USA and the UK have effectively curtailed civic protests and similar activities. Civil disobedience, public protest and industrial action can now all be considered as acts associated with terrorism under certain circumstances (Burgess 2003). Legislation introduced in Australia since 2001 has been criticised for breaching human rights, enabling suspects to be held for 48 hours without charge or questioning, and also giving police more powers to search and introduce new offences not necessarily connected to direct threats of violence (Lee 2007).

Clearly, there are multiple perspectives on terrorism and terrorists. The terrorist label often reflects an ideological political bias successfully applied by dominant or ruling groups to minority or separatist groups. Those labelled terrorists are the 'other' – the deviants who are not like us, although they may pass for ordinary citizens. They are often portrayed as members of covert groups or as belonging to particular ethnicities or as religious fanatics. With FBI definitions of terrorism no longer including politically motivated violence such as abortion clinic bombings, some terrorist actions may be misclassified as common crimes. These misclassifications lead to misconceptions about who actually engages in terrorism.

REFERENCES

Burgess, M. (2003) Terrorism: The Problems of Definition. Center for Defense Information. Available at: www.cdi.org/friendlyversion/printversion.cfm?documentID=1564

Chomsky, N. (2002) 'Who are the global terrorists?', in K. Booth and T. Dunne (eds) *Worlds in Collision: Terror and the Future of Global Order*. New York: Palgrave Macmillan. 128–140.

Lee, M. (2007) *Inventing Fear of Crime: Criminology and the Politics of Anxiety*. Cullompton: Willan.

Mythen, G. and Walklate, S. (2006) 'Criminology and terrorism: Which thesis? Risk society or governmentality?', *British Journal of Criminology*, 46: 379–98.

Pickering, S.J., McCulloch, J. and Wright-Neville, D.P. (2008) *Counter-Terrorism Policing: Community, Cohesion and Security*. New York: Springer.

32 Violence/Interpersonal Violence

> **Definition**: *Violence generally refers to intentional acts that threaten or cause physical injury, and violence committed by individuals often occurs between people who know one another. Interpersonal violence refers to violent acts that occur in the context of social interaction, and large numbers of victims of interpersonal violence do not report the crime to police. Violence can also be instigated by corporations, institutions and states.*

Although research into violence has spanned several disciplines, social scientists do not necessarily agree on how violence is best defined. In other words, there is no real consensus on how violence should be defined or on what acts are considered to be violent. Gartner (2011) suggests that violence is often defined as 'physical force intended to inflict injury on others'. However, this definition excludes verbal abuse and threats of force and intimidation that can result in psychological harm. Other definitions of violence include violent acts against the self (e.g. suicide) as well as acts directed at others.

A typology of violence published by the World Health Organization (WHO) (Krug et al. 2002: 6) is useful because it recognises that violence can be instigated by individuals, institutions (e.g. care homes or prisons), corporations, states or state agents (e.g. police brutality) and by the collective (e.g. crowd violence). The typology includes three general categories of violence: (1) self-directed, (2) interpersonal violence, and (3) collective. *Self-directed* violence includes acts such as suicide and self-harm. *Interpersonal violence* refers to acts that occur among family members or partners, as well as community violence that is instigated by people who are not related to the victim (although they may be acquaintances). The third category, *collective violence*, includes 'social, political and economic violence' (2002: 6) committed by large groups of people or by states.

Despite this useful typology, acts that are considered to be violent can vary *across* cultures and can change over time *within* cultures. For example, stoning as a method of execution is acceptable and deemed beneficial in some cultures yet disdained and prohibited in others. Corporal punishment in schools was viewed as appropriate in the USA until the 1970s. Moreover, there is little consensus about the rank ordering of violent acts in terms of their seriousness. For example, which is more serious: verbal threats directed against an elderly person or physical assault directed at an adult male? At times, external factors can escalate or diminish the level of violence – for instance, the proximity of a hospital or the arrival time of an ambulance can differentiate between physical injury/assault and death.

EXTENT OF VIOLENCE

Violence has been an integral part of human existence. In a review of evidence collected from several archaeological digs in different regions of the world, Walker (2001) noted that human remains from ancient eras indicate widespread violence that included serious physical injuries, mass homicides and cannibalism. He concluded that interpersonal violence has characterised human life over the course of history: 'No form of social organization, mode of production or environmental setting appears to have remained free from interpersonal violence for long' (2001: 573). Other historical evidence from Europe has suggested substantial declines in violence since the sixteenth century. Scholars continue to debate whether the extent of global violence declined after the Second World War.

Global estimates from 2000 show that approximately 1.6 million individuals died as a result of violent acts described in the WHO typology (Krug et al. 2002). Controlling for population, violent deaths from suicide exceeded the number of deaths associated with homicide or war. However, the authors observed differences across countries, and noted higher rates of homicide relative to suicide in several African countries and in the Americas. The rate of deaths from homicide among males exceeded that of females, particularly among adults. A similar pattern was found for rates of suicide. The WHO report also found considerable regional differences in rates of violence that did not result in death. Those authors recognised, however, that the availability and accuracy of data on violent acts also varied by country.

Violent victimisation that results in physical injury can lead to long-term disability or death. Other consequences include the impact on emotional well-being and mental health.

Some victims experience depression, anxiety or fear over the long term. Others struggle with post-traumatic stress disorder that can last for years. When individuals are victimised by people they know, these effects can amplify and can further impact on other family members and the family unit more generally.

VICTIM–OFFENDER RELATIONSHIPS

Interpersonal violence (IPV) differs from other forms of violence in terms of the victim–offender relationship. IPV involves offenders and victims who knew one another prior to the violent act. They might be acquaintances, partners/significant others, spouses, relatives or friends. IPV often occurs within immediate or extended families and can involve repeat victimisation, i.e. patterns of violence over time that involve the same offender and victim(s). This kind of victim–offender relationship is also apparent in some property/acquisitive crimes but to a much lesser extent. The gendered nature of IPV is evident in several cultures. For example, rape, sexual assault and child sexual abuse disproportionately involve female victims and male offenders who are related to or knew one other prior to the violent act. This pattern reflects gendered power imbalances in society. Domestic violence is an example of IPV that takes place within families or conjugal partnerships. Once viewed as a private issue in western cultures, domestic violence has gained increased attention by police who have responded with the development of specialised units in larger police departments. Community-based services for domestic violence victims have also increased. However, some victims of domestic violence still face barriers in terms of accessing services. Additionally, the victim–offender relationship that characterises most acts of IPV has implications for reporting violent acts to authorities and tends to influence the way that the criminal justice system responds to the victim's complaint.

EXPLAINING VIOLENCE

Several theoretical explanations of violence have been proposed; however, they generally focus on specific forms of violence. The diversity of violence by individuals, corporations, institutions and nations presents challenges for developing a single theoretical framework that explains violence. To date, most theories of violence are concerned with violent acts associated with 'street crime' or within domestic spheres. Some theories focus on macro-level factors to explain violence or the likelihood of it. These theories emphasise structural issues such as racism and patriarchy. Other social science theories are concerned with micro-level influences, such as the interaction between victim and offender during episodes of interpersonal violence. Early research in this area was conducted by Luckinbill (1977) who was influenced by the work of Erving Goffman. Luckinbill (1977: 177–8) explored 'situated transactions' that characterised several criminal homicides (non-felony murders) in one area of California. These transactions involved a sequence of interactions between victim and offender. Luckinbill also proposed a series of stages that led to most of the homicides he studied. Although the components of these stages have been critiqued by other scholars, his work is important for highlighting the role of the audience who often encouraged the violence or were neutral and observed without intervening. The interplay among the audience, offender and victim is important during violent encounters. More recently, Collins (2008) noted that the audience reaction can affect the length as well as the seriousness of violent acts. Athens (2005) differentiated among *levels* of violence during social interaction and introduced the concept of 'dominance encounters'.

Other kinds of social contexts can contribute to or reduce the likelihood of violence. Several studies by Sampson and colleagues (2002) have suggested that violence is less likely to occur in neighbourhoods that reflect high levels of collective efficacy. Additionally, certain locations can provide more opportunity for violence to occur. Private settings (e.g. homes, prisons) are isolated from the public gaze so that guardians are not available to intervene. Public settings such as the night-time economy often involve the collective use of alcohol. Local regulations around bar/pub closure times mean that large numbers of people who are intoxicated tend to enter public space at the same time. This factor can increase the likelihood of violent acts to which alcohol use contributes.

A subculture of violence thesis was proposed several decades ago. This perspective assumes that violence is more likely to occur in some areas because of shared views that violence is an acceptable way to deal with disputes and confrontations. The subculture of violence thesis was initially explored among individuals from minority ethnic groups residing in inner cities, and with people residing in the southern USA. Critics argued that the thesis contributed to stereotypical views of ethnic minorities and ignored structural factors that contributed to violence. Ethnographic research by Elijah Anderson (1994) suggested that violence is a rational response in some communities that is practised by individuals so that they can generate or uphold respect from others.

Other individuals who engage in violence are motivated by a hatred that derives from prejudice, bigotry or intolerance towards others who differ in terms of race, ethnicity, sexuality or disability. Motivations can also centre on the aim to exert power and control over others. Still other violent acts are motivated by profit, political ideology (e.g. revolutionaries involved in political struggle) and the desire to punish (e.g. state-sanctioned executions and physical punishments in some countries).

PREVENTING VIOLENCE

The World Health Organization has urged governments to develop action plans that focus on preventing interpersonal violence. Several governments have responded to the initiative by developing strategies to improve indicators of IPV, monitor its trends, identify primary prevention strategies and improve services for victims. Country-specific progress will be updated in WHO's *Global Status Report on Violence Prevention* (at the time of writing, due to be published in 2014).

Violence prevention programmes are often targeted at particular forms of violence. For example, some programmes focus specifically on preventing rape or child sexual abuse, or are aimed at youth violence. Other programmes emphasise ways for potential victims to reduce risk or to defend themselves. Although these programme components are important, they neglect ways that might reduce violence by offenders. There are programmes that centre on violence among males; however, the long-term effectiveness of these programmes has been questioned. Violence prevention programmes are mostly aimed at individuals (either victims and/or offenders) and have no impact on the wider structural conditions that can contribute to violence. Additionally, violence prevention focuses almost exclusively on interpersonal violence. Prevention efforts aimed at corporations, institutions and states are nearly always limited to international and national laws and regulations.

REFERENCES

Anderson, E. (1994) 'The code of the streets', *The Atlantic Monthly*, 273(5): 80–94.

Athens, L. (2005) 'Violent encounters: Violent engagements, skirmishes, and tiffs', *Journal of Contemporary Ethnography*, 34: 631–78.

Collins, R. (2008) *Violence: A Micro-Sociological Theory*. Princeton, NJ: Princeton University Press.

Gartner, R. (2011) 'Historical patterns of interpersonal violence', in R. Rosenfeld (ed.) *Oxford Bibliographies Online: Criminology*. New York: Oxford University Press. Available at: www.oxfordbibliographies.com/view/document/obo-9780195396607/obo-9780195396607-0090.xml?rskey=ScuQ40&result=1&q=+%E2%80%98Historical+patterns+of+interpersonal+violence#firstmatch (accessed 27/09/14).

Krug, E.G., Dahlberg, L.L., Mercy, J.A., Zwi, A.B. and Lozano, R. (2002) *World Report on Violence and Health*. Geneva: World Health Organization.

Luckinbill, D. (1977) 'Criminal homicide as a situated transaction', *Social Problems*, 25: 175–86.

Sampson, R.J., Morenoff, J.D. and Gannon-Rowley, T. (2002) 'Assessing "neighborhood effects": Social processes and new directions in research', *Annual Review of Sociology*, 28: 443–78.

Walker, P.L. (2001) 'A bioarchaeological perspective on the history of violence', *Annual Review of Anthropology*, 30: 573–96.

Section Three
Responses to Crime

33 Crime and the Media

> **Definition**: Crime in the media refers to the types of crime that are reported by the media, and the ways in which crime, offenders and victims are constructed by the media. Some media tend to distort news about crime and offenders, and these portrayals can influence the way in which people view crime and offenders.

In western societies, television and newspapers represent the main sources of news. Other platforms, such as online news sites, email distribution and social networking, have expanded the availability of news in a global world, particularly among young people. News items that feature crime, offenders or victims are among the most common types of topics that are reported by news media.

WHAT KINDS OF CRIMES ARE NEWSWORTHY?

In western cultures, patterns of street crime show that property or acquisitive offences are far more common than violent crime. The consistency of this pattern has been demonstrated with different kinds of data, including police statistics, victim and self-report surveys. Media portrayals of crime often differ from the social scientific evidence about crime, and these differences are manifested in several ways. For example, news media tend to highlight violent offences, particularly stories that focus on interpersonal violence. These depictions are further restricted in terms of the victim–offender relationship, whereby news stories about violent crime focus more often on crimes that involve strangers, compared with violence between relatives, friends and acquaintances. For example, a leading reality crime television show in the US called *America's Most Wanted* featured women who had been victimised primarily by strangers (Cavender et al. 1999), portrayals that are inconsistent with findings from criminological research. Additionally, crimes committed by the powerful (e.g. white-collar, corporate or state crime) generally receive less media attention than street crimes. Although reports about property/ acquisitive crime, acquaintance violence and crimes of the powerful might be described by media, they generally receive less attention through the order of a newscast (e.g. highlighted in the middle or at the end), their placement in a newspaper (e.g. sections other than the front page or main section) or the space devoted to the item.

SOCIAL CONSTRUCTION OF CRIME NEWS

Crime news can be represented through particular non-neutral language that is used to describe criminal acts and suspected offenders. The construction of crime stories can at times omit background or relevant information about the crime, the offender or the victim. In other instances, the media can distort news by including details that are irrelevant to the crime. For example, news media have described victims' behaviours prior to acts of sexual violence, and these descriptions can shape the way that readers and viewers understand the crime. Additionally, describing suspected offenders as 'unemployed' or 'homeless' can fuel stereotypical notions about relationships between social class and crime.

Considerable research has focused on portrayals of race and ethnicity in US crime news. In the 1980s and early 1990s, the media depicted crack cocaine to be linked with violence, primarily among African Americans residing in urban areas. Reinarman and Levine (1997) described how extreme forms of conduct associated with crack cocaine use were portrayed by some media as standard or normal behaviour. They referred to this process as the 'routinization of caricature' (see also *Moral panics*). In their study of television news, Reeves and Campbell (1994) outlined three stages of news that covered cocaine use in the 1980s. Although news media initially described cocaine as a psychoactive drug that was used among the wealthy, news media later depicted cocaine as a recreational drug used primarily by individuals from middle-class backgrounds. During the phase of 'siege paradigm', news media highlighted the use of crack cocaine in inner cities and the way that perceived behaviours that accompanied use of the drug served to threaten the dominant social order.

Barlow (1998) analysed the cover stories of two weekly news magazines in the USA (*Newsweek* and *Time*) from 1946 to 1995. She focused on featured stories that portrayed criminals (suspected or known), crime or issues relating to criminal justice. She observed that although crime was featured on covers during the 1940s and 1950s, the offenders were usually white. In the mid-1960s, news items focused on the political violence among African Americans that eventually led to the racialised nature of featured crime reporting in the USA. Other studies have built on this body of work and have shown that African American and Hispanic crime suspects in the USA are often portrayed by news media as more threatening than white suspects.

Crime news can also distort the image of crime victims by elevating the importance of victims who hold social power. Thus, although black and ethnic minority victims are over-represented in crime data, whites are more often featured as victims in news media. Greer (2007: 22–3) observed the 'hierarchy of victimisation' in media portrayals about crime. For example, *ideal victims* (e.g. children, the elderly, women who are pregnant) are considered to be more newsworthy than *undeserving victims* (e.g. an adult male who was robbed during an illicit drug transaction) who receive little or no media attention. Other work has shown that media perceptions of newsworthy items are linked to the characteristics of victims, offenders and crimes (e.g. youth crime).

FACTORS THAT SHAPE MEDIA PORTRAYALS

The discussion thus far has focused on the ways in which crime, offenders and victims are distorted by some news media. This imbalance – between what we know about crime and how it is portrayed by the media – has been addressed and debated by several scholars. One explanation for the inaccuracies of media portrayals has focused on the competition and profit that characterise the news industry. Producers of television news and editors of newspapers perceive that certain kinds of news stories will attract readers and viewers, which tends to increase ratings for television news networks and increase circulation for newspapers. These 'gatekeepers' engage in filtering by selecting items that they perceive to be newsworthy in an effort to boost profits.

A second explanation focuses on dominant societal values or ideologies held by the ruling elite. The elite include individuals in powerful positions that are tied to major capitalistic pursuits, mainstream politics and government. These dominant values are not necessarily shared by others, however, and opinions and interests that dissent from dominant views are more likely to be omitted by gatekeepers, creating further imbalance. Dowler (2004) argued that the filtering of crime news by US and Canadian media is influenced by the owners of news enterprises, as well as by advertisers who endorse traditional views about crime. Moreover, a relatively small number of private news companies in the USA own the majority of television, radio and newspapers in that country so that dominant views are likely to be diffused through a range of news outlets.

Journalists rely greatly on police communications as one of the main sources of information about crime. Relationships between journalists and police are carefully fostered because although journalists depend on the police for crime news, the police need journalists to portray crime news in a way that is not overly critical of police work. Crime reporters and gatekeepers often ignore the importance of *investigative journalism*, a strategy that aims to educate and inform the public by delving critically into crime phenomena. Although some news outlets (e.g. *Guardian* in the UK and *National Public Radio* in the USA) regularly practise this form of journalism, most mainstream news media avoid it entirely. Investigative journalism has the potential to dispel stereotypes about crime and offenders. Moreover, investigative journalism may be more effective than laws in deterring or preventing corporate corruption.

IMPLICATIONS OF DISTORTED MEDIA PORTRAYALS

Inaccurate portrayals of crime in the media can contribute to fear of crime among the public. For example, news reports in mainstream US papers have exaggerated the likelihood of school violence and blamed schools for the failure to prevent it (Kupchik and Bracy 2009), which can create anxiety and fear among adults and, in turn, children. Another implication is that distorted links between crime and race/ethnicity can encourage a disdain for 'the other' and foster a 'we versus them' mentality, while, at the same time, fuelling prejudice and discrimination. Although some debate has centred on the influence of the biased reporting of crime, several scholars have concluded that people's interpretations of crime and the meanings they attach to it are shaped greatly by the way in which crime is reported by news media.

REFERENCES

Barlow, M.H. (1998) 'Race and the problem of crime in "Time" and "Newsweek" cover stories, 1946 to 1995', *Social Justice*, 25: 149–83.

Cavender, G., Bond-Maupin, L. and Jurik, N.C. (1999) 'The construction of gender in reality crime TV', *Gender and Society*, 13: 643–63.

Dowler, K. (2004) 'Comparing American and Canadian local television crime stories: A content analysis', *Canadian Journal of Criminology and Criminal Justice*, 46: 573–96.

Greer, C. (2007) 'News media, victims and crime', in P. Davies, P. Francis and C. Greer (eds) *Victims, Crime and Society*. London: Sage, pp. 20–49.

Kupchik, A. and Bracy, N.L. (2009) 'The news media on school crime and violence: Constructing dangerousness and fueling fear', *Youth Violence and Juvenile Justice*, 7: 136–55.

Reeves, J.L. and Campbell, R. (1994) *Cracked Coverage: Television News, The Anti-Cocaine Crusade, and the Reagan Legacy*. Durham, NC: Duke University Press.

Reinarman, C. and Levine, H. (eds) (1997) *Crack in America: Demon Drugs and Social Justice*. Berkeley, CA: University of California Press.

34 Moral Panics

Definition: *The concept of moral panic has been used to describe how certain phenomena (e.g. riots, new drugs or types of drug use, immigration, hooliganism) and specific 'outsider' groups (often youth subcultures and/or immigrant populations) are presented as an exaggerated threat to society and how this 'panic' is instrumental in their repression. Exaggeration, misconception and distortion of the perceived threat amplified by the media are seen as producing a hostile and disproportionate reaction and as resulting in calls for new (often punitive) policy measures to resolve the threat. Despite remaining an important casual lay concept, it has nonetheless been subject to a range of criticisms in recent years that suggest its utility is more limited than once thought and that its influence as an explanatory concept is waning, although some researchers have sought to revitalise it.*

INTRODUCTION

The term moral panic is now everyday currency. Almost any 'problem' where it is believed that there has been a strong, disproportionate media and social response to it can now have the label of moral panic applied to it. This relatively casual and lay use (often by the media itself when accusing other parts of the media) means that the term has shifted from some of the specificity of meaning initially applied to it, to a term of general usage that most people would understand to mean mostly (1) an over-reaction, and (2) something where more perspective and less judgement or prejudice needs to be applied. In recent times, the label of moral panic has been given to various social and other phenomena, from fears around various drugs and drug use and fears of sexual predation on children to fears around the emergence of GM (genetically modified) crops/foods. In some senses, the relatively casual way that moral panics are now attributed to a range of issues that become social problems (i.e. they become 'social' problems even if they are fears of new technology or natural events because of the way they are reported and responded to socially, culturally and politically) is also reflective of the way the concept has expanded in the social sciences. Moral panics have shifted academically from a relatively well-bounded concept in its early days to one that is now more diffuse. As real-life examinations of the concept have revealed various limitations or contradictions within it (e.g. When does concern become a 'panic'? Where does a panic come from? Who judges if something is an over-reaction? Do moral panics sometimes work against the powerful?), social scientists have seen it as increasingly in need of revision or critique. However, testament to the fact that many social scientists continue to see the core ideas – stigmatisation of a group or behaviour at a specific moment in time; exaggeration and distortion of the risk a stigmatised group or behaviour present; amplification of this through public media and the consequent social/political lobbying for change – as having genuine credence, it remains an influential way of trying to understand moments of conflict and change. This means that revision or critique rather than wholesale rejection has been the main trend and continues to be so. Too casual a usage of the term (by academics and lay observers both), however, remains its biggest weakness.

THE ORIGINS OF THE CONCEPT

The term was originally coined by Jock Young (1971) in his early discussions about the way that drugs and drug users were stigmatised and persecuted in the 1960s, and developed most famously by Stanley Cohen in his 1972 book *Folk Devils and Moral Panics*. These early works established, through sub-concepts such as 'deviance amplification', 'folk devils', 'scapegoating', 'disproportionality' and 'media amplification and diffusion', the idea of how a moral panic works. Famously, Cohen summed it up thus:

> Societies appear to be subject, every now and then, to periods of moral panic. A condition, episode, person or group of persons emerges to become defined as a threat to societal values and interests; its nature is presented in a stylised and stereotypical fashion by the mass media; the moral barricades are manned by editors, bishops, politicians and other right-thinking people; socially accredited experts pronounce their diagnoses and solutions; ways of coping are evolved or (more often) resorted to; the condition then disappears, submerges or deteriorates and becomes more visible. Sometimes the object of the panic is quite novel and at other times it is something which has been in existence long enough, but suddenly appears in the limelight. Sometimes the panic passes over and is forgotten, except in folk-lore and collective memory; at other times it has more serious and long-lasting repercussions and might

produce such changes as those in legal and social policy or even in the way society conceives itself. (Cohen 1972: 9)

Early moral panic positions were embedded with a broad set of ideas around social control (see also *Social control, governance and governmentality*) and were strongly influenced by the symbolic interactionist school, functionalism and the concept of labelling (see also *Social construction of crime and deviance*). Broadly, this encapsulated the idea that social control in society is maintained, and threats to social norms managed, in modern societies through a range of methods – one of which is to create anti-social folk devils (drug users, paedophiles, witches, etc.) to divert attention away from serious social problems such as economic and other crises, crises that may threaten the whole social order if not contained. Early versions of moral panics were thus strongly about how one group (the powerful, the elites) managed periods of conflict by diverting attention to lesser or even imaginary problems.

Essentially, the concept involved:

- a focus on a group, subculture or event that appeared to threaten established social norms in some meaningful way;
- an exaggerated and distorted representation of the level and type of threat (especially violence) through the media – media reports are sensationalist and dramatic and designed to garner an emotive response;
- otherwise independent events being symbolically linked (e.g. people with similar hair or clothes involved in otherwise unrelated events) and the issue appearing bigger and more problematic than it really is;
- the creation of an amplification spiral, whereby those stigmatised are persecuted by the police (and picked on) and this new visibility creates more headlines – those labelled react in various ways that the police and/or other agents of social control (including the media) respond to, and so on;
- outcomes such as the escalation of police and other interventions, sometimes leading to new laws or powers for the police (or social workers or the army or teachers, etc.) to help deal with the threat.

HOW THE CONCEPT DEVELOPED

Over the years, the concept has been revised by others seeking to develop, improve or strengthen it, including by both Young and Cohen themselves. Goode and Ben-Yehuda (1994), for example, in an attempt to clarify the model, provided specific criteria that need to be met for a moral panic to be considered as such. They listed these as:

1. *Concern*: there is an emergence/existence of awareness that a group/behaviour is a threat to society.
2. *Hostility*: there is an emergence/existence of hostility towards the group/behaviour in question; this hostility will produce stereotyped 'folk devils' who are differentiated from normal people who pose no threat.

3. *Consensus*: the threat is relatively widespread and accepted – this will be demonstrated by various 'moral entrepreneurs' (conservative and other leaders/authorities) and the media agreeing on the nature of the threat and that the problem can be perceived as emanating from the constructed folk devils.
4. *Disproportionality*: the responses (e.g. police force/punishments/new legal sanctions/control) are excessive compared to the actual threat posed.
5. *Volatility*: there is a sudden focus and panic around a problem that, sometimes just as quickly, then subsides.

PRIMARY CRITIQUES AND CONTRADICTIONS

Conceptual difficulties have arisen around the specific meaning of the terms 'moral' and 'panic' and how both are difficult to measure in reality, and how they also involve a normative judgement about what is a disproportionate and/or inappropriate response. Similarly, what constitutes a disproportionate and/or inappropriate response to a problem is difficult to resolve. Numerous commentators have argued that the issues raised by many moral panics are not 'free-floating' or simply made up. Many of the problems are 'real' or of genuine concern. What then is the correct level and type of response? This leads to another issue: rather than creating/amplifying moral panics, the media may be simply (or to some degree at least) mirroring public attitudes and presenting ideas and positions already found in the public at large. Recent critiques have also pointed out that moral panics might not always be bad (e.g. if powerful groups of elites are revealed to be acting in ways that need curbing) and can be 'bottom up' as opposed to simply 'top down'. Other research has revealed that the media itself often works against moral panics, demonstrating that the media is far more complex than was previously the case and thought; that the media doesn't always target scapegoats or folk devils when raising the spectre of a social problem; and that the media audience is involved in various forms and levels of resistance and absorption when consuming media information and imagery – in other words, even when there is a consistent media line on an issue, this doesn't guarantee a consistent audience reaction or that policy change is even likely. Mostly, moral panics are presented as emerging with little explanation of how and why they emerge when they do. Arguably, this sites a moral panic as though it is relatively divorced from preceding historical conditions and contexts related to the issue there is a panic about and thus it tends to be recounted ahistorically, as a useful topic for diverting attention away from something more serious. Related to this, Furedi (2013) has pointed to the way that some morally focused issues, around which there is much ongoing furore, such as paedophilia, both endure over time and, rather than produce quick policy responses, produce 'moral crusades' and crusaders and lobbying for extensive change.

The focus on the kind of issues a moral panic can be said to revolve around has also changed. No longer do these necessarily involve clear 'moral' threats but may indeed be threats to health or welfare or be about the emergence of new technology – in this sense, moral panics may be argued to be part and parcel of general forms of fear now permeating (post)modern society (see also *Fear and the fear of crime*).

FROM SOMETHING CLOSELY BOUNDED TO SOMETHING WITH EVER-EXPANDING PARAMETERS?

Rather than being a hint at desperation, it is perhaps a sign of the perceived worthiness of a concept (able at least to approximate to something that the academic community feels has relevant insight) when it is conceptually expanded to retain its relevance. Moral panics are now, as stated above, being applied ever widely and – taking into consideration the various critiques and attempts to revise the concept in line with real-world complexities – the boundaries as to how a moral panic might be understood conceptually are also widening. What constitutes a moral panic is thus contested and expanding, and while it has historically had the status of a 'big' theory, used to explain social reaction and change at the policy level (as opposed to so-called grand theory or narratives used to explain constancy or changes at the level of society as a whole), it may be the case that moral panic's continued utility lies in describing and analysing micro changes within broader theoretical positionings such as that of 'fear'.

THE FUTURE FOR MORAL PANICS: A SUBSET OF FEAR?

Recently, Steve Hall (2012) declared the concept of moral panics to be theoretically redundant because it is itself originally a product of a time where fear and reaction to change were all around and those (usually on the political left) in fear of this process constructed a thing (moral panics) to explain it, yet this thing does not exist beyond being a fear of fear itself. While this position has some real credence and moral panics are not 'real', it perhaps ignores the conceptual utility of something that has broad explanatory inference. We may not have moral panics around drugs (although we can have events that strongly approximate to them) but a drug scare can be overblown, to the extent, for example, that many aspects are later disproven or shown to have been exaggerated or even made up, such as in the case of mephedrone (bubble, drone, meph, meow-meow), and the idea of a misconstrued panic provides a better cue to events than does simply referring to a scare. Moreover, 'fear' is increasingly important in the social sciences as an explanatory concept in its own right (see also *Fear and the fear of crime*) and it has a more nuanced and historical application to social problems/phenomena. The broader concept of fear provides a way of interpreting complex feared events and is less hamstrung by either specific criteria and/or a legacy of revisionism to make events 'fit' the concept than moral panics. It does, however, provide an opportunity for a moral panic approach (albeit at a diminished sub-concept level) to consider certain events specifically – perhaps as one symptom – but then be strengthened or liberated through recourse to a broader conceptual framework able to cope more fully with the kinds of critiques that continue to plague simpler moral panic approaches (Coomber 2013).

REFERENCES

Cohen, S. (1972) *Folk Devils and Moral Panics: The Creation of the Mods and Rockers*. London: MacGibbon & Kee.

Coomber, R. (2014) 'How social fear of drugs in the non-sporting world creates a framework for policy in the sporting world', *International Journal of Sport Policy and Politics*, 6 (2): 171–93.

Furedi, F. (2013) *Moral Crusades in an Age of Mistrust: The Jimmy Saville Scandal*. Basingstoke: Palgrave Macmillan.

Goode, E. and Ben-Yehuda, N. (1994) *Moral Panics: The Social Construction of Deviance*. Oxford: Blackwell.

Hall, S. (2012) *Theorizing Crime and Deviance: A New Perspective*. London: Sage.

Young. J (1971) 'The role of the police as amplifiers of deviance', in S. Cohen (ed.) *Images of Deviance*. Harmondsworth: Penguin, pp. 27–61.

Young, J. (1971) *The Drugtakers: The Social Meaning of Drug Use*. London: Judson, MacGibbon & Kee.

35 Police and Policing

> **Definition**: *The police, normatively, are the formal public government-funded organisation tasked to uphold the law of the state, maintain order within its boundaries and prevent crime. Policing, normatively, is the act of upholding the law, maintaining order, preventing crime and offering a range of support services to the public congruent with the aforementioned tasks of the police. In the western world, the nature of the police and policing continues to evolve and it is increasingly the case that who and what the police are and what policing consists of are shifting and blurring as different (non-public) bodies/personnel take on roles previously provided by public police forces. Globally, police forces differ substantially in terms of role, authority, purpose, organisation and practice, with some of the biggest differences being between states based on democratic and pluralistic aims and those based on more authoritarian models. Legitimacy of authority is the key issue for police and policing.*

DEFINING POLICING

In its most basic form, the police could be said to be (usually) formally authorised public agents/agencies of government, empowered to enforce the law and maintain public/social order through the use of force, if and when necessary (see also *The criminal justice system*).

Formal, that is governmental and institutional (the police themselves), and academic/critical definitions, however, unsurprisingly focus on different aspects of the police and their role. Formal definitions tend to present the role of the police and the nature of policing as simply providing trustworthy and legitimate security and protection to a populace. Fathomably, these definitions are presented as neutral free and indeed many police forces in formally democratic countries, such as the UK, Germany, Australia, Canada, France, New Zealand and the USA, would see themselves as directly independent of political influence and as such carry out policing on the basis of upholding a fair system of law and order. Critical academic definitions are more circumspect for the role of the police, even in democratic societies, and vary from seeing the police as simply instruments of the state that exist mainly to protect the interests of the elite to those that, while accepting the police have a relative autonomy from political interference and do much to sincerely protect the population from specific threats, have a primary role that mostly involves 'maintaining order' in the public and private spheres of everyday life, where the 'order' that is maintained is inflected with norms and values that are commonly conservative in nature and where the police are always, in some way, agents of social control (see also *Social control, governance and governmentality*).

A BRIEF HISTORY OF THE EMERGENCE OF MODERN POLICING

Historically and globally, police and policing have evolved from different starting points reflecting different contexts and cultures (Mawby 1999). How order has been maintained historically and how wrong-doing has been punished have depended on numerous factors. For sovereigns, warlords and other authorities in control of land and regions, order was maintained through a spectrum of methods as diverse as local self-policing where towns and villages maintained order themselves, often through established cultural norms and practice, through to military-controlled repression.

Prior to the institution of the first modern police forces in the late eighteenth and early nineteenth centuries around Europe, basic 'policing' beyond that of severe militaristic repression had varied enormously in terms of structure but its basic rationale and organisation was similar in many locales around the world: the protection of travellers/trades people on linking roads and tracks from brigands and robbers and protection of locals from those breaking accepted laws. Variations of sheriffs or marshals (by many different names) or 'watchmen' meant that authority was often given or delegated to such individuals and their deputies to maintain basic order. Delegation of the maintenance of order usually depended on how centralised the state was and the extent of its reach into isolated areas. In ancient China, for example, the 'prefecture system' utilised networks of locally based magistrates to appoint prefects and sub-prefects to maintain the law. Magistrates in turn reported to regional governors who were themselves responsible to the Emperor. The prefecture system existed for thousands of years. In ancient Rome, Emperor Augustus instituted the system of Vigiles, initially to protect the huge (at that time) city of one million people from fire outbreaks but also to act as watchmen for robbers and runaway slaves. The Vigiles were allocated to seven city-wide *cohorts* comprising originally of around 500–560 men to be vigilant over specific parts of the city. The force was funded by a central tax on the sale of slaves.

Urbanisation and the emergence of cities, along with an expanded and increasingly intrusive state apparatus, produced a new context whereby crime was more concentrated and diverse than ever before and the state feared decreased control over its populace. Rapid urbanisation in particular can produce impoverished circumstances (see also *Gangs*) where criminal gangs flourish and disenfranchised/excluded groups seek to survive using methods outside of the law. Urban centres thus need different approaches to the maintenance of order to those operating in sparsely populated rural areas and policing has had to evolve to accommodate such changes. The specific political, economic and cultural background of any one nation state or locality has also affected the evolution of policing over time. War and invasion often created contexts anew as victors used elements of their legal systems or approaches for order maintenance, and the development of political ideologies such as democracy, freedom and the separation of state from religion (secularism) also strongly influenced how both the police and policing developed over time in any one place up to the current day.

If modern policing is a predominantly 'western' model, understood as an organised, uniformed (mostly), civilian force paid a salary to uphold the law, protect the public and organised by principles of command and relative autonomy from political interference, as found in many countries around the world, then its origins are to be found within the early French and English forces of the eighteenth and nineteenth centuries. Although drawing on some structural components found in even ancient enforcement approaches (such as the Prefecture and Vigile), the centrally organised French police force created in Paris by Louis XIV was the first uniformed force to be organised in ways similar in many senses to the way national forces are organised today. The French police, however, were normatively understood as more plainly instruments of what was initially, but then effectively – post-revolution – an absolutist state. The shift towards principles of policing based on greater political neutrality was found in late eighteenth and early nineteenth century England, initially with the emergence of the Thames River Police in 1800. By demonstrating the efficacy of prevention (largely by the visibility of personnel) and through the introduction of full-time salaried officers who were forbidden to take extra payments for protection or police work, a sense of credibility, legitimacy and trustworthiness and the prevention success of this experiment had worldwide influence. So much so that this later influenced the emergence of what has been termed the world's first modern police force set up by Sir Robert Peel in 1829 – the (London) Metropolitan Police Service. The 'Peelian principles', which the new service was established on, were that the force be professional, full time, civilian, politically neutral, trustworthy and accountable. Some of this was achieved, for example, by providing each officer with a distinct number visible on their uniforms – a standard practice in any police force open to accountability today.

THE ROLE OF THE MODERN POLICE FORCE

The role of the modern police force today has changed from that imagined by Peel. It has grown, developed and evolved – often as a direct reaction to the changing shape of crime itself. Specialisation is now a key aspect of policing. There has been a proliferation and specialisation of both activities and roles. Many modern police forces are multi-agency. In the UK, for example, the National Crime Agency (NCA) is a specialist police unit dealing with threats from organised crime nationally and internationally. In the USA, policing has many separate specialist agencies such as the Federal Bureau of Investigation (FBI); the Drug Enforcement

Administration (DEA); the Bureau of Alcohol, Tobacco, Firearms and Explosives (ATF); and the Department of Homeland Security (DHS), to name just a few.

Apart from agency specialisation, there is role specialisation within police forces. In the UK, where the police are not routinely armed, Authorised Firearms Officers are trained and called on to undertake specific types of engagement; there are teams of officers that specialise in crime related to information technology but even here specialisation is created, with online crime (see also *Internet crime*) having both its own sub-division and sub-divisions within that (e.g. teams focusing on fraud/scams and others on sex-related crime). Policing has not only adapted to the shape of crime and criminality but also to the changing nature of society and its attendant needs. Some police officers are now almost exclusively 'community' or 'liaison' officers, whose jobs are to be the outward face of the police to a public that demands more than just a penal response to being a victim (or a possible victim). Others such as the plain clothes' Criminal Investigation Department (CID) investigate serious crimes such as murder, rape and serious fraud, while regular officers provide uniformed support and investigate less serious or routine crime. Many police forces, or their agencies, such as the NCA are less bound by national borders than ever before and see it as part of their role to work closely with other countries' police forces and/or international forces such as Interpol, Europol and Ameripol.

POLICING APPROACHES

If the setting up of the Thames River Police in 1800 signalled the beginnings of the preventative approach to policing, as opposed to the former 'reactive' or responsive model, the advent of newer models such as 'problem-orientated policing' or 'intelligence-led policing' offer further incremental reform that continues this into the modern age. Although a great deal of policing remains, and will always be, responsive, intelligence-led policing is a conceptual approach to policing that is now firmly embedded in the practice of many international police forces such as those in the UK, the USA, Canada and Australia, and it continues to be adopted and developed. In essence, the approach seeks device strategies for reducing crime through analysing an array of intelligence/evidence and then putting a plan into operation, as opposed to the traditional method of responding to a crime and using information from that to produce intelligence that is then used mostly to account for the crime, not understand it. Intelligence-led policing is thus about managing risk effectively and efficiently rather than responding to events as a form of deterrence (Tilley 2003). An example of this approach relates to the occurrence of violence outside fast-food restaurants in inner-city areas after local bars have closed at weekends. Rather than respond to this by either closing down fast-food outlets (which may increase conflict due to smaller numbers of outlets and thus more crowding) or simply providing police responses to each event, one study found – through analysing the related data, strategising from it and reducing fast-food trading hours by two hours, from 5.00 a.m. to 3.00 a.m. – that there was a 37% reduction in associated violence (Kypri et al. 2011). Through the application of intelligence-led policing to numerous areas of crime control, prevention strategies are becoming increasingly effective.

key concepts in
crime and society

LEGITIMACY AND AUTHORITY

The key issue that any authority that uses force, or has the delegated authority to use force, against a civilian population has to deal with is that of *legitimacy*. A police force that is seen as corrupt in terms of legitimacy loses the trust and ultimately the support of those it is authorised to control. Modern police forces are constantly feeling the tension between maintaining authority and exercising what they consider to be legitimate force and the accountability of public authority and retention of public trust demanded of advanced democracies (Haberfeld and Cerrah 2007). Flashpoints, such as the killing of a civilian that is seen as the result of unjustified force or long-term policies such as 'stop and search', where disproportionate targeting of non-whites over many years raises questions of institutional racism, highlight both the difficulties of contemporary policing and also where bias and the use of force and authority may be being used illegitimately. Where the police are seen too strongly as the 'arm of the state' or as upholding dated or prejudicial values, then their authority is undermined and conflict against them can escalate. Escalation of violence and mistrust of the police are often characteristics of 'riots' or urban unrest.

NEW DEVELOPMENTS – CIVILIANISATION, OUTSOURCING AND PUBLIC CONFIDENCE

The proliferation of police roles in developed nations, many of which have been said to be akin to social work, and also growth/developments in technological personnel, equipment and enforcement/detection, have meant that policing has grown in scope and responsibility (Joyce 2011). Modern police forces are thus more inclusive in what they do and thus more costly to run/resource intensive. In times of resource constraint and cost-cutting, this has meant that many governments and forces have chosen to deliver 'policing' in a less centralised fashion and diversify their product. In essence, this has meant the use of three primary mechanisms: (1) reducing bureaucracy where possible, giving serving officers more time for 'police work'; (2) using civilians in previously key police roles, particularly those that are 'out-facing' or in direct liaison with the public, to enable rationalisation of resources and so that police officers can focus on roles deemed more effective/appropriate; and (3) using private commercial providers for certain security undertakings (such as the use of private security forces during the London 2012 Olympics). Some of these measures, especially those designed to put more officers 'on the street', can be popular with the public and civilian officers can be more effective in liaising with the public. The extent to which the public is comfortable with and trusting of private security firms, however, is less clear.

CONCLUSION

Police and policing in the modern world have developed into an increasingly refined operation that has to present itself as a legitimate authority in using force to uphold the law; transform itself/change and adapt to modern criminal circumstances while negotiating how to maintain the trust of the public; and remain appropriately accountable and adopt new roles to provide 'support' to a public that stretches its resources.

REFERENCES

Haberfeld, M.R. and Cerrah, I. (2007) *Comparative Policing: The Struggle for Democratization*. London: Sage.

Joyce, P. (2011) *Policing: Development and Contemporary Practice*. London: Sage.

Kypri, K., Jones, C., McElduff, P. and Barker, D. (2011) 'Effects of restricting pub closing times on night-time assaults in an Australian city', *Addiction*, 106: 303–10.

Mawby, R.I. (1999) *Policing Across the World*. London: UCL Press.

Tilley, N. (2003) Problem-Oriented Policing, Intelligence-Led Policing and the National Intelligence Model. Jill Dando Institute of Crime Science, University College London.

36 Deterrence and Prevention

Definition: Deterrence is any action which reduces or inhibits the likelihood of an event occurring. Crime prevention is defined as a set of actions intended to reduce or remove the risk of crime and harms associated with the commission of crime.

Quite simply, the idea of deterrence is to create barriers which constrain deviant and criminal behaviours, and, by extension of this logic, to facilitate or encourage conforming and law-abiding behaviours.

There is no concept so pervasive in criminology than *deterrence* because it is implied in every theory and perspective about crime ever constructed. In fact, deterrence pre-dates the development of criminology as a scientific field of theory and empirical inquiry, with many scholars citing the work of eighteenth-century thinker Caesar Beccarea, among others, who early on wrote about crime and punishment.

GENERAL AND SPECIAL DETERRENCE

There are two forms of deterrence – general and specific. The former refers to any kind of initiative which seeks to inhibit the commission of crime among the general population, hence it is presumed to apply to everyone. For example, a mandatory sentence stipulating a minimal time in prison for the physical and sexual abuse of a child under the care of parents or other guardians (e.g. teachers, youth leaders, sport coaches) is designed to deter such abuse. Publication of this law, or media coverage about the punishment assigned to an offender, strengthens the social order and deters such actions. The effect of general deterrence, therefore, is a collective, vicarious experience (Pratt et al. 2006).

Specific deterrence is directed towards a particular offence or a specific offender. It is not so much that the crime and related punishment are any different than the example described above, but that those who are at risk of engaging in or have been arrested for a type of criminal behaviour, such as child abuse, will find the punishment sufficiently severe or costly to likely never repeat their offence. Unlike a vicarious experience, the source of a specific form of deterrence is a personally felt sanction (Pratt et al. 2006).

DETERRENCE AND CRIMINOLOGICAL THEORIES

Deterrence theory in criminology is related to a number of other criminological theories, but especially social learning theory (see also *Crime and theory*). As Akers (1990) has observed, deterrence theory is based on the idea of differential rein-forcement, a fundamental concept of social learning theory as well. In this case, when individuals calculate that the costs of engaging in a criminal action are too high relative to the benefits derived, crime is deterred. Obeying traffic rules, such as a traffic light when there is no cross-traffic, is a deterrent because drivers calcu-late that waiting until the light changes so that they can proceed legally is less costly than crossing over in violation of the light and possibly incurring a fine or revocation of their licence, should they be so unlucky as to be observed by a police officer. In this example, the costs are direct to the violator, and for those who obey the traffic laws the deterrence effect is avoidance of punishment.

There are also indirect experiences associated with punishment, such as know-ing someone who has been punished for an offence. In relation to the traffic light example, therefore, an indirect experience of punishment is the example of having a friend who leaves a pub at 2.00 a.m. in the morning, did not obey a traffic light, was 'pulled over' by the police and lost his licence for six months, must now use public transport to get to work every day and incurs the inconvenience of con-tinuously asking friends for a ride to go shopping, for travel, etc.

Besides social learning theory, the concept of deterrence shows up in several other forms of contemporary criminological theory (Pratt et al. 2006). The first is a consideration of costs other than court-imposed fines and jail sentences. For example, Braithwaite's (1989) shaming theory defines deterrence – either to com-mit an offence originally or as a form of re-integration for those who have already offended (see also *Poverty and exclusion*), – as posited on the notion that when individuals have established bonds with a society and with groups within, they avoid actions which would cause them to lose these connections, that is, to be shunned or thrown out. Shame is more than a self-perception of guilt, for the idea that others with whom an individual interacts will also be shamed or stigmatised (i.e. family, friends, etc.) if one violates the law is presumed to be a powerful form of restraint. Based on Braithwaite's (1989) shaming theory, a series of actions can be proposed which attempt to clarify for the offender the social costs of illegal behaviour, and the actions necessary for offenders to be re-integrated back into the community. Hence, shaming theory helps provide a conceptual basis for forms of restorative justice that allow victims to recover social, economic and other costs imposed on offenders, and for other conditions imposed on offenders by courts and various criminal justice officials – or, in the case of Indigenous communities, for the authority and recommendations of the elders or tribal leaders – to help make victims whole again.

A second set of contemporary theories which include aspects of deterrence that are related to perceptions of the situations in which offending may occur comprises situational crime prevention and routine activities theory. Both theories attempt to consider the specific contexts or situations in which offenders and victims converge in space and time to create a crime incident. By redesigning the physical environment to create better surveillance by law-abiding citizens and other measures which increase the perception of offenders that they may be seen and subsequently arrested, crime is deterred. Aside from arguments that these actions merely displace crime to another location or another time, the idea is that some crimes are highly situational or opportunistic, therefore they would not otherwise occur if forms of deterrence, especially the probability of being detected or seen, were initiated.

A variation on these theories is the 'broken windows' thesis (Kelling and Coles 1996). This view of crime is based on perceptions of physical and social disorder at particular places. It assumes that small signs of disorder, such as graffiti or a broken window, can lead to additional deterioration of the physical, plus the social environment of an area, hence contributing to the increased occurrence of crime there. Eliminating signs of deterioration and improving the liveability of an area deter the commission of crime. Related to this is the idea of re-establishing norms of law and order in an area. For example, enforcing a minor crime, such as someone who jumps a turnstile to avoid paying a small sum to ride on a subway or metro, especially if the enforcement is public or visible, encourages citizens who witnessed the enforcement action to be empowered and to informally enforce norms of order themselves, hence deterring even more crime (see also *Social control, governance and governmentality*).

CRIME PREVENTION

Even though there is much criticism of the logic of various forms of deterrence theory, and of empirical tests which question the strength of specific deterrence actions on crime, the theory will continue to form an integral part of criminology as a science and of policies related to policing and justice (Pratt et al. 2006). Likewise, a discussion of crime in any society will always include notions of *crime prevention*. Like deterrence, crime prevention is a concept that pre-dates the development of criminology as a science; with commentary and suggestions by Henry Fielding in the mid-eighteenth century and Sir Robert Peel in the first half of the nineteenth century as England industrialised and urbanised (Lab 2007) (see also *Police and policing*).

An oft-cited and rather basic definition conceptualises crime prevention as any kind of action based on an assessment or appraisal of crime risk, and the initiation of various actions to remove or reduce the risk, hence preventing crime (Brantingham and Faust 1976). Crime prevention is not so much a criminal theory as it is a classificatory scheme related to a large set of actions presumed to reduce crime through policies that have a basis in criminological concepts and theories. Brantingham and Faust (1976) identified three levels of crime prevention, all of which include aspects of deterrence. First, there is primary prevention, which is directed at modification of the physical and social environment. This can include anything from increased security hardware for residences and businesses, to improved street lighting and the establishment of neighbourhood or block watches. Secondary crime prevention is geared towards early identification and intervention in the lives of individuals or groups at risk of becoming criminally involved (Brantingham and Faust 1976). Secondary prevention can include everything from sports leagues and summer jobs training programmes for at-risk youth, to attempts at educational programmes in schools, churches and other societal institutions aimed at teaching both juveniles and adults appropriate pro-social behaviours. Finally, tertiary crime prevention has at its heart the goal of reducing recidivism among offenders.

Hunter (2010) divides crime prevention into three levels in a different way from Brantingham and Faust (1976). In fact, at each of his three levels, he cites specific forms of primary, secondary and tertiary level preventative actions. At the micro level are types of prevention 'designed to address individual or specific site vulnerabilities' (Hunter 2010: 212). For example, primary types of micro-level prevention include the reduction of target vulnerability, from self-defence training to residential and business security. Secondary forms of micro-level prevention include training programmes to increase awareness among persons about vulnerabilities and recreational, social and educational programmes which provide alternative activities for individuals in specific locations who might otherwise become involved in crime. Tertiary forms of micro-level prevention include a reduction in victim trauma from crime, compensation paid to victims and restorative and restitution programmes for offenders and victims so that offenders are less likely to offend again and victims feel a sense of justice.

Meso-level prevention efforts are focused on targets and victims within a larger context, such as programmes designed or tailored separately for urban, suburban and rural environments, convention centres, parks and tourist sites, sporting events, etc. (Hunter 2010). Primary prevention programmes at the meso level mainly involve strategies related to the multi-jurisdictional coordination of efforts. Secondary and tertiary forms of prevention at the meso level are designed around issues of common vulnerabilities for communities and groups of people within localities who are potential victims and for communities and groups of people who are potential offenders. Hence, meso-level prevention programmes might focus on the prevention of crime against targets within high-poverty rural or urban communities or on populations within these areas who are at risk of becoming involved in criminal behaviour.

Hunter (2010) extends macro-level crime prevention to cover even larger areas, which can go beyond national borders to include international efforts to prevent certain kinds of crime, such as environmental crime, human trafficking, drug production and trafficking, and terrorism. At the macro level, primary prevention comes in the form of legislation which enables law enforcement and other criminal justice agencies across the world to coordinate actions which prevent and deter crime. Secondary and tertiary prevention efforts, whether focused on potential victims or offenders, are identified by Hunter (2010) as actions at the meso and micro levels that first require legislation to empower enforcement agencies and appropriate levels of funding by government entities so that their efforts can include strategies and actions which are national and international in scope.

REFERENCES

Akers, R.L. (1990) 'Rational choice, deterrence, and social learning theory in criminology: The path not taken', *Journal of Criminal Law and Criminology*, 81(3): 653–76.

Braithwaite, J. (1989) *Crime, Shame and Reintegration*. Cambridge: Cambridge University Press.

Brantingham, P.J. and Faust, F.L. (1976) 'A conceptual model of crime prevention', *Crime and Delinquency*, 22(3): 284–96.

Hunter, R. (2010) 'Crime prevention: Micro, meso and macro levels', in B.S. Fisher and S.P. Lab (eds) *Encyclopedia of Victimology and Crime Prevention*. Thousand Oaks, CA: Sage, pp. 211–13.

Kelling, G.L. and Coles, C.M. (1996) *Fixing Broken Windows: Restoring Order and Reducing Crime in Our Communities*. New York: Simon & Schuster.

Lab, S.P. (2007) *Crime Prevention: Approaches, Practices and Evaluations*, 6th edn. Evanston, IL: Anderson.

Pratt, T.C., Cullen, F.T., Blevins, K.R., Daigle, L.E. and Madensen, T.D. (2006) 'The empirical status of deterrence theory: A meta-analysis', in F.T. Cullen, J.P. Wright and K.R. Blevins (eds) *Taking Stock: The Status of Criminological Theory*. New Brunswick, NJ: Transaction Publishers, pp. 367–95.

37 Punishment

> **Definition: Punishment** can be defined as a socially sanctioned activity to control deviance or crime. Sanctions can be either normative or legal. The nature and administration of punishment are highly variable, both culturally and historically.

Changes in punishment have been linked to changing conceptions of crime, which, in turn, have been linked to changing political and institutional arrangements. Emile Durkheim was one of the first sociologists to speak of punishment in *The

Division of Labour in Modern Society in the late nineteenth century. He perceived punishment as progressing historically from retributive to restitutive systems. For Durkheim, punishment is instrumental in securing social solidarity, which he considered as shared mores and norms integrating society and producing social order (see also *Crime and theory*). Comparative criminologists have also noted that punishment tends to be more expressive and violent in developing countries. For example, stoning and beheading tend to be more common ways of carrying out execution in developing countries and prison sentences in such places can appear extreme and harsh to observers from the developed world. Leniency can also be highly culturally and historically variable.

While philosophy has tended to be interested in examining moral justifications for punishment, most sociological accounts have instead examined how punishment is politically contested between different groups in society. Thus, a central focus of sociological accounts of punishment has been power or 'social control' (see also *Normalisation*). A central question underpinning any discussion of the sociology of punishment is: who gets punished or, more specifically, which social groups get punished? From here, it can be asked: how are they punished and why are they punished in the ways that they are? (see also *Crime (definition of)* and *Deviance (definition of)*).

MARXIST THEORIES OF PUNISHMENT

Punishment is linked to social hierarchies, especially those relating to class, gender and ethnicity. For example, in terms of social class, people of low socio-economic status are more likely to be incarcerated or subjected to other formal procedures of social control. Marxist analyses of punishment emphasise how economic structures inform social control practices. Early theorists, such as Rusche and Kirchheimer in *Punishment and Social Structure* (1933), drew historical links between the forms that specific punishments take and the economic requirements of various modes of production. In this way, rates of imprisonment may be linked to varying economic conditions, with the prison itself developing as a primary response to crime in capitalist societies.

In social terms, punishment has a fundamentally symbolic character, oriented towards public denouncements of socially repugnant or harmful behaviours. It functions to establish what is right and wrong through complex rituals which resonate psychologically and emotionally, and provides a focal point for public expressions of deeply held emotions. Punishment draws and maintains social lines and boundaries in terms of identifying appropriate rules and conduct, reaffirming specific visions of social order. At an ideological level, Marxists (such as Rusche and Kirchheimer, cited above) argue that punishment in capitalist societies reinforces capitalist values, especially those associated with private property.

PUNISHING MINORITIES

When considering ethnicity, minority groups tend to have high rates of incarceration (see also *Race/ethnicity and crime*). This is true, for example, of African

Americans in the USA and is also evident with regard to Indigenous populations in settler societies such as Australia and Canada. Such differential treatment might be explained with reference to power imbalances between various social groups. However, gender presents an interesting counter-point, in that men represent about 90% of the prison population in most countries, but also hold significant social power when compared with women. Explanations for this fact should consider how male power provides opportunities for criminal activity and the distinct patterns and types of male and female offending (see also *Crime and theory*).

The higher rate of male incarceration also highlights the fact that men are generally subjected to greater levels of formal punishment by states, whereas women are subjected to a greater extent to informal social controls administered by men. Female social infractions are often perceived as deviant, as opposed to illegal activities. Indeed, male violence, including domestic violence, has traditionally been understood as an informal, and often socially sanctioned or tolerated, form of punishment for female norm or rule breaking. Women and their bodies have also been pathologised with informal medical practices playing a greater role in their social control. Women's ability to control their own fertility is a prime example of the informal and formal social control of female bodies.

HISTORY OF PUNISHMENT

The earliest forms of punishment sought retributive justice in accordance with the biblical notion of an 'eye for an eye'. This approach to punishment sought to provide visible and enduring deterrents to crime, regardless of whether or not they were proportionate to the crime, and relied on practices of capital and corporal punishment directed against the body. Punishments were public events and involved shaming processes where offenders would be subjected to a number of degrading public acts. For example, offenders could be paraded in the streets with church bells ringing before an execution and the corpses of select offenders displayed in public spaces, as a means of deterrence.

The early modern spectacle of punishment was unambiguously instructive in an age in which limited communications (for example, lower literacy levels) and geographic barriers presented challenges to the enforcement of moral and normative boundaries. The spectacle of shame and suffering was designed to instil fear in the community of the vastly greater terrors of hell and damnation. Public confessions facilitated quick and relatively painless deaths, reinforcing normative expectations of the moral good.

With the emergence of the nation state, which claimed a monopoly on the use of coercive force, and an assumed power to punish on the part of secular and spiritual authorities, new institutions of criminal justice arose. The spectacle of torture and death, initially an event patronised by the lower classes, was so routine that it became distasteful and an offence to new sensibilities about pain and bodily integrity. As punishments began to conflict acutely with the moral sense of communities, people started to identify with the condemned and executions became occasions for expressing public revulsion and a mocking of the law. Rather than promote social order, punishment began to incite disorder and challenges to traditional authorities.

One response to this was to remove punishment from public view, so that it was politically discreet and largely occurred behind the closed walls of correctional institutions. Scenic and collective forms were increasingly eclipsed by coercive and solitary controls (Cohen 1985). It took only a few decades for spectacles of torture, branding, dismemberment and amputation to vanish. In England, hanging was widely practised throughout the seventeenth and eighteenth centuries. Nobert Elias' (1969) work, in documenting the modern aversion to public displays of violence and the demand for a more calculable and ordered bodily culture, offers valuable insights into how broad and longer-term social changes impacted on punishment.

ENLIGHTENMENT AND PUNISHMENT

Early histories of punishment were inclined to view the shift from spectacular to more subtle forms of physical and psychological punishment as a break from the barbarism of pre-modern times and a move to more rational and humanist systems of punishment where scientific knowledge gradually defeated prejudice and irrationality. Enlightenment thinking moved from ideas of original sin to the idea that man was not inherently sinful. In this way, the environment became the key to understanding crime and punishment (see also *Crime in pre-industrial, pre-modern and post-modern societies*).

Enlightenment theorists Montesquieu, Voltaire, Howard, Bentham and Mill all advocated for punishment to be rationally administered and made positive in its results, so that it developed a preventative focus to deter, reform and retrain (see also *Rehabilitation*). These thinkers advocated for the rights of man and the rule of law (see also *The criminal justice system*). They argued that punishment should not be destructive, but measured. Beccaria and others saw capital punishment as inefficient in dealing with the problem of crime, and drew attention from crime to the criminal (Garland 1985).

THE NEW INCARCERALS

The seventeenth century marked a watershed in the history of punishment across Northern Europe. During this period, thousands of deviants were confined in special institutions designed to remove them temporarily or permanently from mainstream society. The new powers to discipline extended beyond deviant populations. Foucault (1977) argued that while such measures were designed in part to control crime, they were also a cost-effective form of social control that extended throughout the social body. Thieves were thrown into prisons, lunatics into asylums, workers into factories, conscripts into barracks and children into schools. Thus, the new forms of incarceration were directed at significantly different populations. While the medieval jail had primarily been a place where prisoners were held awaiting trial and punishment (such as execution or deportation), in the modern prison the deprivation of liberty was itself the punishment.

Imprisonment came to be viewed as a viable penalty option as it provided a form of punishment which could be based on precise calculations of time. Moreover, it removed people from the contaminating influences of the community, and provided an environment in which the prisoner could be reformed. The deprivation of liberty would also serve as a continuous reminder to others of the consequences of non-conformity.

During this period, monetary penalties also became a standardised means of punishment. Fines payable to the state replaced the practice of private restitutive settlements. Monetarisation of the economy made it possible to apply this practice broadly, instead of just for wealthy offenders. To this, a more dispersed network of supervisory practices was added in the twentieth century, such as probation, suspended sentences, parole and community supervision (Garland 1985: 185) (see also *The criminal justice system*).

THEORIES OF PUNISHMENT

The two rationalisations for punishment are reduction and retribution. The aim of reduction is clearly the prevention of future crimes. Its strategies include: deterrence by discouraging and/or denouncing crime at an individual and group level; rehabilitation by treating offenders in order to 'fix' their criminal tendencies; and incapacitation which protects society or potential victims by removing offenders from the community altogether through incarceration, and thereby circumventing their ability to commit future crimes. Retribution, on the other hand, acts as a deterrent by punishing offenders for crimes already committed, with the message being that others committing such crimes will suffer the same fate.

Principles of punishment can be contradictory. For example, a concern with retribution and administration of punishment can undercut any attempt at rehabilitation. Similarly, expressions of public disapproval may serve to alienate offenders from communities and hinder rehabilitation processes (see also *Rehabilitation*).

CLASSICAL CRIMINOLOGY

The classical approach in criminology, which emerged during the Enlightenment, is concerned with issues of retribution, deterrence and justice. It is premised on the notion of humans as rational, hedonistic agents seeking to maximise pleasure and minimise pain. The focus is on rational free will, and crime is seen as a consequence of individuals abusing their free will, by consciously calculating to violate the law (see also *Crime and theory*).

According to these theories, since offenders are entirely responsible for their actions, they deserve to be punished with punishment fulfilling a universal desire for retribution. As well as 'just deserts', punishment should also serve a utilitarian purpose by promoting the greatest good for the majority in society. In practice, this translates into a preventative focus, with the law acting as a deterrent through the threat of inflicting pain via punishment. Thus, punishments should offer more pain than transgressions of the law reward. In other words, the imposition of punishment should outweigh the benefits of committing crime. Hence, the emphasis is on the equality of legal protections and legal treatments which accord with the rule of law, so that like cases are punished alike.

PENOLOGICAL MODERNISM

According to Garland (1985), penological modernism was closely linked with the rehabilitative ideal, emerging during the nineteenth century and dominating criminal justice thinking until the late twentieth century in western countries (see also *Rehabilitation*). Under this tradition, retribution was viewed as a disutility, a product of emotion, instinct and superstition. Effective and humane punishment required individualised corrective measures using expert scientific knowledge and flexible instruments of intervention (Garland 1985: 187). It followed the rise of technical professionals such as doctors, social workers, psychologists and psychiatrists utilising scientific understandings of crime and criminality.

Penological modernism rejects the idea of human beings as free moral agents, arguing instead that human behaviour is predisposed or determined by extraneous factors and forces beyond individuals' immediate conscious control. Crime, then, is not a product of individual choice, but a product of individual pathology or deficiency (see also *Crime and theory*). Offenders are perceived as diseased or dysfunctional in nature and therefore cannot be held fully accountable for their deviant actions, with treatments to be tailored to each offender's needs and personality and amenability to correction. Treatment (punishment) expires when an individual is cured. Punishment is justified not on the basis of the past offence, but in regard to the attainment of a future goal of reform.

PENAL DISILLUSIONMENT

During the 1960s, there emerged widespread disillusionment with the criminal justice system and suspicion of state institutions. There was a collapse of grand narratives of penal reform and progress and a questioning of traditional histories of punishment emphasising advances in humanity and reason. The Enlightenment or Modernist project was considered a systematic failure, which was intrusive and authoritarian (see also *Crime in pre-industrial, pre-modern and post-modern societies*).

French philosopher Michel Foucault (1926–84) criticised progressivist histories of punishment in *Discipline and Punish* (1977) by documenting the rise of 'disciplinary' practices of power (see also *Social control, governance and governmentality*). Foucault juxtaposed the old system of retribution with rehabilitation or the replacement of repression with ideals of normalisation (see also *Normalisation* and *Rehabilitation*). His critique aligned with civil libertarian criticisms of punishment, expressing concern regarding the abusive potential of the treatment being administered. Treatments were often found to be overly intrusive, inhumane and unjust, and were claimed to infringe on the rights of due process because of the arbitrary nature of individualised sentencing.

From a practical point of view, penal modernism had failed to reduce recidivism. As a consequence, classical models of justice were reinvigorated in the latter part of the century, and 'back to justice' movements came to focus on offenders' responsibilities for their deeds as opposed to their needs. Accordingly, the act not the actor forms the basis for rationalisations of punishment. 'Back to justice' critiques have been particularly influential in areas of juvenile offending, where there have been shifts from so-called welfare models to justice models.

NEW PENOLOGIES

According to Cohen (1985: 31), punishment was decentralised in the last few decades of the twentieth century, taking corrections out of state control. This partly involved a weakening of institutional forms of social control, with their attendant professionals, and a push for more open controls based within communities. Community-based controls include a pre-trial period with family group conferencing and community panels. Incarceration was also modified with release for weekends, work and study, supervised and unsupervised. Incarceration took place outside the traditional penological sphere, moving to private homes, foster homes, group or half-way houses and day centres. Other forms of partial detention include community service orders and reparation schemes. These moves were not only a response to the failure of prisons to control recidivism, but also to the costs of supplying a state-dominated criminal justice system (see also *The criminal justice system*).

The four Ds of the new penologies are depenalisation, diversion, deinstitutionalisation and decarceration:

1. *Depenalisation* refers to efforts to expand the range of non-imprisonable offences, making prisons the last resort of courts and applicable only in the most dire of cases. It may include decriminalisation, which seeks to narrow the scope of the criminal law and allow civil remedies in many instances of social conflict.
2. *Diversion* seeks to divert offenders from formalised punishments. However, in practice diversion often involves intervention of a less formal nature, including police cautions, community aid panels and family group conferences.
3. *Deinstitutionalisation* seeks alternatives to traditional institutional care and imprisonment. While a person may not be incarcerated, they are kept under some form of control and surveillance. Typical community-based controls include probation, bonds, suspended or deferred sentences and community service orders.
4. *Decarceration* aims to remove individuals from prison environments by minimising the time they spend there. While deinstitutionalisation diverts people from prison, decarceration shortens their length of stay in the prison environment. Typical forms of decarceration include things such as parole, day-leave schemes, conditional releases and specialist camps.

RESTORATIVE MEASURES

John Braithwaite pioneered the idea of restorative justice in his book *Crime, Shame and Reintegration* (1989), arguing for positive ways to deal with offenders and victims (see also *The criminal justice system*). He argues for a need to produce self-sanctioning cultures through internalisation of social controls. For Braithwaite, the response to crime must be to utilise the least restrictive measures possible and undo the harms committed. His focus is less on punishing offenders and more on maximising the personal dominion of victims.

Braithwaite also argues that offenders should be re-integrated into society, so that their dominion can also be reinstated. This may be achieved through the practice of re-integrative shaming, which involves offenders being publicly rebuked for the harm they have caused. They are forgiven and, in theory, re-integrated back into mainstream society. Re-integrative shaming seeks to acknowledge harms while also respecting victims, the shaming being finite and offenders being given the chance to re-enter communities through a recognition of their wrongdoing, apologising and being repentant.

REFERENCES

Braithwaite, J. (1989) *Crime, Shame and Reintegration*. Cambridge: Cambridge University Press.

Cohen, S. (1985) *Visions of Social Control: Crime, Punishment and Classification*. Cambridge: Polity Press.

Elias, N. (1969) *The Civilizing Process, Vol. I: The History of Manners*. Oxford: Blackwell.

Foucault, M. (1977) *Discipline and Punish: The Birth of the Prison*. London: Allen Lane.

Garland, D. (1985) *Punishment and Welfare: A History of Penal Strategies*. Aldershot: Gower.

Rusche, G. and Kirchheimer O. (1939) *Punishment and Social Structure*. New York: Columbia University Press (edn.) (1968).

38 Prisons

Definition: *Prisons are places that house individuals who have been sentenced for violating the criminal law. In some jurisdictions, remand or pre-trial detainees are also incarcerated in prison. Elsewhere, pre-trial detainees are held in jail as opposed to prison. The vast majority of inmates are eventually released from prison; however, prisons provide few rehabilitative opportunities, making re-entry into the wider community very difficult.*

Sentencing is a stage of the criminal justice process that follows a guilty verdict or conviction. Criminal codes usually specify the sentencing options that are available to judges and juries. The range of criminal penalties varies by country but can be broadly classified into custodial and non-custodial sentences. Prison is a custodial sentence whereby individuals are placed in the legal and physical custody of the state for the purpose of punishment. Prison sentences incapacitate the individual for the protection of society, attempt to deter the individual and others from committing crimes and, to a lesser extent, aim to rehabilitate offenders (see also *Punishment*). Some criminal codes stipulate the minimum and maximum length of a prison sentence, and in several countries prison sentences are designated for individuals convicted of the most serious crimes, as perceived by the state.

HISTORY OF PRISONS

Confinement and other forms of forced separation from wider society have long been used as tools of social control that are designed to instil moral values and to provide distance between society and its deviants. Historically, these mechanisms of social control have included the forced quarantine of people who have been infected with disease (e.g. the quarantine islands off the coast of New Zealand; Grosse Île in Canada), the forced migration of an estimated 160,000 'convicts' by Britain for more than 100 years, indentured servitude for people who had been convicted of petty crimes, and confinement in European workhouses. These policies disproportionately affected ethnic minorities and people from impoverished backgrounds, similar to the characteristics of contemporary prisoners housed in institutions located in a number of countries.

In the eighteenth and early nineteenth centuries, prisons in the UK and the USA either lacked cells altogether, opting instead for chains, or consisted of collective holding units in which prisoners were held together, regardless of age, gender or other vulnerability. Conditions in the USA and Britain were highlighted by observers in written accounts that appeared in local newspapers and other public documents. These prison reformers highlighted the importance of treating prisoners with dignity and advocated for better prison conditions. Organisations were formed in the UK (Howard League of Penal Reform) and in the USA (Pennsylvania Prison Society) for the purpose of addressing these goals. These organisations continue to exist today.

In the USA, the philosophical focus of prisons was altered substantially in 1829, with the opening of Eastern State Penitentiary, located near Philadelphia. Influenced by Enlightenment thinkers, the objectives of the penitentiary extended beyond punishment. Prisoners were encouraged to focus on remorse and spirituality. Isolation was believed to enhance spiritual reflection and, in turn, rehabilitation. Prisoners were accommodated in individual cells with little opportunity to associate with other inmates. They were stripped of individual possessions, other than a Bible, which reflected the role of the Christian ethos in the structure and philosophy of the prison. Although the Eastern State model was adopted in several other countries during the nineteenth century, it was not extended to all prisons in the USA.

Several other prisons avoided the principle of isolation in order to exploit prison labour for private profit (McLennan 2008).

TYPES OF PRISONS

Contemporary prisons are usually classified in terms of the level of security, which often determines prisoners' accommodation, privileges and freedom of movement within the prison. In the UK, prisons are designated as open or closed where placement is determined largely by sentence length and assessment of escape risk. In the USA, minimum-security prisons generally house inmates who have received relatively short sentences or who are approaching the end of their sentence. Several prisoners are housed in dormitory-style accommodation, as opposed to individual cells. The majority of prison camps, boot camps or farms are minimum-security facilities. Freedom of movement is more restricted in medium-security prisons, although prisoners might be permitted to engage in work and other activities within the prison. High fences often surround medium-security prisons, and prisoners are usually accommodated in cells.

Maximum-security prisons (known as Category A facilities in England and Wales) house inmates who have long sentences or who are deemed to be escape risks. These institutions are characterised by a high number of security staff (referred to as correctional officers in some countries and prison officers in others), relative to the number of prisoners. Death-row inmates in the USA are also incarcerated in maximum-security prisons. They are generally housed one to a cell and have very little, if any, contact with other prisoners. Super maximum (supermax) prisons (or super maximum/highly secured units within maximum-security prisons) provide intense security and are generally reserved for prisoners whom the state has determined to be the most violent. Prisoners are often deprived of visual stimulation and association with other people and remain in their cells for 23 hours per day (Mears and Watson 2006). The principle of extremely isolated accommodation has its roots in the ethos of Eastern State Penitentiary, described above. Although supermax prisons are found in nearly every US state, the number of prisoners housed in these facilities is unknown due to limited monitoring at the national level. Supermax prisons have been highly criticised for the impact on prisoners' mental health, the very limited opportunity for rehabilitation, the dehumanising conditions and violation of human rights (e.g. Haney 2008). Although contemporary supermax prisons originated in the USA, the model has been adopted in other countries (Ross 2013).

Prisons are also used for pre-trial detention, although in some countries (e.g. the USA) pre-trial detainees are housed in jails rather than prisons. Outside the USA, pre-trial detainees are known as 'remand prisoners' or 'prisoners on remand'. In some countries (e.g. Northern Ireland), remand and sentenced prisoners share the same living space. Alhas (2010) found that large numbers of people are on remand in several African nations, and some remand prisoners are incarcerated for several years. In some Latin American countries, upwards of 70–90% of prisoners are held on remand (Hafetz 2002). Several pre-trial detainees in the USA remain in jail because they cannot afford bail. Lengthy pre-trial detention can impact negatively on subsequent criminal proceedings because incarceration makes it difficult for individuals to prepare their case (e.g. locate witnesses, have regular meetings with lawyers).

Globally, males and females are usually housed in separate prisons or in different sections within the same prison or prison complex. This designation poses difficulties for transgender prisoners who are at risk of violent victimisation in prison. International data on prisoners indicate that the majority of prisoners are males, although the proportion of female prisoners is increasing in several countries (e.g. Australia, Scotland, the USA). The highest rates of female prisoners have been found in Bahrain, Maldives and Hong Kong, where the percentage of females in prison ranges from 18 to 20% (Walmsley 2012). In general, female prisoners have substantially more problems associated with mental and physical health. Moreover, there are fewer prisons for women which can negatively impact on the opportunity for visits from family members, including children.

Prison populations are diverse, hence the need for specialised accommodation for some prisoners. For example, young people are perceived as vulnerable and are housed in separate facilities. Prisoners with serious mental health problems and those who have been sentenced for sex offences are generally separated from mainstream prison populations.

PRISON DESIGN

Writing in the late eighteenth century, Jeremy Bentham proposed a panopticon design to regulate behaviour and create maximum surveillance of prisoners, patients in state institutions, factory workers and a host of other individuals deemed in need of regulation and control. The panopticon prison design incorporated illuminated cells in a circular perimeter and a guard tower in the centre. The design allowed for maximum surveillance of prisoners and their cells. The guard tower was darkened so that prisoners assumed they were being watched but were not entirely certain when they were being observed. Although prison designs have altered, contemporary prisons in industrialised nations encapsulate Bentham's ideas through constant surveillance and the regulation of behaviour through formal social control. The French philosopher and social theorist Michel Foucault (1975) argued that Bentham's panoptic design served to create and reinforce the power of the watchers and, in turn, the institution of social control. Foucault observed that former methods of punishment (e.g. torture and being housed in dungeons) reflected the imposition of power through assaults on the body. In contrast, the panopticon design represented a shift in power to a 'daily, structurally coercive one' (Dunning 2010: 71).

PRISON ENVIRONMENTS

Prisons are characterised by closed physical environments, limited ventilation and close contact with hundreds of other individuals. These conditions can promote the spread of communicable disease, thus the need for disease-prevention efforts in prison. Prisons in several countries have experienced massive overcrowding, consistent with a 'get tough on crime' approach that is reflected in policing strategies, determinate sentencing and increased penalties. For example, prison populations in several countries (e.g. Australia, the USA) greatly exceed the available accommodation in some institutions. Overcrowded prisons can increase the likelihood of violence directed at prisoners and staff. Most inmates are eventually released from prison and prison-related violence can negatively impact on rehabilitation and re-entry into society.

REFERENCES

Alhas, M. (2010) 'The Challenges of Overcrowding and Correctional Programming.' Paper presented at the African Correctional Services Association biennial conference, Accra, Ghana, September.

Dunning, E. (2010) 'Wrongful incarceration: A Foucauldian analysis', *Journal of Theoretical and Philosophical Criminology*, 2: 69–99.

Foucault, M. (1977) *Discipline and Punish: The Birth of the Prison*. London: Allen Lane

Haney, C. (2008) 'A culture of harm: Taming the dynamics of cruelty in supermax prisons', *Criminal Justice and Behavior*, 35: 956–84.

Hafetz, J.L. (2002) 'Pretrial Detention, Human Rights, and Judicial Reform in Latin America', *Fordham international Law Journal*, 26: 1753–1777.

McLennan, R.M. (2008) *The Crisis of Imprisonment: Protest, Politics, and the Making of the American Penal State, 1776–1941*. Cambridge: Cambridge University Press.

Mears, D.P. and Watson, J. (2006) 'Towards a fair and balanced assessment of supermax prisons', *Justice Quarterly*, 23: 232–70.

Ross, J.I. (2013) *The Globalization of Supermax Prisons*. New Brunswick, NJ: Rutgers University Press.

Walmsley, R. (2012) *World Female Imprisonment List*, 2nd edn. London: International Centre for Prison Studies.

39 Rehabilitation

Definition: Rehabilitation is one of the key objectives of criminal justice systems and aims to bring about positive behavioural changes within offenders, encouraging a cessation of offending. The individual is thus transformed in the public and/or private perception from having the identity or image of a criminal to that of a non-criminal or 'normal' citizen. In contemporary rehabilitation programmes, offenders participate in a range of therapeutic interventions such as employment and skills programmes and drug and alcohol counselling, either in the community or in prison (Prenzler and Sarre 2009: 260–1).

(Continued)

(Continued)

Proponents of rehabilitative strategies claim that rehabilitation can 'improve' individual offenders, increase social participation by making offenders employable and reduce or eliminate re-offending (Robinson 2008: 430). A blurring of boundaries between punishment and rehabilitation has sparked debate about the objectives of rehabilitative interventions (Robinson 2008).

THE DEVELOPMENT OF REHABILITATION

In his work *On Crimes and Punishments*, the classical criminologist Cesare Baccaria (1738–94) argued for a codified, rational and calculated approach to law and punishment which would make punishment commensurate with the gravity of the crime (Daly 2012; Vold et al. 2002) (see also *Crime and theory*). Baccaria's work was premised on the notion of deterrence, which assumes that human actions are the result of rational decisions and choices. He proposed that offenders make decisions about crime based on a 'just deserts' principle which takes a highly rationalist and mathematical approach to punishment (Daly 2012: 401).

According to the just deserts principle, offenders can choose whether or not to offend but if the penalty is harsh enough the offender will make a rational calculation that the risk of punishment is not worth the pleasure that can be derived from the criminal act. Therefore, penalties must slightly outweigh the benefits or gain made from crime to deter potential offenders. When a punishment is administered, it should be certain, swift and severe enough that the offender will learn his/her lesson and be deterred from further crime. The severity of the crime should also serve as an example to other potential offenders, however it should not be so severe that it prevents the offender from living an honest life once they have been punished. Punishment therefore should be for the good of the offender and the community (Vold et al. 2002: 17–19). Baccaria's concern with the common, communal good was in part consistent with the utilitarian philosophy of Jeremy Bentham (1748–1832) which forms the basis of the contemporary notion of rehabilitation. Utilitarian perspectives propose that punishment should prevent more harm than it creates, and be useful and purposeful. From this perspective, punishment is a pragmatic state response to crime that looks to the future benefits of reforming offenders (Daly 2012) (see also *Punishment*).

By the nineteenth century, with Cesare Lombroso's development of positivist criminology, the focus of punishment had shifted significantly from deterrence to reformation and rehabilitation (see also *Deterrence and prevention*). Influenced by the evolutionary theories of Charles Darwin, Lombroso proposed that criminals belonged to an inferior gene pool, and argued that they needed to be segregated to prevent them from offending (Daly 2012). Rehabilitation derives from the positivist idea that criminal behaviour is inherited and determined by individual traits such as

key concepts in
crime and society

abnormal physiology, or biology. Positivist approaches encourage the rehabilitation of criminals through the intervention of medical and psychiatric expertise. Because rehabilitation is based on a medical view that offenders are sick, there is an emphasis on 'correcting' the individual and retraining them to become law-abiding citizens, rather than simply focusing on punishing the criminal act (Daly 2012; Platt 1977).

REHABILITATIVE SENTENCING PRACTICES

Rehabilitation of offenders has historically been framed in terms of welfare and punishment. From the emergence of penal welfarism in the early twentieth century came the notion that offenders require rehabilitation for their own welfare and the collective interests of society (Robinson 2008: 430). This idea framed the 'rehabilitative ideal' during the 1950s which aimed to serve a therapeutic function in order to effect changes in the behaviour of offenders and in the interests of social good (Allen 1959: 226).

Rehabilitation is at the heart of indeterminate sentencing practices, which evolved in western nations from the second half of the nineteenth century. Indeterminate sentences allow the incarceration of offenders for unspecified periods until it is determined that they are rehabilitated. In Britain during the 1950s, persistent offenders who were deemed to constitute a danger to society could be detained for 'preventative detention' for a period of between five and 14 years. Those who were 'not yet beyond hope of correction' by treatment were required to undergo corrective training for a period to be determined by the court of between two and four years. The purpose of the training and treatment was to establish in prisoners the 'will to lead a good and useful life' through becoming a moral, responsible and involved citizen (Fox 1958).

Rehabilitation as a model of sentencing remained popular until the 1960s, but support for it had waned by the 1970s in favour of a punitive law-and-order approach which gives priority to goals of retribution, incapacitation and deterrence (Brown and Hogg 1996; Garland 1996). Deterrence continues to underpin punitive sentencing principles of criminal justice systems in contemporary common law countries, and is the basis of get-tough policies and justifications for harsher penalties which have been enacted in many western nations (Akers 2000: 27).

Following the disillusionment with rehabilitation during the 1970s, a new strand of rehabilitation emerged in the 1990s, encompassing a suite of interventions based on cognitive-behavioural principles and methods for use in both probation and custodial contexts (Robinson 2008: 431). Underpinned by a utilitarian rationale, contemporary rehabilitative programmes are promoted on the basis of their benefit to the greatest number. With their potential to protect communities and future victims, the welfare of offenders is no longer a primary consideration (Robinson 2008: 432). These forms of rehabilitation are, in effect, forms of punishment that take place in the community or within penal sanctions. Hence, contemporary sentencing practices endorse an eclectic approach, encompassing a concern with retribution and proportionality in punishment, yet, at the same time, there is a focus on individualised rehabilitation (Potas 1991). Despite the punitive aims of much current sentencing legislation, correctional administrators invest substantial resources in the development of rehabilitative programmes for moderate- to high-risk prisoners (Heseltine et al. 2011).

In contemporary sentencing practices, the severity of a crime is weighed against the potential for rehabilitation of the offender, and penalties are decided within a range of minimum and maximum discretionary options to meet the individual's rehabilitation needs. The sentence is, in effect, indeterminate, because the parole board makes a final decision about the prisoner's release date. The decision is typically based on prison reports and assessments from a range of professionals such as parole officers, psychologists and social workers. These extra-judicial decision makers are assigned power beyond the court to determine the individual's risk of re-offending and the success of their rehabilitative activities.

CONTEMPORARY REHABILITATION

Robinson (2008) argues that in spite of claims by international penal commentators that rehabilitation is dead, it has survived into the twenty-first century by transforming and re-marketing itself. The contemporary model of rehabilitation assigns personal responsibility to the offender for their rehabilitation and reformation of their anti-social behaviour (see also *Punishment*) (Garland 1996). An example of this type of rehabilitation is restorative justice which is practised in various forms in many western cultures and a number of other jurisdictions including South Africa, India and Thailand. Restorative justice includes a range of initiatives designed to encourage the offender to acknowledge their wrongdoing and take responsibility for repairing harm to the victim and economic disadvantage (Day et al. 2004).

Rehabilitation also encompasses the use of diversion from the criminal justice system, and treatments and programmes such as Drug Courts in Australia, the USA, England and Wales (Makkai 1998) (see also *The criminal justice system*). There is a focus on resources being allocated to offenders who are most at risk of re-offending to ensure they receive the most intensive rehabilitation (Day et al. 2004). Juvenile justice policy has been especially influenced by rehabilitative goals to allow the courts to act in the interests of young offenders by using punishment as an opportunity to re-socialise the young offender. It has been argued that while rehabilitative programmes have been shown to help reduce the risk of re-offending, there are a number of significant social factors that contribute to offending that need to be addressed in conjunction with rehabilitative programmes. These include educational factors, mental health problems, housing, and family and social issues.

STRENGTHS AND LIMITATIONS

There is evidence that rehabilitation is generally successful in reducing re-offending and may provide a number of other consequential benefits such as improved social networks for offenders (Heseltine et al. 2011). While reports on Drug Courts in the USA, England, Wales and Australia are mixed, there are indications of success in terms of deterring offenders and addressing problematic illicit drug use (Makkai 1998). In Australia, the Youth Drug Court has reported positive effects, including reduced offending, offenders reducing or ceasing drug use, employment and educational opportunities and improved family relationships (Eardley et al. 2004).

Potas (1991) argues that rehabilitation philosophy has contributed to a more humane and individualised sentencing system concerned with the offender's welfare. However, others, such as Garland (1996) and Roberts and Indermaur (2006), argue that some rehabilitative options, especially those that allow for the exercise of discretionary power by courts and parole boards, and extra-judicial specialists such as counsellors, psychologists and parole officers, can result in net-widening and harsher punishments, as was seen in the 1980s when a blurring of the boundaries between welfare and punishment resulted in longer sentences and abuses of power (Carrington 1993).

REFERENCES

Akers, R. (2000) *Criminological Theories: Introduction, Evaluation, and Application*, 3rd edn. Los Angeles, CA: Roxbury Publishing.

Allen, F. (1959) 'Criminal justice, legal values and the rehabilitative ideal', *The Journal of Criminal Law, Criminology and Police Science*, 50(3): 226–32.

Brown, D. and Hogg, R. (1996) 'Law and order commonsense', *Current Issues in Criminal Justice*, 8(2): 175–91.

Carrington, K. (1993) *Offending Girls: Sex, Youth and Justice*. Sydney: Allen & Unwin.

Daly, K. (2012) 'Aims of the criminal justice system', in M. Marmo, W. de Lint and D. Palmer (eds) *Crime and Justice: A Guide to Criminology*, 4th edn. Sydney: Thomson Reuters, pp. 286–406.

Day, A., Howells, K. and Rickwood, D. (2004) 'Current trends in the rehabilitation of juvenile offenders', *Trends and Issues in Crime and Criminal Justice*, No. 284. Canberra: Australian Institute of Criminology.

Eardley, T., McNab, J., Fisher, K., Kozlina, S., Eccles, J. and Flick, M. (2004) *Evaluation of the New South Wales Youth Drug Court Pilot Program*. Final Report for the NSW Attorney-General's Department. Sydney: University of New South Wales.

Fox, L. (1958) 'The sentence and rehabilitation', *Federal Probation*, 22(15): 15–18.

Garland, D. (1996) 'The limits of the sovereign state: Strategies of crime control in contemporary society', *British Journal of Criminology*, 36(4): 445–71.

Heseltine, K., Sarre, R. and Day, A. (2011) 'Prison-based correctional rehabilitation: An overview of intensive interventions for moderate to high-risk offenders', *Trends and Issues in Criminal Justice*, No. 412, May. Available at: www.aic.gov.au/documents/D/3/F/%7BD3FCEAF3-7E16-4180-A3F2-507B1052C734%7Dtandi412.pdf (date accessed 06/10/12).

Makkai, T. (1998) 'Drug courts: Issues and prospects', *Trends and Issues in Criminal Justice*, No. 95, September. Canberra: Australian Institute of Criminology.

Potas, I. (1991) 'The principles of sentencing violent offenders: Towards a more structured approach', in S.-A. Gerull and W. Lucas (eds) *Serious Violent Offenders: Sentencing, Psychiatry and Law Reform*. Proceedings of a conference held at the Australian Institute of Criminology, Canberra, 29–31 October. Available at: www.aic.gov.au/en/publications/previous%20series/proceedings/1-27/~/media/publications/proceedings/19/potas.pdf (date accessed 06/10/12).

Prenzler, T. and Sarre, R. (2009) 'The criminal justice system', in H. Hayes and T. Prenzler (eds) *Introduction to Crime and Criminology*. Sydney: Pearson Education Australia, pp. 259–73.

Roberts, L. and Indermaur, D. (2006) 'Timely intervention or trapping minnows? The potential for a range of net-widening effects in Australian drug diversion initiatives', *Psychiatry, Psychology and Law*, 13(2): 220–31.

Robinson, G. (2008) 'Late-modern rehabilitation: The evolution of a penal strategy', *Punishment and Society*, 10(4): 429–45.

Vold, G., Bernard, T. and Snipes, J. (2002) *Theoretical Criminology*, 5th edn. New York: Oxford University Press.

40 Alternatives to Imprisonment[1]

Definition: *Imprisonment is one of the primary tools for the punishment of serious crime in most countries around the world. Custodial sentences, however, are not the only punishment option for the courts and many argue that alternatives to imprisonment can be more effective in reducing criminality and providing better social justice outcomes for both offenders and victims. Increasingly, alternative approaches to sentencing reflect an acknowledgement by the criminal justice system that crimes and offenders differ in severity and intent and may benefit from more nuanced approaches to punishment, whereas in other cases (e.g. mothers) prison may be deemed unreasonably harmful to connected others and thus should be avoided for such reasons. Opposition to alternative sentencing is variable but being 'soft' on crime and criminals is a populist criticism often targeted at those in favour of it.*

INTRODUCTION

For some, it is the broader social benefits of including non-custodial sentences in the options for punishment that provide a strong rationale for why less incarceration is the way forward. Unrelated to cost, perceived benefits include providing punishments that are: less stigmatised; less likely to embed a criminal within an even stronger criminal culture (within the prison setting); less damaging to family structures and interpersonal relationships; likely to reduce crime/recidivism and avoid some of the institutional inequalities (race, gender, class) deemed to be embedded within the prison system.

There are numerous types of alternative punishments, from well-established supervisory roles relating to probation and parole, and various forms of community participation/work schemes, to the use of technology (electronic surveillance and tagging; drug tests) to monitor and constrain those subject to curfew and geographical and behavioural restrictions. Each of the interventions has a variety of forms and is implemented variously. Each has its problems and benefits. What follows is indicative of the kind of interventions currently in use.

FORMS OF COMMUNITY SENTENCES AND RESTORATIVE JUSTICE

In recent years, a multitude of forms of community sentence structures has developed internationally. Table 40.1 broadly categorises these forms and those developments.

Table 40.1   Examples of community sentencing

Emphasis is on ...	Traditional alternatives	Newer forms
Supervision and support	• Probation • Conditional imprisonment • Suspended sentence	Intensive probation
Restrictions of liberty in the community		• House arrest/electronic monitoring • Other restrictions of movement
Community ties and integration (+ work)	Public work	Community service order
Social work/social training	• Probation • Juvenile corrections	• Social training courses • Juvenile corrections
Treatment (psychological/ psychiatric/medical)	Treatment orders	Contract treatment
Restitution/ compensation	Criminal damages	Compensation orders
Restitution/mediation/ community involvement	Different forms of informal out-of-court settlements	• Victim–offender mediation • Community mediation • Family group conferences • 'Healing circles'

Adapted from Lappi-Seppälä (2003: 66–7)

BALANCING PUNISHMENT, VICTIM RESTITUTION AND COMMUNITY OUTCOMES

In essence, at the time of writing in 2014, many countries are trying to manage non-custodial sentences in ways that satisfy a number of competing demands. To satisfy a general trend towards punitive populism (see also *Punishment*), community sentences increasingly need to be seen as genuine/appropriate punishment, while, at the same time, providing restitution (compensation) to either the victim, the community or both, as well as aiming at reducing re-offending.

EFFICACY OF COMMUNITY SENTENCING

Imprisonment, punishment apart, doesn't in general achieve the desired outcomes of preventing re-offending and/or rehabilitating offenders. In fact, due to the

criminogenic milieu it provides, prison can increase re-offending, especially in relation to short-term sentences. By and large, this is because what is an already
expensive punishment approach rarely has, in any country, the additional resources
required to provide specialist intensive rehabilitation in conditions conducive to it.

What then of the effectiveness of community sentencing? The Howard League
for Penal Reform sees incarceration as a 'blunt instrument' and that 'Community
sentences and programmes that are outcome focused are the most successful penal
intervention at preventing reoffending and have the support of victims' (2011: 5).
In support of this claim, they refer to UK-based data that show that re-offending
rates for offenders who receive community sentences rather than prison sentences
is upto 14% lower. They acknowledge, however, that community approaches that
do not try to address the issues relating to individual offenders will likely be no
more effective. A RAND review (Davis et al. 2008: iii) of the available research on
the effectiveness of community orders largely concurs with this analysis and concludes that:

> in two areas – cognitive/behavioural programming and drug treatment – rigorous
> research exists that points to a reduction in the odds of re-offending. In four other
> areas – programmes for domestic abuse perpetrators, unpaid work, education and
> basic skills training and intensive probation – existing studies have not suggested that
> the programmes have a positive effect on recidivism. Finally, in four areas – anger
> management, probation, and alcohol and mental health treatment – the question of
> impact on re-offending remains unsettled.

CONCLUSIONS

The real costs and checks and balances of prison compared with non-custodial
sentences are not as simple as often presented and this is why two trends – increased
prison and increased community sentences – in a context of (broadly) falling crime
rates can co-exist.[2] Neither form is necessarily successful – implementation and
approach clearly matter. If a country simply cannot afford its prison system (now
or in an expanded future), it will deliver an overcrowded service likely to reproduce
the worst of interpersonal conditions for offenders and prison officers; provide living conditions that contravene United Nations and other international standards;
and provide a criminogenic context that works against resolving crime in the long
term (Lappi-Seppälä 2003). Likewise, if community sentences are implemented
without sufficient care or reference to the appropriate evidence base, then (apart
from avoiding the pitfalls of a poorly provided prison context) few aggregate gains
will be made in relation to recidivism or the extant criminogenic context.

NOTES

1. This chapter is concerned with alternatives to prison, excluding the death penalty (least
   prevalent) and punishments of a lesser level such as fines and/or reprimands (including public
   shaming) which are most prevalent.

2. In the USA and the UK, for example, this has happened because of longer prison sentences, parole 'triggers' that automatically send the parolee to prison and increased numbers of people sent immediately to prison. Another (not uncontested) factor may be that imprisoning recidivist criminals reduces crime rates.

REFERENCES

Davis, R., Rubin, J., Rabinovich, L., Kilmer, B. and Heaton, P. (2008) A synthesis of literature on the effectiveness of community orders, RAND Europe. Technical report prepared for the National Audit Office.

Howard League for Penal Reform (HLPR) (2011) *Response to Breaking the Cycle: Effective Punishment, Rehabilitation and Sentencing of Offenders*. London: HLPR.

Lappi-Seppälä, T. (2003) 'Enhancing the Community Alternatives: Getting the Measures Accepted and Implemented', in the Annual Report for 2002 of The United Nations Asia and Far East Institute for the Prevention of Crime and the Treatment of Offenders (UNAFEI): Resource Material Series No. 6. Available at: www.unafei.or.jp/english/pages/RMS/No61.htm (accessed 05/01/13).

Walmsley, R. (2012) *World Prison Population List*, 9th edn. London: International Centre for Prison Studies. Available at: www.idcr.org.uk/wp-content/uploads/2010/09/WPPL-9-22.pdf (accessed 05/01/13).